The Metaphysician

Memories of a Psychic Operative

by E. M. Nicolay

Forethought Publishing

Copyright © 2024 by E. M. Nicolay
Cover & Text Design by FTC Group

This is a semi-autobiographical work of creative nonfiction. It represents the author's perspective, interpretation and present-day recollections of events over time. Some names, characters, characteristics, dates, locations, corporations, companies, organizations, descriptions and other identifying details have been changed or modified to protect privacy, maintain anonymity and ensure creative literary effect. Some characters, locations and events represented have been compressed, modified, supplemented or fictionalized, and some dialogue has been recreated and is not intended to represent exact conversations or precise descriptions or remembrances. The author has attempted to creatively retell his story in a way that preserves privacy and anonymity, but still evokes the unique feeling, meaning and essence of what he personally experienced and remembers.

ISBN 978-1-7334182-5-6

Forethought Publishing
P.O. Box 7023, La Quinta, CA 92248

Metaphysician: *[medəfə'ziSH(ə)n]*

An expert in the fundamental and energetic principles of a super-reality, particularly an understanding of abstract concepts related to the Multidimensional Universe and the nature of Being.

Contents

1. Oak Lane

At first glance, I could have been driving through any mid-century, upper middle-class suburb in America. The Philadelphia Main Line had a reputation for attitude and snob appeal, but in my opinion, it wasn't a bastion of individuality.

Maybe the sameness was intentional. The monotony of so many similar suburban homes packed together in tight succession was strangely relaxing. Sometimes a house or two would do its best to stand out, but the tidy neatness of all those well-manicured lawns and the uniformity of endless painted perimeter fences, quickly betrayed them. Commonality lay like a blanket across entire swatches of land.

This was a version of America left behind but still straining to be relevant, where everything looked familiar because it was so relentlessly homogenized. As I kept driving, it dawned on me that I had spent years living abroad trying to escape this brand of modern American life. Now, here I was making endless right-hand turns, looking for Oak Lane in a labyrinth of Oak Lanes, each as perfectly mundane as the last.

Turning onto the street I had been trying to find, suddenly something was different. The sameness remained, but there was a strange stillness that permeated this street unlike any of the others.

It made you squint as if to look for something you thought your eyes were missing, but couldn't quite identify. I shrugged it off telling myself it was just one of those streets where everything gets quiet around midday, with everyone at work, school or out running an errand at the Mall.

Still, the sensation stuck with me as I continued, and the feeling grew more and more demanding. Why was this street, unlike the many others I had already driven down, deserted? Could there really be no cars coming or going down this one lane?

There wasn't a car parked on the street or in any driveway either. In fact, the houses all looked deserted and empty, as if everyone had suddenly drawn the blinds and disappeared in some rapture-like event. It was unsettling.

I shook my head back and forth in a soothing gesture, as if to tell myself nothing was wrong here, then turned my attention to the street numbers emblazed on the mailboxes. But the further I went, the more that odd sensation tugged at me.

How could I be driving down a prosperous, suburban dead-end street with no noticeable signs that anyone lived there? House after house, beautifully maintained, almost unrealistically pristine, with a stillness and silence that hovered over the entire neighborhood, screaming at you to pay attention.

No neighbors looking out from their windows, no kids playing in the yards, no garage doors open, no one out taking a stroll or walking the dog. In fact, there didn't even seem to be the prerequisite squirrel or two chasing each other around the old Oak trees that gave the street its name.

It was as if every house on the block had gone up for sale simultaneously, and at the same time every inhabitant had moved out. But there were no signs posted anywhere and no indication of that.

Then I realized something even more strange. There were no cleaning services, garbage trucks, plumbers, electricians or repair people anywhere. No cable or utility trucks, no postmen and no deliveries.

For an upper middle-class neighborhood as well-kept as this, those services are a stronghold of daytime activity. Isn't that how they stayed functional and alive? Where was the army of landscapers, pool men, tree trimmers and gardeners essential to daily life in a neighborhood like this? There was no one, anywhere.

The stillness followed me as if it was looking over my shoulder, and it seemed to watch even more closely the further I got down the lane. The street culminated in a cul-de-sac that vaguely felt like a giant boomerang intended to turn you back in case you stumbled on the location by mistake. But before it could sling me back around, there on the last mailbox at the furthest point on Oak Lane, was the house number I was trying to find.

I stopped the car at the curb before passing in front of the driveway and sat there gathering my thoughts, looking up at the house where I was expected momentarily. It was a fairly non-descript 60's or 70's wood and stone-façade structure, the kind they once called a Rancher. The house was painted a dark olive green with brown shutters, and it was neither an attractive nor unattractive house, although it vaguely looked as if it were actively trying not to be noticed, and disappear itself into the background.

Thick hedges and flowering Rhododendron had grown up all around it, and although well-maintained, they hid the front walkway and front door. You could see high bushes reaching up to almost the eaves of the building, and, except for a few structural elements that peaked out from underneath the vegetation, the house was almost completely camouflaged.

To the rear of the structure was an unclimbable, almost mountainous hill, which rose up behind it blocking access from any side but the front. You couldn't calculate where the house ended, since the entire building seemed to bury itself into the steep hillside at the rear.

I had imagined the meeting would take place in a small office building, or, at least, in some commercial location, so I checked the address one more time just to make sure I hadn't made a mistake. I hadn't. According to the map sitting on the passenger seat next to me, I was in the right place. This was the address I had been given on the phone a few days earlier.

Like most people in those days, I didn't answer calls when the Caller-ID box sitting next to the phone said "Unknown", but for some reason I picked up this time and took the call. I was in the middle of emptying out my suitcase, having just gotten back from Hong Kong, so I probably picked up as a distraction and to take a break from unpacking.

In a slow-paced, officious, almost mechanical voice, the man on the other end introduced himself and asked if he could speak with E. M. Nicolay.

"Speaking," I responded casually.

I didn't catch his name at first, so I listened rather than speak. He began by saying he was an Executive Recruiter and he had heard good things about me.

Holding a wrinkled-shirt I had just pulled out of my valise in one hand and the phone in the other, I was only half listening until his flattery got my attention. I looked out the bedroom window of the Pennsylvania farmhouse I had just finished restoring a few months earlier, and wondered who had been talking to him about me. Then, I started listening in earnest when he added that he thought I would be a great fit for a company he recruited for.

He had my full attention now, and I was curious to see where this would go.

"I know of a full-time career position that might be of interest to you," he teased. "With your experience and particular skills, we think you could even write your own ticket as a member of this company's International Division. Would you be amenable to finding out more?"

When you're in your 30's, as I was then, you're more adventurous, less cautious and not as inquisitive or concerned with details, particularly when someone uses the magic phrase, "career position". Then again, all of us were probably fairly naïve in the 1990's, and we weren't as distrustful of people and situations as people are today. Yes, the Internet was starting to exist, in bits and pieces, but verifying things with Search Engines wasn't that common yet, so mostly people relied on what they were told, after it was analyzed through basic instinct and street smarts.

Besides, recruiters called all the time to scout for multi-national companies trying to keep up with globalization trends. The call seemed normal enough, even if I didn't know who it was exactly, how they got my name or why, specifically, they were calling.

"Of course," I said, after he set the scene a bit more telling me it was a privately held, high-tech company operating internationally. "I'd be interested in finding out more."

"Good," he said, "Let's start by meeting up. Can you come to me at Noon the day after tomorrow?"

After explaining that he'd rather not mention the name of the company just yet, mixed in with a few other unimportant comments, he passed the phone to his assistant, and I was given a street address and a phone number. The male assistant told me to only use it in the event something came up and I couldn't make it. No need to confirm otherwise.

I was a little surprised when he didn't give me any exact location directions, and he sounded more like he was giving orders rather than arranging an interview. But I decided to let that go, and didn't bother to question anything further. Hanging up, I even wondered if by not giving precise directions, this was some kind of strange initiation to see how well I complied with orders, or to test my resourcefulness.

It was an interesting thought, and even if true, the whole thing sounded like an amusing challenge. I have to admit I was also somewhat intrigued by the idea of a new international career opportunity, especially one that sounded like it was right up my alley.

It wasn't hard to brush off the idea that this might be some strange test, concocted by an eccentric professional recruiter.

Testing like that by Recruiters in those days wasn't that uncommon, since they were always looking for ways to vet you before introducing you to their clients.

At the same time though, my head filled with questions, any of which I would have asked if I had been invited to or if someone had lingered on the phone just a bit longer. For starters, anyone probably would have asked themselves who the Hell this was, and why were they calling? But, true to character, I meandered down a completely different line of questioning.

Why didn't he ask me more about myself and what I could offer, I wondered? Did he know enough about me that he didn't need to ask anything else, and if he did, how was that possible? And why didn't he want me to send over a resume or a reference of some kind before we met?

LinkedIn and online references weren't a thing yet, so I wondered if he had gotten his hands on an old resume from someone. And he certainly never asked my salary requirements, which is the holy grail of initial questioning by a recruiter. Their commission usually hinged on that.

And why didn't he ask if I had any experience or interest in high-tech? I didn't, so if he had heard about me from someone, he probably already knew that.

I was getting exhausted asking myself questions. With one last hoorah, I asked myself if this was some elaborate prank, or if it would turn out to be a monumental waste of time. After all, the address I was being sent to was over an hour and a half away by car. I hadn't even been told where the company was based, or asked if I was willing to relocate.

God knows, I had received mystery calls in the past asking me for things some would consider strange. It seemed to be my line of work these days. But I could feel something was out of the ordinary with this one, so it made me hesitate. Still, after all was said and done, I put the questioning aside and decided that finding answers in person is always more of an adventure. Besides, I'd gone much further distances as recently as a month ago in search of lesser possibilities.

In fact, I wondered if this could somehow be connected to the project I had just completed overseas. That project had me in Hong Kong and Macau three weeks before, and that project came in a similar way, via an out-of-the-blue phone call from someone who said they were a friend of a friend.

I had been working as an independent contractor for some time by then, and as long as the airline ticket was waiting for me at John F. Kennedy Airport in New York, which it was, I was game. It turned out to be a completely legitimate consulting project, one unlike any other I had ever done.

Calls like the one I had just received from the recruiter were starting to be routine. Since I didn't have anything else pressing on my calendar, I decided to entertain the possibilities. If it didn't pan out, I was only an hour and a half from home.

To be honest, it felt like the Universe was pushing me in a new direction, and all I needed to do was sit back and say, "Yes." After I hung up, I tossed further trepidation aside, and diligently printed out a fresh copy of my resume, as any good "corporate" person would. Then I put the whole thing out of my mind, until I was sitting there parked in front of the driveway on Oak

Lane, ready to walk up and go inside.

It always feels awkward when you reach a front door and can't find the doorbell. I looked up and down both sides of the door frame, but there wasn't one I could find. No door knocker either.

For a second, I stood there wondering how hard I would need to knock to make sure whoever was inside heard me, without knocking so loud it would be considered obnoxious. No sooner had I clenched my fist to go for it however, then the door suddenly opened without the need to lay a hand on it.

I was greeted by a tall young man in his mid to late twenties, who introduced himself as Matthew, the assistant who had given me the address and phone number the day before. Once he verified who I was, he acknowledged that I was expected.

Matthew was fairly average looking, with angular features, closely cropped light brown hair and hazel eyes. He clearly wasn't the type who liked to chat or banter beyond what was necessary, so he didn't offer me much by way of introduction or explanation, and I decided not to sound like I was going to interrogate him.

I took note that standing there, dressed in his dark grey slacks and wearing a fitted white Oxford shirt with collegiate stripped tie, he looked more like a student from the local private Catholic high school than an executive assistant. His All-American appearance worked well for him though, and it also seemed a perfect fit with the neighborhood and the house.

He politely asked me how my drive out had been, as he motioned me into the house. I smiled and responded that it was painless enough, then, moving slowly forward, I glanced from left to right as I entered the large foyer of the Rancher. I could feel the brow over my eyes arch because of what I saw next.

In a manner of speaking, I literally saw nothing. The house was completely empty. There wasn't a stick of furniture in the large sunken living room to the left, not a single chair, lamp or table in the entry, and no server, dining room table or chairs in the empty dining room to my right. For as far as you could see, there was absolutely nothing.

And it wasn't just that there were no furnishings or decoration anywhere. There wasn't a desk, a chair, a box, a filing cabinet, a lamp, a typewriter, a computer, a copy machine or a garbage bin anywhere to be seen. Nothing. From the ceiling, to the walls, down to the floor, I was following Matthew deeper and deeper into what looked outside to be an average, suburban Ranch house in a banal neighborhood, that was utterly, completely and devastatingly empty inside.

I always had a talent for being perceptive with little to no outward reaction, almost to a fault. As a child, people thought I must be a little slow, until they realized the bulkhead of information that was perpetually processing inside my silence.

This unnerved family members to no end, and teachers would stand me in the corner endless hours for staring at them "too intensely" without speaking. I was thought to have a "behavior problem". But, did I have a choice? I was picking up a barrage of information and it was confusing, especially when people seemed to become unhinged if they heard me spout their deepest thoughts, or say things they were hiding from the world out loud for everyone to hear.

At the time, I didn't understand what it all meant, and I don't think I ever really rectified the many punishments I endured for providing truths and revelations about people that seemed to just pop into my head unannounced. It took me a long time to realize that there were things unspoken, which were considered secret that people did not want to share.

Perhaps because of that, I appeared to be a stoic child, and I did eventually learn to separate it out from what was acceptable to talk about day to day. Like it or not, my natural intuitive, or psychic abilities were being honed by that observational intensity and silence. As I grew slightly older, it was particularly pronounced when it combined with an ability to leave my physical state on-demand, and return to myself with information I saw from a perspective that no one else could see or understand.

I was the kid who saw and heard things no one else did, which I was told repeatedly was not there. Alone, I had to navigate a learning curve for knowing how to distinguish between the two forms of reality I experienced, as well as when to bottle it up and remain quiet.

How clear I can recall at the age of six, sitting outside on the front steps and seeing my Uncle Don approach me, walking slowly up the long sidewalk. When he reached me, he asked me to tell everyone he was just fine and to not worry about him. I ran inside and told my mother that Uncle Don had just visited, and told me to tell her he was doing fine.

My mother smiled and gave me a pat on the head. Then she

said, "That's very nice honey, but you know Uncle Don lives in another state and isn't outside. You shouldn't make things like that up."

Then she added, "And don't tell your father. He'll explode if he thinks you're making up stories or lying about things. Now go outside and ride your bike."

When the phone rang that evening, I could hear the adults down the hallway from my bedroom moaning as if in pain. Uncle Don had unexpectedly and suddenly died that afternoon of a massive heart attack at the age of 52.

A therapist looking for explanations to all this, probably would have attributed it to the emotional abuse I received from a father who was withdrawn, overly critical and in constant competition with me. I survived by developing the skill to disappear, launching myself into an out-of-body state where time stood still and other dimensions seemed to open me to insights not apparent to the rest of the world.

Seeing things from a unique and different perspective was normal for me, even before I had any real sense of who I was. Without realizing it, by the time I was seven I was already an initiate into a metaphysical world that offered unexplained mysteries most considered to be fiction.

In fact, the more severe and stressful the situations I encountered as a child were, the quicker I learned to control that exit from my physical body, and "journey", as Shamans say, to investigate what was happening from outside day to day existence. As a youngster, it became a game to delve into the hidden meaning of things.

In no time not only did I master the art of controlling the protective measures I had discovered, but I developed special talents for understanding people and life from the higher dimensional perspective that came with it. Now I could protect myself from an emotionally and sometimes physically abusive parent, while also gaining truths and insights into others and the world that no one else seemed to have and few could fathom.

Standing in the foyer of that house on Oak Lane, I disappeared myself once more, doing exactly what somehow came naturally to me. Without saying a word, but unafraid and acting as if this was entirely normal, I resolutely followed Matthew through an empty building, almost hovering outside myself.

As I looked out from that semi-altered state, I had a sense of calm, and immediately knew that all was well. In fact, it felt like I had more control over the situation, than the situation had over me.

2. The Colonel

Matthew and I walked straight down a long passage to the rear of the house where we both stood in front of a closed and locked door. He knocked twice, and we waited until you could hear footsteps approaching from far off, and then the door being unlocked from the other side.

As the heavy wooden door swung open, I could hear Matthew say my name to the man standing there. With that, I was pulled into the room by the force of someone shaking my hand vigorously, while Matthew vanished behind me and was no longer anywhere to be seen.

I had met several people with the name Colonel before, who were not in any way, shape or form connected to the military. So, I hadn't really thought about the fact that he introduced himself on the phone as Colonel McCormick the previous day. Actually, I thought I heard him say Virgil, or maybe Cyril.

For a second time though, I ignored his name and just assumed it was a first name and not a rank, particularly since he spoke with what I thought was a time-eroded Southern accent. In the South, Colonel was a common proper name for his generation.

The man ushering me in was probably somewhere in his late 60's, to early 70's. He was agile and young acting, dressed in an expensive tailored wool brown pinstripe suit, a custom-made white pima cotton shirt and a solid red silk tie. I paid only slight attention to his dress and manner however, because I was now fascinated by the fact that suddenly, I was in a very large room filled to the brim with furnishings and objects.

Unlike the rest of the empty house that I had just traversed with Matthew, this was a comfortable, upscale executive office, and it felt as if I had walked through a looking glass into a completely different world. The office was hyper-masculine, outfitted in expensive walnut paneling with a large desk and chairs at the far end in front of you.

A small meeting table with chairs sat to the right, and a couch and club chairs created a sitting-area to the left. Built-in wooden shelving encircled the room, filled with books, manuals, awards and photographs everywhere you looked. The room seemed stately, but somewhat somber and old fashioned because of the wood paneling.

It was also the result of the fact that there didn't seem to be any windows in the room. Lamps and recessed ceiling lights illuminated the office space evenly, so the lack of windows wasn't overly disturbing. But I had the distinct feeling I was now standing slightly underground, perhaps buried halfway within the steep hill behind the house.

McCormick motioned with his hand, inviting me to sit on the orange-toned, Danish-style couch, as he took a matching club chair in close proximity that was sitting catty corner to the couch and coffee table. Taking my place as directed by him, I momentarily glanced at a series of framed photographs lined up on the shelving behind the couch. There, in dozens of large and small black and white as well as color photographs, he was photographed together with political and business leaders of varying degrees of importance.

Those that registered were the really famous ones, where I recognized who he was standing with immediately. There was the one with Lyndon and Lady Bird Johnson at an event, the one with him, Ronald and Nancy Reagan, together with Walter and Lee Annenberg, at another event. Several on Capitol Hill with Bob Dole, Tip O'Neil and various other Congressional leaders. There was even one of him and a group with French President Francois Mitterrand, not to mention the photo of him standing with a group of British military officers, with Queen Elizabeth II and Prince Phillip standing in the center.

The largest framed photos were of him, at various points in time, with George H. W. Bush. There was even one with him and Bush climbing the boarding stairway to Air Force One together. Then there were the miscellaneous photos of him with various high-ranking military officers, from various branches of the Armed Forces, as well as a small black and white combat shot of him as a much younger man holding an M-16 over his head, and walking through waist-high water in what looked like a jungle in Vietnam.

He wore military attire in all those shots, which made me realize Colonel was a rank and not a first name. It all went by a little too quickly to distinguish much more. But I continued to be struck by the fact that this gallery represented a potpourri of some of the most important political, military and industry leaders of the past several decades. It was an impressive display, to say the least.

As we sat down, the Colonel, as I now called him in my head, wasted no time on pleasantries.

"Thank you for coming by to see me," he said. "As I mentioned on the phone, we hear good things about you."

It was safe enough, until he elaborated.

"Officials at the Portuguese Mission in Macau seemed very pleased with your work," he said in a matter of fact way.

I was stunned. How did he know about the project I had just completed and whom it was for? Certainly not from me. I hadn't said anything to anyone, not even family or close friends. To the best of their knowledge, I was just off on another International Marketing project, this time in Asia. No one except two other people knew about that project, and one of them was the friend of the friend who picked me up at the airport in Hong Kong and did everything but swear me to secrecy.

She was the one that had arranged the meeting with officials reporting to the Governor at the Mission, and had organized our excursion to Macau. Together with one other person that I had been working with in Hong Kong and elsewhere for over a year, she was the only one who knew that the "project" entailed being asked, months in advance, to analyze how the turn-over of Macau, and the years earlier turnover of Hong Kong to the Chinese, would ultimately turn out when remotely and psychically viewed by me on the future timeline.

Keeping my composure, I acted nonchalant hearing him mention Macau, determined not to give away any details about that project. I had learned never to kiss and tell, as they say, on these projects. It would have jeopardized what I was offering corporations and their officers, and I think my discretion was a hallmark that gave them the confidence to hire me again and again, as well as refer me privately to their close colleagues and friends. No matter what he said or did, I agreed in my head to only confirm that I had recently worked with government officials there, which somehow, he seemed to know already.

These projects had been growing in popularity the past year or so. I had fairly impressive real professional credentials working in the field of International Marketing and Communications, but somehow, I was becoming quietly known far and wide for a side talent I never really marketed, let alone discussed. The secret "analysis" projects I was doing under the cover of corporate marketing and strategic planning had grown exponentially in a very short period of time.

It worked rather simply and was very straightforward. A company Executive, Director, Executive Team or Brand Manager would call me in, and hire me on the spot for what they described as a special "marketing" project, which they intended to incorporate into their strategic 3, 5 and 10-year planning. The projects mostly consisted of a series of management questions, and I would conduct a strategic analysis and generate a Brief or Report. The only difference was that these "Briefings" were done from a psychic, or metaphysical perspective, offering a glimpse of the future timeline based on current trajectory of the company or executives involved.

Sometimes it looked at general market trends, sometimes it was what the competition was doing or could be expected to do next, and sometimes it was simply a forecast of where the company or brand was going in the future and what to expect. A few times it was about what would happen after a proposed merger or acquisition.

What was almost never discussed was how these strategic planning Reports, or Briefs, were being accomplished, and no one ever seemed to want to know the answer to that question. Regardless, the work was all based on my ability to step outside myself and "Remote-View" the company, as well as the key events I saw coming up for it on the emerging timeline.

Remote Viewing as a secret science, to psychically look at targets, as well as what energetically and metaphysically could be seen in the future on the prevailing timeline, had been sponsored and used by various international spy agencies beginning as early as the 1970's. Governments far and wide, including the US, were known to have small groups of talented psychics, or "Remote Viewers", working clandestinely in this way to uncover certain secrets or map out future events. But I wasn't connected or keyed into those groups in any way, and barely knew of their existence at the time.

I simply considered myself an international corporate marketing executive who happened to have a very rare skill that could be applied for companies that hired me on a project-to-project, consulting basis. Depending on what I saw there, and the metaphysical component of the corporate mission and the company or brand's energetic state and expression, as I saw it, I would generate a simple report.

Candidly, I coined the term "Briefs" or "Briefings" for these reports. I imagined myself performing a function something like the one performed in ancient times by the Greek Oracle in Delphi, where pronouncements, revelations and prophecies were given to Greek rulers, the executives of their time.

The Briefings defined exactly where the company or brand would find itself in the near term, as well as in the distant future, and I felt it was up to the end-user to understand the Briefs or not. Usually, what was mentioned in the reports was well heeded, and executives were grateful. At times however, the feedback was so quiet it was deafening.

Companies that ignored things presented to them in these Brief-ings, usually did so at their peril. Many a Company President or Manager would call months and even years later to say, "Do you remember that *item* you mentioned in your report? Could you provide us with another look at it?"

Whenever I got those calls, it was clear that what had been re-ported had been discounted in some way, but was now begin-ning to materialize.

My Intuitive Briefings also answered specific questions for management, such as the impact of various executive's personal involvements, personnel decisions, as well as looking inside a whole range of business agreements, liaisons and other accords. Actually, this was usually my favorite part of most projects, since a good question about *what* was happening usually yielded a great report as to *why* something was meant to hap-pen in the future.

Analyzing the impact of a person's life mission on the corporate or brand mission and vice versa, as well as the metaphysical rea-son for the interaction in the first place, was a specialty of mine. Companies, like people, have life missions related to their en-ergetic purpose in the world, so you need to understand all the metaphysical, energetic and hidden influences and interactions that are brought to the table.

It can get complicated, but it can also be the difference be-tween navigating through to success or facing endless chal-lenges. Briefings, usually prepared by me for the benefit of a small group of executives only, provided a glimpse of all con-tributing interdimensional, metaphysical and energetic factors.

They also highlighted expected and unexpected events seen affecting the company when its trajectory was remote viewed on the prevailing timeline.

Since I was doing this under the auspices of International Marketing Communications, I had always convinced myself I was essentially doing the corporate work I was good at, but with a twist that few really had to offer or could understood. To date, I had worked this way in hospitality, consumer goods, fashion, the automotive industry and banking, to name only a few.

That fateful call from "a friend" in Hong Kong however, had definitely opened up new avenues I didn't anticipate. Until the day I was standing in the Portuguese Mission in Macau, I hadn't realized I was now being asked to size up the future of international political and diplomatic affairs using my talents as a Psychic and Remote Viewer.

I could feel McCormick waiting for a reaction and response to his mention of the Macau briefing, but the most I was willing to offer was, "Thanks. That's very flattering. I think they were happy with the results."

It was then that I expected a full grilling, or at least a list of questions, but there were none. Frankly, McCormick seemed please that I didn't divulge anything further, and he cut straight to why he had called me there.

"I represent a large, privately held company founded in 1959 and operating in the global high technology industry called, Quantrolics, Inc. The company is Chaired by its founder and owner, Aaron Spivak, a physicist and scientist who helped the

US government develop certain types of transistors, semiconductors and other technology in the mid to late 1950's."

Nothing sounded out of the ordinary in all this, and I listened attentively as he continued the well-rehearsed monologue.

"One division of the company, which is directly under Aaron Spivak himself, invents, develops and manufactures Transistors and Semiconductors for electronic and related telecommunications equipment. The second sells and outfits businesses and entire buildings around the world with high tech telecommunications equipment and complete building control systems, employing the semiconductors they make in all manner of commercial audio-visual, security, communications and lighting equipment. The third division heads up all International marketing, analysis and strategic planning for the company worldwide."

It seemed as if he knew this all inside out, and continued with his explanation without stopping.

"The company is run by an Executive Team that reports directly to the Founder and consists of a President, a Chief Executive Officer and a Chief Marketing and Operating Officer. You would be reporting directly to the Chief Marketing and Operating Officer, who heads up the third division in charge of all global operations, corporate marketing, strategic planning and communications."

Again, I felt obliged to throw in some acknowledging comment. "Sounds structured in a way similar to some of the privately held European companies I've worked with in the past," I said.

The Colonel seemed wound up now, so he continued without

pausing as if he was giving me an assignment.

"Your role will be to provide international marketing and strategic communications and analysis for corporate purposes, communicating with company offices around the globe, acting as a liaison between foreign offices and corporate, providing whatever materials or project requests sales or corporate might have, and providing corporate with reports forecasting national trends, international situations and any other areas of opportunity requested by the Executive Team. You'd strictly be overseeing global marketing and communications, since currently there is someone in charge of national marketing. Officially, you'd be based at the company's headquarters in Reading, Pennsylvania, but you'd be expected to travel extensively and constantly, wherever and whenever you were needed globally."

McCormick handed me a Post It note with something written on it, and said, "This is the salary you can expect the first year, with a minimum annual bonus of 10% of salary, and an additional 3% of salary dependent on the company's minimum sales figures for the year. Naturally, the company offers full health insurance benefits, as well as a lucrative 401K where the company matches contributions 100% up to 10% of your salary."

I glanced at the ample number, but refused to visibly react. It was the late 1990's and the figure I was shown was way above scale or anything I would expect, so there was no need to negotiate anything further. I remained stone silent.

To someone that had traveled worldwide since the age of 16, spoke several European and at least one Asian language fairly fluently, had gone to school in Switzerland and College in France, and lived throughout Europe and Asia, it sounded as if they were inviting me to take a dream job. If I had fabricated it from scratch in my imagination, it couldn't have been a better fit.

Besides, for the most part at the time I was unattached, had little family and was free to travel anywhere, for however long was needed. There was no reason I wouldn't be perfectly happy, employed full time in such a role, so I just shook my head in agreement with whatever he said from that point on.

Since my newly restored farmhouse in the country was about 30 minutes from Reading, all that remained was to ask for the address of the company's headquarters. When he gave me the address, I was shocked to see that it seemed vaguely familiar. If I was correct, it was very close to my house, in the middle of nowhere with extremely poor access by seldom-used, old country lanes.

If the same, I knew that to be a rural lane that was low lying and somewhat sunken land, densely wooded on three sides, with acres and acres of high corn and other things growing on the only approachable side. Even more astonishing, it couldn't be more than a 10-minute drive from my house. I started to question the validity of this whole thing again, silently wondering how this could be possible.

"I've been past there a thousand times," I said, slightly confused, "But to be honest, I've never seen a building or even a large barn nearby, let alone a corporate headquarters, office complex or company campus."

Before thinking carefully whether or not it might sound like I was questioning his rationality, I added, "That address is just a cornfield!"

The whole thing was slightly off-putting, and suddenly I was feeling uncomfortable again as the Colonel grinned sheepishly at me.

"Oh, it's there, I assure you," he said.

Then his grin became a smile, as he added, "You'd be surprised what you can find hiding in a Pennsylvania Dutch cornfield."

Synchronicity, when the Universe offers you something easy and highly compatible that coincides with your desires or your needs, should never be dismissed easily, so I knew enough not to discharge the whole thing out of hand. But seeing that I was still looking confused, the Colonel offered further explanation and told me the complex was somehow located in, or near, Mr. Spivak's hometown, and he owned several thousand acres throughout the region. He told me the buildings had been de-signed to blend into the environment, in an effort to make them "environmentally compatible with the surroundings."

"Objective achieved," I said, smiling.

Oddly, after a little additional small talk, I could tell our brief time together was nearing an end. Since the Colonel had made it sound like this was a legitimate International Marketing and Communications role with the company, without bringing my other side talents into the discussion, I suddenly realized that we hadn't talked at all about my professional experience or qual-ifications. I took out the freshly printed resume that I had kept in my portfolio and handed it to him. He took it obligingly, and without looking at it, placed it in the folder sitting on the coffee table in front of him.

For the first time since we sat down, I noticed that the folder had my name on it in bold type. The surprise to me was that the folder had to be at least an inch thick. I couldn't quite tell if seeing the thick file with my name on it made me apprehensive or angry, but I didn't let my feelings show.

Before I could gain the upper hand and give my own elevator speech about my professional qualifications, the Colonel said, "I'd like for you to meet the man you will be reporting to as soon as you can get in there."

He handed me a business card with a name and number on it, and said, "Call this number and tell them you've met with me, and would like an appointment to see Mr. Ron Mallick."

"Now, do you have any questions for me," he asked, beginning to draw our meeting to conclusion. I had many, but I knew from his tone that we were almost done here, so I weighed everything carefully trying to identify the one most important thing I wanted to know.

"How did you hear about me?" I asked innocently. "And what made you think of me for this particular position?" I knew where I was going with this, even if the Colonel was going to pretend he didn't.

A strange look came over him, as he carefully considered what to say. Then, he grinned again, as if he had decided to let me in on something.

"We've known about you for quite some time," he said. "Years ago, you had an association in Switzerland, France and England, with a colleague of ours. Do you recognize the name Steve Moreau?"

"Oh, my God," I blurted out in astonishment. "Yes, I know that name. He was the brother of a very good friend of mine at Boarding School in Switzerland. But that has to be going back 20 years ago, or more, when I was in my teens. I recognize the name, but to tell you the truth, we never actually met in person, although I spoke to him on the phone a few times."

"Well," he said, cocking his head to one side, "You may not realize it, but you were a help to him in the past, and he let us know about you some time ago. Are you still in touch with his brother?"

"Yes and No," I answered. "We exchange an occasional postcard or Fax, but I haven't spoken with him since seeing him for dinner in New York City a few years back."

I met Anthony Moreau in Switzerland when I was 16, at the American Boarding School I was attending there. My father was anxious to send me as far away as he could at the time, since I had just revealed to my parents that I thought I might be gay.

After I told them, my father stood clutching his heart and, as dramatically as he could, said, "If you had stabbed me in the back, it would have been better than this. What will all my friends say?"

The performance deserved an award, as much for being ridiculous as for being insensitive and narcissistic. After that, he decided that sending me to Boarding School in Switzerland was just the ticket. You couldn't get me much further away than an isolated Boarding School outside a small mountain village up in the Alps.

Like many other things, what my father thought would be punishing, alienating and emotionally traumatizing for me, turned out to be the biggest favor he could have done for me in life. It formed the basis of my ability to quickly rebound and adapt to nearly any situation, culture, language or group. I never looked back - duck to international water, you might say.

Both Anthony and I were new to Switzerland at the time, and we bonded quickly. The school didn't have enough dormitory space, so the two of us were put up in adjoining rooms at a local small hotel. We spent the next several months there, and quickly became inseparable. After that, Anthony moved into a four-bedroom Chalet close by, with extraordinary views that looked out on the Alps as far as the eye could see.

When he invited me to move in, free of charge, and share the Chalet with him, I jumped at the opportunity. He never said where he got the money for such an extravagant lifestyle, but between the Chalet, the fast, expensive cars, that seemed to change every few months, and the constant restaurants, cafes, nightclubs and trips abroad, where I was always invited to accompany him, school quickly became the best experience of my life.

I don't know what it was, but from the first second I met him, Anthony became the brother I never had. I may have had a slight crush on him at first, but that was submerged in our friendship soon after we met, and never expressed or acted upon. Although I suspected he was also gay, Anthony seemed as close to being truly asexual as you could get, so we never talked about sexuality unless it was in reference to someone other than ourselves.

Anthony had a thick Slavic accent, but for some reason I could understand what he said without him repeating himself and without giving me any explanation. Sometimes, we literally didn't even have to express words.

Cliché as it might sound, it was as if we could read each other's minds, and feel whatever the other was feeling. He was tall, refined and sophisticated, with long dusty blond hair, and from the very beginning I felt like our meeting and our friendship was some sort of cosmic intervention, planned before we were born, or, at the least, intended years ago by some outside force unknown to us.

Watching Anthony was like watching a Mountain Lion, nonchalantly but purposefully examine everything around him as he sauntered through a room. People could never quite tell if he was satiated and going to pass without incident, or if he was going to pounce and devour them. I can't quite say what he saw in me, except that we thought alike, were both outsiders and seemed to have the same psychic and metaphysical gifts. Both of us were naturally intuitive, and we had the same talent for seeing into the secrets that made people tick.

Endless conversations formed around knowing those secrets, as well as what we "felt" was coming up for someone, and when we were together it made us seem otherworldly to observers. Whenever we would go somewhere, from the smallest café to the swankiest metro hotel, you could feel a hush come over the place when we walked in, and people who didn't know us seemed to back away. We never really understood it, but enjoyed it, as if it were a strange power we had finally discovered and were coming into, individually and together, after years of insecurity, isolation and abuse.

Like me, Anthony had been emotionally abused and bullied most of his childhood. But his abuse also had a disturbing sexual component to it, and it went far deeper and was more recent than mine. We compared notes once, and agreed that it was highly probable that our talent for removing ourselves during abusive childhood situations was precisely what also gave us access to a type of higher wisdom and the metaphysical realities we had to teach ourselves to understand.

Even so, whenever he would mention his brother, Steve, it was with a combination of awe mixed with utter disdain and hatred. In fact, he seemed to shake for several minutes whenever he would hang up from a call with his brother.

It turned out that his much older brother had sexually molested him on a regular basis since he was a very young teen, and except for telling me this once during a brief moment when he broke down after speaking with his brother, it was never mentioned again. I sometimes wondered if the cycle of incest and abuse was continuing even then, especially when he would be called off on a moment's notice to meet his brother at some luxury hotel, where I was specifically instructed not to join him. Every time he returned from such a visit, the trauma, which was palpably lodged in his eyes, brought us closer.

Truth be told, he was terrified of Steve, whom he described as a high-powered business man who had gone from Yugoslavian immigrant to one of the richest men in England in less than two decades. Steve was self-made, and everything in Anthony's life, from his tuition, to the Chalet, to the townhouse in London, to the apartments in various cities throughout Europe and in New York, to the yacht in Saint Tropez, to the many new, expensive cars, were all thanks to a brother whom he admired, but feared and detested at the same time.

In my mind, Steve sounded like the quintessential thug, who had risen quickly through the ranks to become head of an entire crime syndicate. At least that's how I fictionalized him based on the limited impressions I got from Anthony. But to be truthful, nothing as specific was ever discussed about Steve's life, business or otherwise, and there were no pictures or details about him anywhere.

I took it as a forbidden topic, and never mentioned it unless Anthony opened up about it first. It was also front and center whenever I was asked by Anthony to help him solve some dilemma or current upheaval caused by Steve.

Foremost among those frenzies were the many errands Steve would send us out on throughout Europe on a moment's notice. Together, we would pick up packages in Munich, drop them in London and be back at class by Monday morning.

Then there were the luxury cars, including Rolls-Royce Corniches, Mercedes and Porches, that we would drive back and forth from Geneva to Monaco, or deep into the Pyrenees. And we were always given the same instructions -- Do it immediately, do it without stopping, do not ask any questions and do not open anything locked in the car, especially the trunk.

Other than that, Steve was an unwelcome subject. Could these forgotten incidental errands performed by naïve teens decades before, be something the Colonel was referring to as "helping" an associate? I didn't know I was helping Steve; I was just helping Anthony avoid any new trauma imposed by his erratic and demanding brother.

Coming full circle so many years later, I sat there pondering how Steve Moreau, or my schoolmate Anthony, had anything to do with Colonel McCormick, Quantrolics or this job offer.

How was it even possible he had forwarded my name to the Colonel? How old was that file? Had it been sitting around somewhere for decades?

It was all just too much to figure out or consider in the few moments I had before the Colonel ended our meeting.

"This has been very worthwhile," he said in a declaratory way, standing, "I think you're going to find your true calling working for Quantrolics. Contact Ron as soon as you can, and give Matthew a call at the number you have to let me know when you start the job."

He picked up the file, and I stood and shook his hand. Matthew appeared at the door, ready to see me out, and I followed him back through the empty house. As I left, I thanked Matthew and told him I would be in touch with him soon. With that, I retraced my steps and made my way back to the car, anxious to leave as quickly as I could.

I was excited, confused, and then excited again the entire way home, and I tried to distract myself by fidgeting with the radio, going from preset to preset station. Again, and again, I questioned how any of this had happened, who these people were and what was this company, hidden in a cornfield in the middle of Pennsylvania Dutch country, practically unseen and unknown.

The ride seemed as fast as I had ever made it out to the coun-tryside, where years earlier I had carefully chosen that location as a peaceful weekend refuge from a hectic life in Manhattan. As I was going over the 1850 Covered Bridge that led to my place, I noticed a neighbor standing in his yard. I hadn't seen Jacques, who was usually only at his house on weekends and holidays, in quite some time, so I stopped the car and got out to say a quick Hello.

Jacques Durand, who was Parisian, and his partner Ed, had a highly successful import-export business dealing in high-end leather goods. Jacques was not only well traveled, he knew tons of people in almost every corner of the world.

Seeing him was fortuitous coming on the heels of my meeting with the Colonel. After I told him I had just returned from Asia and caught up about comings and goings in the country, I told him I had just received a lucrative job offer from a company called Quantrolics, which, surprisingly, seemed to be located less than ten minutes from us.

Jacques thought for a moment, and then scratching his forehead said in his perfect English with a heavy French accent, "Non, does not ring a bell for me, but perhaps I may have seen some warehouse or buildings near there once or twice in the past."

He laughed to himself and added, "They appear at certain times of year, when the crops are just planted or just harvested. Tu as raison, they are in the middle of nowhere."

Then he asked me again, "What did you say was the name of the company?"

I took out the card I had been given, and showed it to him. He muttered the name several times, as if to think about it carefully or remember something.

"Non…Je'sais pas," he repeated, "But I know people who might recognize it. I'll give them a call and ask about it for you."

Jacques was like that. He had a good nature combined with a global network of contacts that cultivated such connections. They were their own pre-Google, Google, and if anyone could find out something, I knew he could. I waved and thanked him as I got back in my car and headed home.

The peace of being home again after such a long, strange day felt grounding and good. I opened an inexpensive bottle of Cabernet as soon as I got back, and settled in for the evening. Around ten o'clock the phone rang.

It was unexpected being so late in the evening, and the Caller ID let me know it was a name I didn't recognize calling from a Boston area code. Curious though, I picked up the phone, and said Hello.

"Hello?" questioned the woman on the other end, "Can I speak with E.M. Nicolay, please?"

"This is he," I said.

"Oh, Hi," she continued. "I'm Cynthia Logan, a friend of Jacques Durand."

"Great to meet you," I gushed, happy to hear the connection. "I just saw Jacques a few hours ago."

"Yes," she said, "That's why I'm calling. Jacques called to ask if

I knew anything about a company that he said you've just been offered a position with. Congratulations, by the way"

I was somewhat pumped up, so I smiled to myself, and said thanks, then added another piece to the story.

"I'm excited about the possibility, and they've made me a terrific offer. But to tell you the truth, I don't know much about the company other than it sells high tech electronics globally. When I was speaking with Jacques, he said he would ask around."

"Yes, exactly," she said, sounding more serious as we got deeper into the call. "That's why I'm calling, but perhaps I should explain something to you first."

She sounded as if she was treading carefully.

"You see, I'm an Investigative Journalist at the Boston Globe," she continued.

"I'm currently working on a piece about Alphabet Agencies in the US, including the CIA, DOD, DIA and DARPA, among others, that are operating worldwide through privately held companies with black budgets as a way to avoid Congressional oversight or scrutiny. They're essentially front companies doing the bidding of intelligence agencies without anyone realizing it."

She paused as I pieced together what she said, and began speaking more slowly as if to impress on me the importance of what she was going to say next.

"The company you mentioned to Jacques, Quantrolics, is one of the companies we're investigating for our report," she said.

There was a slight pause, and then to break the silence she asked, "Do you understand what I'm saying?"

I remained silent. I knew something was up, and I had my suspicions. My mind flashed to the vacant neighborhood, the empty house, the photos of Colonel McCormick in uniform with all those political dignitaries and the too-good-to-be-true offer coming out of the blue just days after returning from an Embassy project in Asia. The pieces were falling into place, and all the threads floating around in my head were suddenly finding a match.

"Yes, I understand," I responded, after the pause.

"Good. Then that brings me to the reason for my call," she said, in an even more serious tone.

"We'd like to know if we could pay you to go undercover for our report, and act, confidentially of course, as a Whistleblower from inside the company to confirm or deny rumors about its operations."

I was no longer confused by any of it, but I could still feel my throat tighten from what she had just asked. This explained everything, except one important fact – How and why was there an existing, one-inch thick file with my name emblazoned on it, sitting in front of the Colonel on that table?

"I'm very sorry," I said, apologetically, "I really don't think I can help you."

Then I hung up the phone without saying Goodbye.

3. Knock Once for Yes, Twice for No

"What are you doing!?" my mother asked frantically, bursting into the Den of my childhood home in Westchester, New York.

"Nothing," I responded meekly, like the shy eight-year-old I was. "We're just talking with spirits."

"Nonsense," she admonished. That's mice in the attic.

"Everyone out," she commanded to the group of kids who had gathered there, and now hurriedly scattered in every direction.

The Den, which was my father's domain in a separate wing of the house, was generally off limits to unaccompanied children. It was a dark paneled room, with a large mahogany desk that dominated the space. Antique sabers hung crisscrossed on the wall behind the desk, giving the room a slightly menacing air, and overstocked bookshelves were flanked by gilt-framed etchings of famous racehorses from the 19th Century.

Somehow, I had figured out a way to quietly infiltrate the space when adults were not present, entering through an unlocked patio door that opened into the room from an outside breezeway. For over a week, I sat there almost every day talking to something not physically present that would rap strongly on the ceiling above -- once for Yes, and twice for No.

At first it was just me and my younger sibling. Then she told one of her little friends what was going on, and they wanted to hear it too. Bit by bit, every kid in the neighborhood had heard what was happening, until the group was at least 7 kids, sneaking into the room with me after school and sitting quietly in a circle on the floor, as questions were asked to the air.

The questions that came from the neighbor kids were pretty typical for the age, with, "Will I be rich when I grow up?" or "Will I get married?" being the most common. They would direct their questions to me, and then I would repeat it loudly looking up at the ceiling. Nervously, everyone waited for the response – one thump for Yes, or two thumps for No.

Remarkably, these ceiling thumps seemed to correspond to our young lives in amazingly accurate ways, especially for questions we knew the actual answers to. What was more amazing was that no thumps were heard unless there was a question that had been asked, and the one or two raps would sound within seconds of a question being asked by me. So, at least to us, there was no possibility this could just be "mice".

On the heels of this incident, my mother determined it was probably time to have a "talk". After the last child spectator had cleared out, she sat me down and became very serious. I remember her nervously fidgeting with her hands, as she tried to find a way to begin.

"Why do you keep a radio on all night long?" she asked coaxingly to begin.

She was referring to the transistor radio that was tied to my bedpost, right next to my ear when I slept. I had mentioned the reason to her before, without knowing if she understood or not.

"To drown out the people talking in my room and down the hall at night," I said.

Although I didn't understand it at the time, whenever I would lay down to go to sleep as a child, I would begin to hear people talking in my room and just outside my door in the hallway. It didn't scare me at all, and seemed as real a part of the room as anything else, but it was bothersome because sometimes it was so loud it would keep me awake.

It was like having a TV constantly on in a nearby room, where you couldn't make out what was on, but you knew from the muttering that conversations were taking place. They were never inside my head, but always came from outside of me, like when people on the other side of a door are conversing, or when you hear the muffled sounds of someone talking loudly through a thin building wall. The problem was, there was no one actually there.

My remedy to all this was simple. I tied a transistor radio to the bedpost, and turned it on low as soon as I would get into bed. That way, I could fall asleep at night to the voice of Deejay Cousin Brucie on New York's WABC Radio, instead of the muffled sounds of people whispering from the corner of my bedroom.

"Yes, that's right," my mother said, slowly shaking her head in agreement.

"That's what I want to talk to you about," she continued, in a serious tone.

"You see, when I was a little girl, I could hear the same people talking the same way in my room. Sometimes, I use to see them too. I used to close my eyes and hum so I couldn't see or hear them."

I looked at her in amazement. She had never mentioned any of this before, and I wondered why she was admitting it now. She continued to explain.

"Your grandmother heard the same thing when she was a little girl too. So, you probably got it from us," she said, almost as an afterthought.

"Got what," I interjected excitedly.

"Some people have a rare talent for knowing, seeing and hearing things that other people can't. There's nothing wrong with it, and it's perfectly natural. In fact, lots of people think it is a gift from God to be able to know things other people do not know, or speak with loved ones who are no longer alive and are in Heaven. But lots of other people think it is a bad thing. Some people even think it's kooky, or that something might be wrong with you, like an illness," she said.

"But it's not kooky or an illness! It's a rare talent that runs in our family where you have a sensitivity and an ability to see and hear things other people do not."

I was mesmerized.

"That's what I want to talk to you about now," she continued. "When I was growing up, my mother, your grandmother, told me that she had this special talent, just like you and I do. And she told me it can be disturbing to other people who don't understand it, so she decided that it would be much better never to tell anyone about it. So, I did like she did and I ignored it, until it went away."

"You mean you didn't tell anyone about it, and it went away?"

I questioned, curious to know more, but apprehensive at the idea of losing a part of myself.

"No, it never really goes away. This is a talent that will always be inside of you, just like some people have a talent for sports and others are gifted at math their whole life. It may fade into the background as you grow up, and you will be able to choose whether or not you want to hear it or use it, but the talent will always be inside of you whenever you really need or want it."

She continued explaining, choosing her words carefully.

"Since other people don't have this kind of special talent, they don't really understand it at all, so it is best to keep it as secret as you can, and not tell anyone the things that you know or hear, especially if you think it is something coming from some-one or from somewhere no one can see. Think of it as seeing or hearing an Angel that came down from Heaven, just to speak with you. But imagine that the Angels would like this to be our little secret, since they don't want others to feel they aren't special too. Do you understand what I mean?"

I didn't, but I could see how stressful this conversation was for her. To calm her, as much as appease her, I agreed not to tell anyone about it again, and I promised I would try to ignore these things when they happened. That included speaking with anything in the attic by rapping on the ceiling. If that's what it took to keep her happy, I did so willingly and decided to keep it all to myself, even ignore it from then on, in the hopes it would go away.

That promise to my mother guided me through to my teenage

years, at least until I met Anthony Moreau at Boarding School. For the first time, here was someone just like me. We could hear and see the same things, and, with hormones raging, it created a unique bond between us that, because of the intuitive nature of our talents, no one else could duplicate. As friends, we identified and confided in each other, without ever making it official that we were exploring a range of metaphysical and psychic talents we had both forcibly buried in childhood.

To be truthful, I'm not certain we actually knew the real nature of what was buried inside of us at that point either. We had no name for it and no way to define it, so each of us remained cautious, speaking about these things in riddles mostly.

Keeping it bottled up wasn't really all that hard anyway, since we were unfamiliar with the actual language to use, or how to talk about what was, essentially, the philosophy of metaphysics. I don't even think we knew what a psychic or intuitive was then, or what being that way actually entailed. In any case, our focus at the time was on the elite group of friends we were forming at that small Boarding enclave in the Swiss Alps.

There were very few Americans at school, which I found comforting since I was misunderstood by kids my own age in the States. For the first time I was comfortable and happy in my skin, and I felt more of a connection with the European, Arab and Asians friends I was making than to anyone I had ever been associated with before.

Despite growing up well-off and fairly privileged, I was never a snob, so the sense of connection was not because this was an elite group, even if many of them came from celebrated and princely families. It was because I identified with the fact that they were naturally more philosophical, spiritual and mysterious, as I had always been. They also knew how to keep secrets as well as I did, although, except for Anthony, I don't think any of them had the special inner talents my mother had lectured me on long ago.

The other main focus we had was on pleasing Anthony's brother Steve, so Anthony would be able to live in peace. To me, it seemed easy, and in retrospect, it certainly was, since I didn't have to deal with the possible incest and abuse, which it seemed Anthony was still experiencing at Steve's hands. As a naïve teenager, being asked to drive a luxury auto through Europe without opening the trunk was a no-brainer. Why would we ever have thought it odd at the time?

Similarly, sitting in the back of a stretch Phantom Rolls-Royce limousine driven by a Chauffeur through London, making deliveries of double-sealed envelopes to various offices and buildings was no great effort at all. These things seemed like a normal and inconsequential exchange for the all-expenses paid trips we took courtesy of Steve. That included London weekends in his private townhouse in Knightsbridge, holidays in Monte Carlo at his mansion overlooking the Mediterranean, and excursions at Christmas to his reserved suite at the Palace Hotel in St. Moritz, among so many other things.

And why in the world would anyone question Anthony and I being asked to write "essays" on various innocuous world events and subjects that his brother would send to us? Requests went something like this: Steve would send a statement that he was producing a movie on, say, Basque separatists, and needed us to think about it and write a short summary of what we thought would happen to them, how many there would be, where they should hide out and if we thought they could be caught. It was for the "movie script," of course.

There was the time he asked about the oil tanker he owned, wanting us to look into its current voyage from South East Asia, and deliver him an essay with our advice on what would be the best possible route for the tanker going from Indonesia to Europe, to avoid detection by "terrorists". Or, the one where a secret group in Rome was planning to kidnap an Italian government official, and he wanted to know what would happen as an outcome. We were told to keep that one particularly secret, and never mention it again.

There was also the one about restoring the Russian Monarchy, which I remember seemed especially strange to us at the time, since everyone knew the communists who were running the USSR would never allow that to happen. Or would they? And then there was the one where he said he was planning to buy a diamond mine, but needed us to write a summary of where in Africa we thought the best diamonds could be procured, and who might be involved in mining or potentially stealing them from him.

No, he specifically didn't want us to do any actual research for this. He was clear that he only wanted scenarios and summaries that came straight from our imaginations. After all, as Anthony would explain, he was a well-known financer of French and Italian Indie films.

Our scenarios and imaginings were being turned into scripts by his team of "professional" writers, or so he told Anthony. That was enough for us. Did his story line questions parallel world events? In retrospect, perhaps. But we were kids isolated and living in a Swiss mountain-village at boarding school, what did we know? And why would we question anything?

We accommodated him on dozens of these strange requests, each time sitting down, thinking about the parameters we were given, which often included names we didn't know, minor details and specific places. Then we'd write down what we "imagined" would or could happen there. As far as we were concerned, we were writing about fictitious people, events and locations that popped into our heads.

We never questioned the reality of it all. Comically, in doing so we were led to think of ourselves as future screenwriters, putting the depths of our imaginations about this or that scenario down on paper.

If we were being played by Steve, we certainly didn't know it at the time. And we certainly had never heard of "Remote Viewers", so how could we know what they did, or that what we were doing had eerie parallels.

To be sure, I was as yet wholly unfamiliar with any real definition of our talents, and I don't think it ever crossed my mind to investigate its nature. That is until I met Lisa, during my first year at University in Paris.

Anthony and I remained close and in constant contact by phone, but at some point, the Alps had become too small, and I longed for a metropolitan-style change. It may have been a desire to branch out in the world and meet more people, and although I asked Anthony to join me, the fear of his brother's wrath was just too overwhelming. He stayed in Switzerland and attended University there, while I gained admission to University in Paris, France

Lisa was an exchange student from UCLA. We met the first day of classes, sat afterwards for several hours in a café discussing our lives, and then walked to my apartment in the Seventh Arrondissement together, where we continued to talk well into the night.

Lisa was savvy, intense, philosophical, excited and calm all at once. She had a worldly air about her that was beyond her years, despite this being her first year as an American living abroad. We connected on an intellectual, artistic and esoteric level, and became best friends almost immediately.

The first thing I noticed was how well read and sensitive she was. She may not have had the same talents that I hid inside, but she had a unique understanding of who I was, almost before I was aware of it myself. That included being aware, almost from the start, that I was suppressing a potentially extraordinary gift.

What was most attractive to me was her ability to discuss metaphysical subjects based mainly on how well read she was on the subject. I listened to her for hours with fascination and wonder as she detailed and introduced me to the many books she knew of and had read on the subjects of metaphysics, reincarnation, mediumship, prophesy, energetics, extraterrestrials, chakras, spirit messages, and so many more related topics.

Shortly after first meeting, Lisa gave me a copy of "Seth Speaks" by Jane Roberts. Despite the off-putting image on the cover of a woman in trance with eyes rolled back in her head, channeling a spirit named Seth, which we laughed about frequently, I quickly read it, then read it again. It was like nothing I had ever seen before, but everything in the book made complete sense to me.

All the things detailed in it about how the universe and reality really worked, how your personal reality was attracted to you based on your Soul's desires as well as your thoughts and fears, and how a long chain of interfacing lifetimes led to all your current interactions, karmic, familial and otherwise, I knew to be true. It was a revelation, since I had kept quiet about and buried the same thoughts for most of my life.

I realized, perhaps for the first time, that everything I instinctively knew about the Universe, which was quite different from what I was taught in Sunday school, or what the majority of people I met thought and felt about life, was true. It was overwhelming knowing that Anthony and I were not isolated geeks, needing a place to hide out from the rest of the world. There were many, many others like us, and there were even books written about the philosophies I intrinsically understood and held close to my heart, submerged though they might have been after promising as a child to deny them.

In part, Lisa's interest in these subjects came from a difficult upbringing where her father had died when she was a child, and, more recently, her brother had taken his own life. The trauma of these events had cultivated in her an awareness and understanding of death and hidden metaphysical realities that most people do not have. I understood her immediately based on my hidden connection to such things.

Secondarily, her mother, who was perhaps one of the strongest and most intuitive women I ever met, was a fairly well-known child Psychologist. She had instilled in Lisa a deep appreciation for the hidden mysteries of life, while also being part of the world and raising a family of three children singlehandedly after the death of her young husband, Lisa's father. It was inspiring, to say the least.

Though I had worked for years to disappear myself, deny my hidden talents and avoid the "kook" moniker, Lisa was now inviting me to express myself as outwardly and forcefully as I could. Suddenly, I could be myself in a way that I had banished from existence after the "talk" with my mother at the age of eight. I was now, more or less, ready to learn who I was and what existed beyond the veil of life. But even though I shared this fully with Lisa, and a select group of friends, I was not ready to be outed to the world yet.

Then before I knew it, life as a student came to an abrupt ending. Forced to return home to New York following graduation, I was suddenly back in the clutches of a father who had disliked me throughout childhood. Fortunately for me, life had changed him somewhat. He was older and therefore mellower, and perhaps I had grown to the point where he no longer thought of me as direct competition or a social threat. Still, he was as demanding as ever, and since he was a successful developer who had retired by the time he was 50, he was not about to leave me any slack.

His major concern, which is understandably the usual concern of most parents whose young adult children have just graduated University, was what I would now do to earn a living. Working that out became my priority, so, for the moment, any further investigations into my metaphysical "hobbies" had to take a back seat in focus. I tried my hand at a variety of things, as most recent grads do, and tended to follow the path of least resistance. With a University Degree in Philosophy, based on my interest in exploring life's meaning and journey, and a Minor in Communications and Languages, most opportunities led me into fields related to the Arts.

I was hired as an Associate Producer and Copywriter for advertisers on a syndicated Talk Show on AM radio. Next, I toured the East Coast, first as Assistant and then as Stage Manager for a successful traveling theater group. Then I worked for a short time for UPI, assigned to the department that wrote about children's issues.

Eventually, I opened a small Art Gallery in New York with an eclectic stable of young, emerging lower East side artists that I had met along the way. Renting an empty space belonging to my father, my natural marketing and communications skills brought the gallery immediate press and local notice.

Financially however, we struggled, and although I could pay all the requisite bills, which were substantial, I couldn't realize a livable salary for myself. I soon embarked again looking for other avenues to pursue.

Since I had discovered a particular talent in the field of integrated communications, combining advertising, public relations and promotional programs into unified programs for the Art Gallery, it only took a minor effort to start receiving job offers from Advertising and Design agencies. I leaned towards corporate in-house marketing agencies, since I preferred the vast diversity of personalities working in a corporate environment, with specialties in a wide range of areas for various industries.

I was also particularly good in-house with corporate clients, working closely with top level executives and management conducting all manner of the business. Once they knew me, most kept me close by, quickly realizing I seemed to have an uncanny way of describing and accurately mapping out the consequence of their actions as it impacted the company or the brand's future.

I did so usually as a means of solidifying my position with the company, and selling this or that marketing program that I wanted to implement and manage was a simple task based on the confidence I fostered once they knew me. Deep inside, I knew I was using my hidden talents to further personal goals, but I pushed that idea down and decided to credit my acquired expertise and professional marketing skills instead.

Over a decade and a half passed, and to be honest, time flew by. I was focused on my career, making money and successfully continuing on a corporate path. As a serious and dedicated corporate marketing and communications professional, and based on my language skills and international experience, I was offered various global marketing and communications projects for all manner of multi-nationals. I became recognized as a corporate communications officer, brand manager and integrated marketing communications executive specializing in global integrated marketing programs for fashion and apparel, food, the Arts, consumer products and financial businesses.

At the beginning, it was mostly foreign based companies looking to market to Americans. They trusted me as a rare American they could relate to, who understood the market they were trying to target, but also could relate to them as well.

Beginning in the 1970's and through the 1990's, American businessmen and corporations had, shall we say, a "reputation" in various countries for being pushy, uncouth, superficial, impatient and, in most cases, ignorant. Similarly, Americans despised the endless bureaucracies, meeting after meeting to discuss the philosophy behind a strategy, and the depth of forethought and logistical preparation required in doing business overseas. Most could never understand why you couldn't just "ram" something past an executive or through a foreign marketplace, as was so often done in America.

My strength was understanding the hidden nuances of various cultures and people to the point where I could patiently tailor international campaigns to specific markets, something globalization required, but few knew how to do. Eventually, I was not only working for international-based companies entering the American market, but I was also working for American companies looking to understand the subtleties of marketing in Europe and Asia.

Occasionally, I would be hired and receive an out and out request concerning what I saw as the future of a brand or company, and I usually didn't hesitate to respond. The most poignant one I remember was when the 47-year old Italian owner and CEO of one of the largest textile conglomerates in Italy stood next to me at a Venice Biennale event his company was sponsoring, and said, "I hear you can predict the future of companies and their executives, so what do you see for me?"

I was taken aback by the question, especially in such a public setting. I liked him, so at first, I tried not to respond to the question directly. He wasn't having it though, so he asked me again, this time in Italian.

Now I knew he was serious, and maybe he really needed to hear the truth I reasoned with myself. Then again, maybe he subconsciously already knew what my answer was going to be, and wanted it confirmed. Something possessed me to blurt it out. As I said it, I felt like the Trojan Prophetess Cassandra, condemned by the God Apollo to predict the truth but not be heeded or believed until it was too late.

"In three years," I said, shaking my head sadly, "You will **not** be the head of the company. And in five years, **this** company will no longer exist."

He feigned being amused, but forced an arrogant, 'I don't believe a word of it', reaction that belied his deepest fears.

"So, you mean I will probably sell the company and retire?" he laughed, trying to make light of what had been said. "Good,

54

I'm so glad to hear that."

His eyes squinted and I could see his brow buckle. I was unsure if he was discounting my statement completely, or just thinking how misguided and deluded I must be, considering his company was currently one of the largest in Italy, with factories in Italy, Germany, Mexico and China. To make matters worse, he had recently released to the Press plans for his company's global expansion stretching through the coming decade.

Three years later, he suddenly and unexpectedly died after a very short major illness. Since he was a bachelor, without heirs and little immediate family, the 150-year old, privately held conglomerate that he had inherited from his father as a young man was sold off in pieces by his surviving cousins. Five short years later, the company he headed no longer existed, just as I had told him.

Regardless of such incidents, I tried to keep dramatic and dire predictions to myself. I was glad to be traveling again globally, and wasn't willing to risk anything now through an ill-timed negative forecast. I was racking up nearly 100,000 frequent flyer miles a year, and I was more than happy to be back in touch with friends who had dispersed following my school days in Switzerland and Paris, looking them up whenever I was passing through their town.

For the most part, friends from school had all gone their separate ways to different parts of the world upon graduation. That was the reason breaking into the corporate world in New York had been more difficult for me than expected. All my contacts and friends were living and working in Paris, Milan, Dubai, London, Tokyo, Singapore or Hong Kong.

I had no Alma Mater, Fraternity or Alumni Associations to help, so I had to start from scratch in New York. When I was finally back in touch with what I considered to be my world, and in my comfort zone, I was grateful, even if it did come to me through what sometimes felt like false credentials, or, at least, by hiding my true nature inside my chosen corporate profession.

I saw Anthony a few times during that period, once in Switzerland, once in the South of France and, the last time, in New York City. Each time, it was as if nothing had changed between us, although he did inform me at our last meeting in New York that Steve had died.

Anthony was vague on details, and only mentioned that mysteriously, a long, lost son no one knew existed emerged after Steve's death. He came forward just in time to inherit the bulk of his fortune, per the instructions of a signed and notarized Last Will and Testament, which surfaced out of nowhere at the exact same time.

Between the two of us, we agreed that this was not possible, and whoever this "son" was, he was not the biological offspring of Steve Moreau, and the "Will" was not legitimate either. We could have gone further into discussing what really happened, but Anthony said he had decided not to contest anything since he had been well provided for in the same Will. I could see however, that even in death, Steve still had an irrational control over him.

Life went on much like this for years, until the day I received another fateful call.

4. Random Act of Kindness

I didn't know the person calling my office, but the pink tele-
phone message slips the receptionist was leaving me began to
pile up. I had been working for a few years by then as head of
an in-house marketing agency for a Paris-based multi-national
company that owned several of the largest apparel brands in the
world, and it was busy.

I was well suited for the job, excusing the pun, since I always had
a good idea of what trends would be coming up globally. To others it looked like I had my finger on the pulse of some secret in-
dicator that would point me towards what would take hold, what
new and seldom-used techniques to employ and which markets
would be viable, years before it was widely known.

Trend-Gurus were becoming popular then, raking in clients by
forecasting what would become the next "it". What they were
doing seemed contrived and trite to me however, and although
trends were marketed as a mystical "brain-trust" discovery, you
couldn't really compare it to the natural abilities I had. I wondered at times if some of those companies had someone like me
on staff, or if I should call and key them into how to use intuitive rather than statistical and analytical techniques, which to
me seemed as risky as they were expensive.

I finally told the receptionist to put the call through to me from
the main number. Even so, whenever I took calls that came in
through the main line, it was most likely someone selling some-

thing, so I rarely let them ramble. The people I needed to speak with regularly knew my direct line, and time was precious, running a staff of four with advertising, public relations and promotional budgets that were in the millions annually.

"Hello, is this Mr. Nicolay?" I heard a woman say on the other end of the line. I didn't respond, probably because I was multitasking, or signing dozens of the same outgoing letter.

"My name is Karen Brown, and I'm a friend of Daniel," she said, fumbling to keep the one-sided conversation going.

Daniel was, for lack of a better term since gay people couldn't marry then, my partner at the time. We had met originally in Paris at the University I attended years before, and then re-met at a massive sit-down Thanksgiving dinner for 24 people that I was invited to in SoHo. I remembered him immediately because the day we met in Paris all those years before, I was with Lisa sitting in an Art History class when he walked into the room.

"Bedroom eyes," Lisa laughingly said describing Daniel, who had just arrived as an exchange student from Tulane.

I laughed back with her. They were definitely bedroom eyes. After class, Lisa made it her goal to meet him, and she brought him over and introduced him.

Daniel was quiet and charming. It was the kind of quiet that made you wonder if something was percolating underneath, and the kind of charming that knocked your socks off with your shoes still squarely on. He had a true old-fashioned Southern gentleman air about him, worn in a youthful, handsome physique.

The herringbone sport coat he was wearing on that first day of classes stood out like a sore, if not reasonably attractive, thumb. His brown eyes were large and dewy, somewhat like a baby deer, hence the "bedroom eyes" label, and his blond hair was neatly combed and gelled to one side, with a long wisp cascading over the left ear. It was a style that looked Aryan and like it came straight out of the 1930's.

We spoke for a few minutes, and I felt a definite connection with him. I knew immediately, from somewhere deep inside of me, that we would eventually become an item. But soon afterwards, we noticed that he had become overly friendly with a female classmate who always looked like she had just stepped out of an Yves Saint Laurent advertising billboard.

The woman was never without a full entourage of loud, flamboyant gay men, and the group quickly became one we avoided whenever we heard them cackling or being dismissive and catty to others nearby. We would marvel at how incredibly superficial and phony they all sounded when together. From then on, Lisa and I would detail events that one of us had overheard, where this woman's capacity for oscillating from certifiable social snob to ruthless Cruella de Vil in the course of a single sentence, was all too apparent.

The definitive event as to whether or not Daniel and I would get together in those days took place when Mademoiselle-YSL and he were sitting together in the Lobby of the main meeting area of the University. As we walked up to them to say Hello, mostly to Daniel, she flung her head to one side and flicked her long silken black hair over her shoulder after it cascaded out from under the Blue Fox ushanka she often wore.

Then, in the most despicably pretentious intonation we had

ever heard, she said, "Have *you* been to Club Seven?"

She was referring to the most popular members-only private gay nightclub in Paris at the time. I smirked. Lisa and I had been numerous times, once with one of the owners.

Slightly annoyed at the pretense, and mimicking her tone without any real malice, I spontaneously shot back, "*Love* your hair."

Tit for tat. I laughed out loud at my uncontrollable response, but she didn't understand what I was laughing at. After witnessing that shameless display, as soon as we were alone Lisa and I spent an hour mocking the poor girl. For decades afterwards, 'Have *you* been to Club Seven,' became our private joke for describing the highest level of fakeness and insincerity someone could achieve.

From then on as a result, I avoided Daniel and we never hooked up. He went on to find what I considered to be a "Sugar Daddy", who was a reasonably disturbed perpetual Graduate student from a very wealthy family that lived in LA.

I stopped saying Hello the day I ran into them both sitting at a café together with a beautiful Borzoi puppy, which the graduate student boasted he had just bought for Daniel. The dog was extraordinary, to be sure, but when they left, the sight of the two of them, long leash in hand, being pulled down the boulevard by an elegant, giant Borzoi struggling to get away, was as cliché as it was laughable. It was just too much for me to stomach.

Despite that initial schoolyard falter, when Daniel and I met again years later as adults at that New York Thanksgiving dinner, we became lovers, and then partners, almost immediately. Within weeks of meeting, Daniel ended his relationship with the older man who had thrown the Thanksgiving dinner in that giant loft in SoHo, and moved in with me into my small apartment on 57th Street.

I gave him credit for giving up a life of luxury as the kept darling of a wealthy older gay decorator in SoHo to live with me on the Upper East Side, which was a world away from downtown Manhattan. Soon after, I paid for him to take courses and get his real estate license, so he could begin to gain his own sense of self-worth and equality. He quickly became highly successful as a Douglas Elliman Real Estate Agent selling expensive and elite Coops in New York City.

"Hi Karen," I said into the phone, sounding out of breath and half annoyed at the distraction.

She continued quickly, sensing urgency.

"Daniel has been so wonderful to work with. He's a real gem", she said.

"He just sold me an apartment on 23rd Street, which I love, and said you might be able to help me out with something."

Now there was a mutual point of reference, and I could relate to the beneficial connection we had, so I decided right then, without knowing what she wanted, that I would try to help her if I could.

It was a rare thought, because I instinctively didn't like people who asked for favors, having learned to be self-sufficient and never ask for them myself. But I felt drawn to her, for some inexplicable reason. If it was within my power to help her, how bad could it be to provide this stranger who had helped Daniel, by performing a random act of kindness?

"I am a Jungian Therapist with a fairly successful practice," she continued.

"I'm making some changes, and want to expand my practice so I can take it to the next level," she said. "But I'm afraid I am not very good at marketing myself, so I need some help creating a plan, a brochure of some kind, and perhaps a website. Daniel said this was your area of expertise, and you wouldn't mind giving me a little advice on how best to do that, or maybe point me to some freelancers that I could work with."

It was probably one of the easiest requests I had received in years.

"Of course, I'd be happy to help in any way I can," I answered.

"Oh, thank goodness," she said. "Daniel told me you were really good at this. But please, I insist on paying you for your time and efforts."

"Oh, don't worry about that. We'll be in touch," I said, hanging up the phone after taking down some of her objectives and background information.

I had no intention of taking any money from her. Taking money for this would have been inconsequential to me financially anyway at that point.

I was mostly glad she had benefited Daniel through a commission on his sale to her of the Coop on 23rd, so I just wanted to please him with my offer to help. In my mind, she had already paid an ample price to have me put together a simple marketing plan of action, as long as she didn't expect me to implement the plan.

I really didn't need any side work, but that evening I was compelled to write up a simple marketing plan, if for no other reason than to be done with it. I even went as far as to design mock ups of a consistent look for an identity system, as well as suggest a possible ad campaign complete with tag lines and copy, a possible website look and a new target audience evaluation that would broaden her reach.

It all flowed out of me effortlessly, as if it was meant to be, and without understanding why, I intrinsically understood the nature of exactly what she did as a Therapist. The exercise also seemed to open me up to the principles of Jungian therapy, without ever having studied them.

That was odd too. Yes, I had taken some required psychology classes in school, but mostly I was skilled at understanding people based on my own hidden gifts. Certainly, I had an aptitude for what she did to the point where one Psychology Professor wrote on a paper I handed in to "Please, Please, Please, consider making this field your career", but I ignored him at the time.

Why would I enter that field, when I could see into someone's life mission from their Soul's perspective? In hindsight, that Professor was right on target, and it would have been a natural fit, but it didn't appear at all like that to me at the time.

I remember looking at his comment on that paper and asking myself why I would need to conduct weekly therapy sessions to "investigate" someone's personal issues through a long lengthy process of analysis. To me, that was a tedious and cumbersome effort, when I could just look at the personality features they had chosen for the lifetime prior to being born and explain the reason they were going through something almost instantaneously.

It was interesting to me, of course, but it just felt like something I could do naturally every day. Didn't everyone have some form of that ability? It seemed too easy to actually turn a hidden talent into a career.

I knew Jungian therapy incorporated concepts of the Soul and consciousness as a guide to higher wisdom, as well as symbolic archetypes, which rang very true to me, but the actual methods or techniques Jungian therapists used to arrive at a union with the subconscious weren't familiar to me. I had never been subjected to them.

Yet, in almost a trance-like state, I created her plan organically, including unknowingly making direct references to the work and symbols of the subconscious used by Jung. I also provided her with some practical resources and tips for getting the marketing plan accomplished. Finally, I offered her the name of a member of my staff who I knew freelanced and could implement the whole thing. Then, I sent the entire package to her by Fax, without thinking about it any further.

Apparently, Karen was ecstatic with the plan. Daniel told me that she raved about it for 20 minutes when he saw her a day or so later, and was particularly taken by how well it understood exactly who she was and what she did. She told him she was going to call to insist that she pay me, but truthfully, I had no interest at all in ever speaking with her again.

I dutifully shook my head, happy that she was telling Daniel what a great job I had done. Any boost to our relationship helped, since Daniel and I were not always as forthcoming with each other as we probably should have been. I tended to be obtuse and was traveling constantly. He tended to be covertly manipulative and aggressively passive aggressive.

Case in point, having a friend, colleague or acquaintance ask their partner for something they would like them to do. Then again, maybe it was just that genteel way of getting things done that those raised in the Deep South, who come from a certain class, seem to have. It may sound smug, but I always knew exactly what was going on, and allowed him to feel he had all the control.

For the time being, it was in both of our best interests to keep my hidden intuitive abilities silent, and I sometimes felt like he was afraid of, or embarrassed by, my inner gift. His Southern upbringing had been highly religious, and he was from the group that thought anything metaphysical was slightly "kooky", if not devilish, so he didn't want anyone to find out I had some mysterious connection to such things.

For my part, I was far too busy to have to deal with domestic upheavals, so I just let it ride. Keeping the relationship alive, which wasn't really that difficult emotionally or intellectually, was enough for me.

It wasn't that Daniel didn't know about my deepest interests, it was just that he had absolutely no desire for it to be openly expressed, or, for that matter, no desire to know what made me, or anyone else, tick. To be fair, I had embarked on a corporate road that for the most part required me to push the truth about that part of myself back inside again anyway, so I didn't feel the need to discuss it publicly either.

Still, friends often questioned our relationship, knowing me to be far more introspective and thoughtful, whereas Daniel was known to be generally more preoccupied with how things looked and superficially felt on the surface. As long as I didn't include him or his friends in any discussion of psychics or metaphysics, it could be allowed as an unspoken inconvenience. For him, it was somewhat like having a partner with an unseen handicap. As long as it wasn't visible or actively discussed, it didn't exist.

So, to make our life together work, I kept my inner thoughts to myself as they related to my gifts, as well as spiritual or psychic topics. This was also a product of me not wanting to look at these things for myself, and sometimes having difficulty clearly seeing higher perspectives related to me personally. Whereas I could see into the life mission and purposes of others with ease, probably because I could remove myself and look objectively at the things happening as they related to their higher purpose in life, my Ego often objected, and looking at myself in the same manner was more challenging.

This seems to be the case with most true psychics, mediums and intuitives. It can be done on a limited basis, especially with respect to your Soul's path in life, but it is more difficult to see what is on the horizon for yourself than it is for others. Aside from my own Ego getting in the way, and refusing to see or acknowledge certain things, I realized early on that this was because regardless of my talents, like everyone else I was also on a personal path of consciousness and Soul growth.

Knowing in advance things that would happen to me could negate my own Free Will, or perhaps even the need for those things to take place. That could conspire to make the current lifetime obsolete, at least from the Soul's perspective, which was animating a lifetime in physical form for the purpose of consciousness and Soul growth. Knowing things in advance for yourself would defeat that purpose.

For reasons unknown to me, I always felt that every person had a life "mission" of some sort, created for them by their Soul, but I was unaware of specific archetypes, such as those investigated by Jung. From what I could feel psychically, each person, including myself, also had defined personality traits that seemed to be cultivated in them from childhood that tempered the way in which they saw and interpreted the world, as well as the things that happened to them.

I knew instinctively that everyone had their own set of personalized "Rose-Colored-Glasses", which caused them to react to the world accordingly. But I had never spent much time deeply investigating the archetypal nature of life missions, or what the corresponding personality features someone carried might be.

Although I could easily Remote-View the upcoming timeline for other people and situations, telling them what to expect or what was coming up for them, I never actually looked within myself or looked at my own hard and true facts or life-events. In that sense, the whole looking- inward therapy approach was new to me.

Other than my life mission, a few other minor things and some past-life connections, I had never spent much time looking into my own personal life information. Up to that point, the trade-off allowed me to live a life uncomplicated and unimpeded by precognition.

Karen called incessantly for a week after I sent her the plan. I would receive message after message, to the point where the receptionist jokingly asked if I was having an affair with her or owed the woman money. I would just roll my eyes and walk away. Finally, it became clear that I would have to speak with her, so I decided to pick up the phone the next time she called.

"I'm so glad to finally get ahold of you," she gushed. "I cannot tell you how great your plan was, and I'm already starting work with the freelancers you referred me to on creating the materials and launching a campaign."

I smiled to myself, and said, "I'm really glad it was useful. Sorry not to be able to come to the phone lately. It's been a grueling month."

"Oh, I understand completely," Karen exclaimed. "No need to apologize. And I don't want to take up your time, but please, you must allow me to thank you for what you did. I am so, so grateful"

Then, as if she had carefully come up with something I couldn't possibly turn down, she said, "I am really good at hypnosis and hypnotherapy. People come to me from all over the country for smoking cessation, stopping unwanted behaviors, relaxation and things like that. Please, let me offer you a hypnosis session or two in exchange for what you did for me. It can be extremely useful, even just for grounding and relaxing."

It was an intriguing idea. I hesitated for a moment, but quickly realized that this was a timely gift sent by the Universe. I was in the process of preparing a major marketing presentation for a high-end fashion label to the management of Henri Bendel's Department Store in New York City. The presentation needed to be made to their buyer's team, consisting of a dozen hardened and icy professionals. If there was one thing I didn't like and was not good at, it was groups, or group presentations.

There was a concrete reason for that, and it was the same reason I shied away from groups of all kinds, especially large groups, my entire life. As anyone who has true extrasensory, psychic or intuitive abilities will tell you, the barrage of invisible information accosting you from every direction when in a group situation can be completely overwhelming.

If you're sensitive, and open, metaphysical information will overtake you like a flood from every angle to the point where it is almost terrifying. Avoidance was always the best policy for me, but it was also a giant hindrance.

"I wonder if a session with you could help me with a presentation I am making next week?" I asked Karen.

She jumped at the opening. "Absolutely, I can give you some hypnotic suggestions for complete calm, and whatever you think would work to help you remain relaxed and in control through your whole presentation."

As we hung up after making a date for the next day, I actually felt relieved. The thought came to me that this might be an opportunity to change something that had long been a thorn in my side professionally.

Having avoided her for days, now I couldn't wait to meet up in person.

5. *Apartment 333*

When I arrived at her apartment building after work the next day, I had the sense something life altering was about to occur. I broke into a cold sweat as the Doorman rang for Karen Brown on the house phone to announce my arrival.

It was hard to understand what was going on inside of me. I hadn't felt like this since telling my parents that I thought I was gay many years ago, right before being shipped off to Boarding School in the Swiss Alps. It was a strange combination of exhilaration and dread, and I knew the feeling was shouting at me to pay attention, telling me that something was about to change me in ways that would never allow me to turn back.

Part of me wanted to leave and forget I was ever there. The other part of me knew this was a fateful event, one of those things highlighted on the timeline that changed your trajectory forever and was planned by the Universe, and your Soul, before you were born.

"Apartment 333," the Doorman said, hanging up the phone and pointing to the elevators.

"333!", I acknowledged out loud, shaking my head in confirmation.

Then, as I walked to the elevators, I mumbled under my breath, "You must be kidding!"

The number had profound recurring symbolism for me. It was my parent's street address half my life. And for the past year, I would wake up at 3:33 AM every night, and glance at the digital clock read-out before falling back asleep. I remarked how odd it was when six months prior, the DMV had allocated a license plate for my newly purchased car that had 333 as the number sequence. Then, two months later, I opened a bank account and was randomly assigned an account number ending in 333.

Years later, 333 would appear and become the notice I received whenever my deceased father was present and wanted to communicate with me. Sadly, in a way, but also thankfully, our relationship after he died was far better than anything we had known in life.

It was only then that each of us could acknowledge his active participation, albeit through moments of terror, abandon and abuse, in creating the childhood environment that would not only bring out my rare clairvoyant and trance medium abilities, but also ultimately make them better. The irony has always been staggering.

Yet in truth, it was the terrified moments of a child who was captive and could not escape, that shaped the techniques I developed for getting out of the way, disappearing myself or leaving my body completely. Our participation occurred by agreement between both our Souls prior to birth, as so many similar Soul agreements are made with those people that seem difficult in life.

'There are reasons that reason can't explain,' I would often tell people seeking insight into their challenging or traumatic life relationships or upbringing.

Here was the 333-symbol resurfacing again, as confirmation to me that something important was happening. It was as if Jung himself, the master of subconscious symbolism, was sending a message.

I knocked on Karen's apartment door as I arrived in front of it, after walking slowly down the long corridor on the third floor. Karen opened the door and exclaimed in a somewhat shrill, high-pitched voice, "I'm so glad you could make it. Please, do come in."

Seeing her now, I disliked her, at least momentarily. I didn't want to not like her, but I couldn't help it. She reminded me so much of "Have you been to Club Seven?" the woman Lisa and I had found laughable so many years before. They could have been twins, albeit much older now, with dyed black hair and enough Botox to smooth out the worst face lines. Actually, more than her looks or personality, it was the overtly superficial over-tones that rang hollow as she plied me with one conversational platitude after another.

Karen gushed some more about how happy she was that I was there, and how pleased she was with what I had done for her. It was over-the-top, to the point where I was embarrassed. I knew she was grateful, but I just didn't like all the fuss. It sounded more like nervous rambling, as if, like me, she too felt something out of the ordinary was about to take place.

I wanted to turn around, say "Thanks, but no thanks", and leave. But something intangible stopped me and my feet stuck to the ground. Maybe I was jumping to conclusions, I thought.

After all, she is a highly successful, licensed Jungian Therapist that gets rave reviews from all of her clients. Those credentials couldn't be that easy to come by. She pointed me over to an overstuffed, comfortable easy chair by the window upholstered in a pastel flowery pattern, which seemed appropriate and well placed amidst the girly-apartment décor.

"Can I get you something to drink, or bring you anything to make you more comfortable before we start?" she asked.

Suddenly, she was speaking in a lower, melodic tone that was not at all shrill or animated. Her tone grew deeper and richer as I began to see a more genuine, professional side of her emerge and prepare to kick into gear.

"No, thanks," I responded, "I'm fine for now."

"So, we can begin then," she confirmed, dimming the room lights before sitting in a small office chair that she wheeled up to my left side.

"I use a combination of techniques in my hypnotherapy practice," she said.

Methodically, she continued to explain.

"I find that works best, because each person is different and one size never fits all. My experience has been that by incorporating various methodologies, including techniques from traditional Hypnosis, NLP and Ericksonian hypnotherapy, the results are more effective and provide better, longer lasting results."

I had no real experience with Hypnosis, and, like most people, I was convinced it wouldn't work on me. But what the Hell, it was a free session, and if it could help me maintain my train of thought at the upcoming presentation and keep me from faltering because of the dizzying array of invisible information flying towards me at lightning speed from the group assembled, then I was game.

Karen continued her thorough explanation of what was about to take place.

"You should be aware that you will be in full charge of what occurs," she said, "And your subconscious will not allow you to do anything you would not do while fully conscious, so if you have any trepidation about being put under or not being in control of your actions, that is not the case and that will not happen."

I had told Karen I simply wanted to feel calm, poised and remain focused at the group meeting coming up. I had not mentioned anything to her about the real reason I wanted this session, which was to curtail the endless distractions I had whenever a group was present due to my inner awareness and intuitive sensitivities. I also doubted Daniel had mentioned anything, considering the subject was pretty much taboo between us. I let her continue without saying anything else.

"Now," she said, continuing, "We talked on the phone about your objectives already, so I will begin by relaxing you so that we may access your subconscious mind. Once we achieve a state of relaxation where your subconscious mind is accessible, I will provide you with suggestions that will be seeded deep within you, that you can call upon whenever you are in this kind of situation."

Her voice had become melodic, evenly paced and relaxing. She was kind and thoughtful, and I was beginning to like her and feel at ease. Karen held an index finger in front of my eyes, and asked me to focus on it as she began moving the finger slowly from left to right, then back again as she spoke. I could feel my breathing change, matching the rhythm of her voice and the finger she was slowly waving in front of me.

"We're going to start by counting," she continued. "One… you're feeling very relaxed. This is a pleasant experience and you are beginning to breath deeply. Two…you are more relaxed, and looking inside of yourself, going down a set of stairs and feeling more and more relaxed with each step you take. Three…"

Something was happening. She was on my left, and I could hear her speaking, but my right shoulder was beginning to vibrate, at the junction of the shoulder and the neck. It was tingling, like a charge of electrical energy pocking at me and trying to push through a small opening in my neck, attempting to make its way into my body. Then the buzzing moved up to my right jaw, and into the center of my head, close to where the pituitary and pineal glands are located. It was warming and pleasant when it hit the center of my head, but it was becoming more and more vibrant and alive by the second.

"Four," she said, "With each step you take down, you feel calm and relaxed, more relaxed than ever before. You are letting go of any worries, fears or concerns…"

My shoulder, neck and the right side of my head were now ablaze with buzzing and quivering. I felt the indescribable sensation of being released, with the world swelling-up all around me. From my head, the warm vibration started moving slowly down into my body, reaching the throat and into my heart, then it moved further down into my root, and then to my legs.

It felt as if I was being released from my physical Being, and the sensation was now traveling up and down my spine. It was expansive and exhilarating, like nothing I had ever experienced before. I possessed a clarity and lucidity I didn't know was possible, and it felt as if the entire world was opening up in front of me for the first time.

Suddenly, I could hear someone speaking softly next to me, on my right side. It sounded like they were standing very close, whispering in my ear. I hadn't heard this kind of voice since I was a child, when I agreed to block it out to please my mother. Every new syllable made the hairs on my arms stand up and twitch.

"Please be quiet," I said rudely to Karen, to silence her and stop the counting.

She stopped abruptly.

"I can't make out what they're saying to me," I said apologetically.

The disembodied voice whispering in my right ear was getting louder now, and I was starting to make out distinct words.

"Someone is standing directly to my right, and speaking to me!" I said nervously to justify my rude behavior.

Karen was still, and went completely silent. Now, I could distinctly hear what the voice to my right was saying. It was as if the words were slowly being chiseled into my brain, and then traveling together with the vibrational sensations I was feeling up and down my spine. I couldn't tell if I was hearing it, or if I was feeling it, or both. The voice had become as real as anything else in the room.

"The time has come for us to work together," it said. "The woman you are with now helps people in the way she has demonstrated to you, but if you are willing, you will be able to help people in ways you have never imagined possible. It is by agreement with your Soul before the lifetime began that you chose to do this work with us, and the time has come for us to begin."

My memory is vague on what happened next. I could hear myself breathing heavily, sounding like I was almost gasping for air. The last thing I remembered was how, all of a sudden, the walls of the apartment building became a waterfall that I could look through. I could see through the walls from where I was sitting on the third floor of Karen's building, and through them I could see the entire Manhattan skyline laid out before me.

Then the walls of the buildings next to where I was looking out did the same thing as the building I was sitting in. Their walls disappeared and evaporated into a liquid stream of energy.

As I kept looking, all the buildings in lower Manhattan began to liquefy and look like a waterfall composed of electromagnetic energy or some kind of static that you could see right through. The shapes were all there, but they had transformed into a quiver of vibration and wave lengths that were ethereal and unreal. Finally, I could see the entire city and all the people in it at once, each a liquefied semi-solid energetic mass, laid out and moving through time right before me, in a kind of super-dimensional way that even now I have trouble fully expressing.

With that, I fell into a deep trance, and lost consciousness.

"I have it all on tape!" Karen said excitedly, as I gained consciousness again and came back to myself.

She was hovering over me and seemed to be shaking, but I couldn't quite tell if it was fear or extreme excitement. Fifty-five minutes had passed, and I had no recollection of it at all. To me, it was as if I had been out cold for only a minute or so, and all I could remember was the energetic liquification of everything around me as far as the eye could see before going under.

"I've got it all on tape!!" she exclaimed a second time, with even more inflection.

As we both regained our composure, Karen brought me a glass of water, and handed it to me before turning towards her chair.

"Drink some water, it will help ground you," she said.

As she sat down, she picked up the cassette recorder that was sitting on the small table between us, and said, exuberantly, "Everything should be here. I hit the record button as soon as you started speaking."

Karen pressed rewind on the recorder, and we both waited in silent anticipation as the tape spun madly, racing against itself to the starting point. When it clicked off automatically, she smiled at me triumphantly, and hit 'Play'.

I could hear myself breathing roguishly on the recording, as if I was in distress. But I knew I wasn't. Then suddenly, there was a voice. It boomed loudly, filling the room.

Karen reached for the volume control, but it didn't seem to lessen the impact of the strange, otherworldly intonation. Elongated words began to form in between the gasps, and as the cadence stabilized you could still hear the bellow that seemed to come from the deepest parts of my body.

I knew it was me, but it wasn't me at all. There was a tonality, a chord, an accent and a style of speaking that I had never heard myself utter, certainly not something that was natural to me. I wondered if this was some strange hoax, and if not, where could such a voice come from and what did all this mean.

I had never "channeled", and certainly, it was not something familiar to me. Was channeling even a real thing? Yes, I knew it existed. The 'Seth Speaks' book that Lisa had turned me onto so many years before was based on that. I remembered how Lisa and I had talked about the strangeness of that kind of experience at the time, and even questioned its authenticity.

I still had doubts years later, until one day by chance I met a woman who told me she was the attending nurse on the floor of the hospital in Elmira, New York, where Jane Roberts was taken by her husband when she was dying. After a short banter about the information in the Seth books, the woman told me that she was working the night Roberts lay there in an unconscious state on a morphine drip for pain.

Suddenly, Seth stepped in and "took over" her physical body, alarming nurses and doctors alike and sending them scurrying around without knowing what to do next. She said the hospital had to clear an entire wing of the hospital for 24 hours because of the booming and unsettling voice coming from this frail little woman.

But the oddest thing was that it was uncontrollable by medical standards. She appeared to be knocked-out, but kept getting louder and louder by the minute. Patients had to be evacuated to other floors because the voice, which was giving detailed, coherent personal messages about the doctors and nurses present, could be heard echoing up and down the hall despite the large doses of morphine she was receiving.

Channeling became real to me after that conversation. I had absolutely no doubt this woman was telling me the truth, based on how she seemed to still be affected by it, and spoke of it only in a hushed tone, as if she was telling me a mysterious secret.

But was it really happening to me now? This was a totally new experience, even considering my long history of dealing with metaphysical and extrasensory experiences by this point.

I didn't say a word, and neither did Karen, as we listened to the messages now beginning to ring out from that tape recorder. The entity speaking began with a salutation.

"We bring you much love and peace…"

It was paranormal in nature, and sounded as if aliens from some other planet had just landed and announced their arrival. But there was something real, comforting and sincere in it as well. I relaxed somewhat as we listened further, and the voice repeated in a slightly different way what had been whispered to me in my right ear before I left my body and went into full trance.

"During this critical time, when Ascension energies are proliferating on the Earth plane of reality," it continued, "We have come forward to begin the work that was agreed upon prior to this entity's incarnation in physical life. He is well known to us at the level of our Souls, and we have acted as Spirit Guide to him on many occasions. We have incarnated together with him in various other physical lifetimes lived on the Earth-plane of existence."

The information was coming at a faster pace now, as the voice modulated and became melodic and soothing.

"His gifts in this life were formulated within him from childhood and intended to culminate in the work that will now unfold. If he chooses, using his Free Will, now begins the time when we will work with him to perform what has been agreed upon by us prior to his current lifetime."

With that, they began a brief explanation of who they were.

"We are a group of seven entities from the mid-causal planes of reality in the Seventh Universal Dimension. As is the mission of Souls residing in the Seventh Universal Dimension, we offer higher guidance to lower Dimensions in many different ways. We assist Earth's Human Angelic Souls incarnated in your physical reality at critical junctions like the one to be experienced now on the dimensional timeline."

"The group that comprises our energetic expression exists on a plane of reality that is physically less dense than your own. We have no agenda and do not adhere to any specific dogma, philosophy or religions. We seek no following. It is our goal to bring Light and provide spiritual knowledge as to the true structure of the universe, as well as the purpose and mission of each Soul's life."

Karen nodded her head as if in agreement with what the voice was saying, as we kept listening to the tape.

"We will assist you by providing insight and prophetic visions of events emerging on the dimensional timeline, in an effort to bring higher consciousness into the world, and help heal wounds and conditions that lower your vibrational integrity and linger in your physical bodies and on the planet. We seek to assist you, the planet and the Dimension as a whole, to reach Universal Ascension, the process whereby all Souls and planetary Beings evolve to higher dimensional awareness."

Karen and I looked at each other in between sentences, wondering where this was going, shocked by the stream of information coming from the recorder. We had heard the term Ascension before, but had never heard it described as the evolutionary process of the Universe.

"You call such guidance "Angelic", or by the terminology "Spirit Guide". Although we do not have a formal name designation in our realm, since we are known to each other by our vibrational and energetic signatures, we invite you to refer to us by the name 'Samuel', as a matter of convenience. This name designation has symbolic significance for us, not only because of its ancient meaning -- Given in the Name of God -- but also by virtue of the fact that it recalls our efforts at other times on the dimensional timeline when we provided prophesy and guidance to Souls over the millennia on Third Dimensional Earth."

The voice went on to explain that monumental confluences of energy that began decades ago, will soon alter the vibrational structure and frequency of the planetary system and the galaxy. We were told that these energies will push the transcendence and evolution of the Dimension, as well as the Ascension of all Human Angelic Souls currently incarnating within it. The guidance being offered will help us understand the evolutionary patterns of our Souls and the Universe.

Samuel offered a cautionary tale as well, and informed us that assistance from higher dimensional fields is warranted because during such Galactic Ascension periods, Ascension is neither mandatory nor assured. Earth, and the planetary system it is part of, is a system of reality that is based on the use of Free Will by the Souls that inhabit it. Because of that, should the enlightened energy of higher consciousness be forcibly curtailed, or should it not crescendo and reach its peak during this period, the entire Dimension risks not achieving the vibrational resonance required for Universal Ascension to take place.

Yet, we were also reassured concerning this by the voice.

"Many others like us have come forward at this time," Samuel announced, "And we will work with you in an effort to assist those willing to raise their consciousness and vibrational quality, through the gift of universal wisdom and enlightenment. We will start our work to do so through the physical work of this entity beginning now, in order to communicate guidance and knowledge to all those who, through prior arrangement, have agreed to be spiritually awakened at this time."

There was so much information being offered at such a fast pace that it was almost impossible to absorb it all. Samuel went on to describe the Universe as being Multidimensional and magnetic and electrical in nature, consisting of what they termed "Twelve Universal Dimensions", each with "Twelve Dimensional Sublevels" nested like Russian Matryoshka Dolls, one within the other. Physical reality in each Universal Dimension formulates at the Sublevel of that particular Dimension down, so, as an example, Earth's physical reality is formed from the Third Dimensional Sublevel down to the first Sublevel of the Third Universal Dimension.

Higher Dimensional sublevels, also exists as part of the Universal Dimension, and these are sometimes referred to as Astral Planes. They are not physically visible to lower Sublevels of the

Dimension, and as a result, when a person passes out of physical existence, their energy is carried forward into the higher Astral Planes, until such time as it rejoins their Soul.

I was becoming uncomfortably aware that everything I thought I knew, which was far different from other spiritual or religious philosophies, was grossly inadequate and limited in its scope compared to the bulk of universal and spiritual information that was now coming from Samuel. I listened intently as the voice went on to describe certain percepts with regard to the life and purpose of what they termed "Human Angelic Souls".

Certainly, I had always known, perhaps better than most, that people chose the parents they did before being born. But now we were being informed that the Soul chooses the environment and the position on the timeline that it grows up in for specific reasons as well. Nothing is accidental, from the Soul's point of view.

Intentional personality features and parameters are formulated in childhood by parents, elders, siblings and the environment, and this becomes the basis for the energy emitted consciously and subconsciously throughout life. Almost all events in life are magnetically attracted to someone as a result of their conscious and subconscious energetic vibration.

Everything that transpires in life becomes an opportunity for consciousness growth built around one's life lesson, or life mission, and the experiential nature of dealing with one's life mission provides your Soul with growth as well. Becoming conscious of that lesson, or mission, is key to mastery of it. Samuel explained that it requires a certain level of maturity to accept that you energetically participate in creating the fabric of your life, electromagnetically attracting to yourself the physical reality that best matches your energetic and vibrational output.

The voice also stressed how a life mission is not a career, a calling or a profession, as we have come to believe, and it has nothing to do with the erroneous standards of merit established by society or culture. Instead, a life mission is a far subtler experiential exploration of Universal precepts and parameters in ways unique to each person and Soul. These experiences are intended to raise their consciousness and improve their Soul's vibrational quality.

Energy, the voice said, always seeks to create, but attracts similar-energy to itself to build upon. In this way, physical reality is composed of what you attract to yourself through your vibrational quality and frequency. That vibrational resonance is a factor of your thoughts, beliefs and conscious intentions, as well as the subconscious underpinnings of your life combined with the Soul's life lesson, which has been chosen prior to your lifetime. This law of reality creation is also applicable on a group basis to form a mass consciousness environment, and this serves as a backdrop on the dimensional timeline, against which each person's personal life mission unfolds.

Samuel went on to discuss a concept referred to as "Spin". Spin, or polarity in more simplified terms, generates scalar waves that magnetically pull reality into existence by "magnetizing" particles into matter and form, as they pass over the fields of dimensional physical existence.

Everything is energetic in nature, and even the physical body has scalar qualities, with two sides of the brain, as well as the two sides of the heart and circulatory system. Blood circulating through two polar hemispheres creates a scalar energy wave of sorts, and this is what generates each person's personal energy field.

The chakras in the body act as vortexes that push the energy along, feeding and communicating with organs and meridians related to that particular chakra. This is the Soul's life force energy, which animates the physical body. We are, as Samuel explained, spiritual Beings experiencing a physical reality through the use of an avatar known as the physical body.

Thoughts and speech are action, not idle dreaming, and imagination is a field of pre-potentiality. When energy fields are charged with conscious intention and the right vibrational quality, people and events are attracted into your life.

Then Samuel explained how your Soul's life mission is experienced through the lessons magnetized and created by you in the sphere of physical reality. The difference in the quality of your experience however, is whether or not you are operating through the negative polarity of your personality, better known as the Ego, or through the positive polarity of your Being, better known as your Essence, or Soul's true path.

This determines if your lessons, or the opportunities for consciousness growth that come to you in life, are achieved through positive experiences, or through negative ones. Obviously, when life is attracted through the negative polarity of experience, events manifested in your life will be more difficult and challenging.

In that regard, free will is more than just picking what hairstyle you'd like to have. It is the ability, through consciousness and growth, to attract life from the positive polarity. This ensures growth through positive experiences, versus attracting life events from the negative polarity, which is comprised of challenges that correspond to that vibrational input.

Yet, the Soul does not necessarily see "negative" or "challenging" as a bad thing, and it follows that a bad or challenging event in our eyes, is not necessarily an inferior way of learning one's life lesson. It is merely the flip side of the same lesson. In other words, from the Soul's perspective, one can learn lessons about "Love" in either polarity, positive or negative, but for us in physical reality, learning lessons of love through positive loving experiences is far superior to learning the same lessons of love through hateful, challenging ones.

Samuel explained that Free Will is truly a divine gift because it gives you the ability to channel your life lessons, better known as your Soul's mission, into the positive pole of experience. Understanding this, and raising your vibrational output through higher consciousness, can alter your life experiences accordingly, since it allows you to attract life situations and opportunities for growth that are learned through positive and minimally challenging adventures.

Samuel then turned attention to the work we would accomplish together in the future. They suggested that a time would come when several manuscripts would be dictated through me containing all manner of universal truths, explanations of universal structure, the nature of the Soul's path and future prophesies. These manuscripts would become published and widely known as the Essence Path materials.

We were also informed that although this information could be provided through the trance state I had just undergone, this would not be necessary in the future. In fact, they cautioned that despite the fact I had the ability to attune myself to their energy, pushing the higher vibrational frequencies of Seventh Dimensional Energy through my Third Dimensional physical body would be akin to constantly pushing a lightning bolt through a thin cooper filament.

Instead, we were told that my abilities were highly enough tuned from my experiences since childhood that they would be able to communicate with me directly through expanded clairvoyance, clairaudience and imagery they would provide. Once I was familiar with their tonality and methods of communicating with me, this would be the chosen method of communication to uncover the higher guidance they would impart.

After that, the voice on the tape suddenly ended our session, saying loudly once again, "We wish you much love and peace."

With that, they were gone. Karen pressed "Stop" on the recorder and sighed, as a new chill ran through me, traveling up and down my back.

6. Off to the Races

The ride home after my evening with Karen was hardly comforting. I was stunned and amazed at the same time, and had no idea where to turn. We were off to the races it seemed, but what races? And where were we racing off to?

I had to wonder if any of this was real. I wasn't a flake, didn't do drugs, didn't meditate or pray wildly every free moment, didn't follow Gurus or spend vacations visiting Ashrams. Yes, I had paranormal experiences since I was a child, and definitely had an interest in metaphysics. But that was all completely natural to me, and for the most part it took place outside of me, rather than internally.

None of this had ever interfered with life, especially once I understood it as a child, and I certainly didn't feel like I was having any kind of psychotic break. I didn't have imaginary flights of fancy, lapses, nightmares, headaches, depression, mania, OCD, ADHD, schizophrenia, brain disorders or other disturbances. Karen, a respected professional therapist by the sound of it, had seen and heard everything as well. Wouldn't she have said something?

The tape was proof that something extraordinary had taken place, but I had no memory at all of the time when I was unconscious. I left with a feeling that a portal had suddenly opened in my life, and I had been lifted-up and thrown into it. The whole thing was disconcerting, and something that had been submerged my entire life now flooded to the gates, screaming for release.

It was getting late, and as I looked out of the taxi window, I noticed that I was suddenly seeing colors emitted like a force field around people walking down the street. They were an array of colors, some intense and rich, some shallow and hardly visible. Some were cooler shades of blues and greens. Some were vibrant shades of red, yellow or orange.

Was I seeing the reflection of street lights, playing unnatural games with my vision? Or were the colors auras, surrounding and emanating 6 to 36 inches from around people's bodies like halos? I had never seen this before.

As we waited at a stop light, in the midst of all the colored glows emanating from the people next to him, I saw a middle-aged man walking slowly with only a somber grey, dusty light circulating around his head and neck. How could any of these glows be light refraction, since they weren't at all consistent from person to person standing next to each other?

"He's preparing to leave the body and experience physical death", a voice whispered inside me.

"Who is that?" I asked myself.

I wasn't talking to myself internally, it was distinctive and separate. Is this what Samuel meant by saying they would send me messages via clairaudience or other methods? I never had that happen before. These things were always outside of me, albeit unseen by anyone else.

There was a high degree of confidence in the message I was being given however, and these new utterances sounded like confirmations more than questioning. Of course, I didn't know if it was true or not, nor could I confirm the statement, but when they emerged in my head, it was as if this could be counted on as certainty. Somehow, looking out onto the street watching the pedestrians, I knew for a fact that the physical death of this man with the grey light shrouding his body was imminent.

Turning my attention away, I said out loud, solemnly, "Go in peace."

"Excuse-me?" the cab driver said looking in the rear-view mirror, as if I had asked him something.

"No, nothing," I answered.

Now my attention became fixed on the taxi driver. All of a sudden, a woman was sitting in the back seat of the cab with me. Not a flesh and blood woman, but the presence of a woman right next to me. She was small, but exceedingly bright and forceful, and she acted as if she knew she could reach me somehow.

I had had these experiences since childhood, but as an adult, I was able to turn them off and control them. Sometimes, they would be overpowering, like when I was with Anthony as a teen, but as an adult, I was always able to sense when a presence or spirit was nearby and I could control and tune it out without difficulty unless I wanted to investigate, which I hardly ever did.

Suddenly, I couldn't. Try as I did, the spirit of this woman was almost in my face screaming at me.

"Tell him I'm OK," she shouted at me.

"Tell him...tell him!!" she insisted. "I'm his wife, and he needs to know that I am OK. Tell him!" she shouted over and over again.

As the taxi pulled up to my apartment building, I took out a twenty to pay the fare. His wife continued shouting at me loudly, even belligerently.

I pushed the bill through the plastic shield, and said to him, "I'm really sorry to bother you, and I hope you won't think this is crazy, but I have a talent for seeing those that have passed away, and someone that says they are your wife is insisting I tell you that she is OK."

I expected the worst, and even thought he might curse me out, as cab drivers in New York can be known to do. Suddenly, he put the car in park and his entire body swung around as he opened the plastic security shield that separated the front and back seat. Tears were beginning to stream down his face and he turned bright red.

"How did you know," he mustered, with his voice cracking.

"My wife died last week, and we buried her two days ago. I have sat in this cab all evening praying for a sign that she is OK. God bless you...you're an angel...God bless you."

With that he pushed the twenty-dollar bill back into my hand, repeatedly thanking me, and telling me I had given him a gift he could never repay. The ride was on him.

I got out of the taxi relieved, happy that I had mustered the courage to tell him what his deceased wife had been shouting the last two-dozen city blocks in the back of that cab.

I didn't mention much to Daniel the next day, telling him only that my experience with Karen was fascinating, and I would definitely be contacting her for several more sessions. What I didn't tell him was that I intended to go back to see her again the next night, and as many as she was willing.

I did just that for weeks afterwards, and even though he was suspicious that something was up, I decided it was best left unsaid. He never asked.

For her part, Karen couldn't wait to continue working with me. She cleared all her evening sessions with clients, and would diligently record and then transcribe our meetings. The information coming from Samuel grew more and more extraordinary by the day, and it was like nothing either of us had ever heard or done before.

The emerging information included detailed descriptions of Universal structure and the Soul's journey through the Twelve Dimensions, using reincarnation, karma and Soul relationships to organize lifetimes on what appeared as spokes on a Wheel. They elaborated on the explanation that each lifetime had a purpose, or mission, and the growth achieved as a result of that lesson would eventually reunify with the Soul. This reunification would bring the Soul an increase in universal consciousness that would augment the Soul's vibrational resonance, and propel it through "Ascension" into higher dimensional fields of awareness.

The information shared how the Pineal gland serves as the Seat of the Soul in the physical body, and, together with DNA, acts as vibratory communication links between the Soul and the individual's physical body. This is achieved through the Earth's electromagnetic grid, which is in fact the planet's chakra system, so that messages and guidance coming from the Soul and higher dimensions are transmitted through this grid constantly, communicating cellular instructions and messages to each individual from their Soul.

 It was explained to us that Black Holes are the energetic recycling bins of the universe, where spent energy that creates reality is magnetically drawn in after it has washed over the fields of dimensional reality, and then recycled to other Dimensions. We were also told how interdimensional portals exists, and are accessed by various extraterrestrial races, and how the timeline of a Dimension is dynamic and always changing.

The knowledge Samuel was imparting was as unique as it was surprising and informative. It was exciting, it was exhausting and it was overwhelming. But it was also awe inspiring, remarkable and exhilarating. Each day we walked away stronger, clearer, more enlightened and more highly attuned than ever before, to ourselves and to the Universe.

Within a day or two, I no longer went into full trance, as so many mediums or channels do. I found that if I tuned in and listened for the particular thoughts and voice of Samuel, words that were not from me filled my head together with thought forms and images that complemented and animated the words, adding innate meaning and, more importantly, visible and tangible understanding. Often two or more concepts would be running simultaneously in my mind, and I could grasp several concepts at once in a multidimensional way.

At times, the information came at us so fast, Karen had difficulty keeping up with her notes, but her grasp of esoteric symbols and concepts, which had facilitated her understanding of Jung in the past, helped her to be open to the new materials being presented by Samuel. Whenever she stopped us, I would explain the concepts to her using an explanation of the visual images and symbols that Samuel had flashed in my head simultaneous with the words.

No matter how complex or esoteric the information was, she did not complain or argue with it, and we would work well into the evenings like this, transcribing messages from Samuel and discussing application of the theories in day-to-day life. For concepts we didn't quite absorb, we would go back and she would formulate questions to be answered for clarification and understanding by Samuel.

We worked like this for hours at a time. There were days when we would put in a full day of work, then meet at six or seven and be up till well after midnight, on a "school night", talking excitedly about the multidimensional concepts of the Universe and the Soul, the ability to find one's Essence Path and the facets of reincarnation, all of which was being imparted to us.

On one particular evening when I walked in, Karen looked frustrated and exhausted. She said that just before I arrived, she had had an extremely rough session with a woman she had been working with. She was discouraged with the results and the woman was back-sliding, and Karen felt that she had hit a major road block and was unsure if she could assist her client any further.

I empathized, knowing Karen's dedication after seeing the efforts we were making with the Samuel Materials. I was also beginning to realize the deep concern she had for her clients, now that I had gotten to know her better. I wondered out loud if there was a way I could help her.

Both of us looked at each other as if we had just had an "Aha" moment. The same thought popped into our heads at the exact same time, and I wondered if the thought was organic, or planted in our minds for some higher, unknown purpose.

"What would happen?" we both wondered out loud, "If we asked for some insight from Samuel on this situation, as seen from a higher, Soul perspective."

Karen was reluctant at first, carefully considering issues of patient confidentiality. But desperate for answers that would help her help her client, she reasoned that only using a first name and no other identifying information would allow her to proceed as if this was merely a discussion of a case study among colleagues. Surely that couldn't be considered a real violation of any trust or privilege. After all, I had no idea or knowledge of who this person was.

After a short discussion, we decided that we would break from our usual evening process, and see if Samuel was able to shed light on Karen's difficult case. Perhaps there was an answer to the problems that wasn't readily apparent until the whole thing could be looked at from the Soul's perspective. It was worth a shot.

As soon as I tuned in that evening, we discovered there was no need to even ask. Samuel was ready to assist with a full overview, based only on a first name and nothing more, of Karen's client and her issues seen from a higher spiritual perspective.

It was as if Samuel had not only been eavesdropping on us for the past half-hour, it seemed they knew precisely what was going to occur and even had full knowledge of the person in question. It also felt like they were anxious to provide a real-life example of how the information we had been talking about hypothetically for weeks now was relevant, demonstrating in real terms methodology for viewing issues in a spiritual and multidimensional way.

Karen had explained to me earlier that her client, Rachel, who was in her mid 30's, suffered from severe depression caused by an obsessive-compulsive disorder that expressed itself through the incessant acquisition of things that she seemed to drag home almost unconsciously. What was even more concerning however, was the fact that all of this was accompanied by a condition of extreme hoarding and the inability to throw or give anything away. The severity of all this had reached a point of no return.

Rachel was on the verge of being evicted by her Landlord for safety concerns and as a nuisance, since the young woman's apartment was by now a maze of very tiny paths leading from the front door to the bed, to the toilet and back. Items she could not part with, many of which were picked up out of garbage cans on the street over the course of years, were literally piled from floor to ceiling, lining either side of the miniscule paths that led through her apartment.

Karen had worked with Rachel through hypnosis and regular psychotherapy for some time now, but with only minor and temporary success. The two had reached an impasse, and Karen was out of answers. She was considering referring Rachel to a psychiatrist for pharmaceutical intervention, which Rachel adamantly opposed, or perhaps even institutionalization.

Samuel began the session with their usual greeting, "We bring you much love and peace," then went straight into answering the question at hand, without being asked.

"The entity under discussion has become lost in the negative polarity of their personality features and their life mission. The condition is deep seated, and stems from a childhood trauma and post-trauma formulated belief system, originally planned by the Soul and all parties involved to assist the entity later in life to successfully achieve their life mission. But the event has negatively impacted them to this day, causing their life lesson's expression to be experienced solely through the negative pole, which has led to the severe challenges you witness. We shall detail this now further for your complete understanding..."

Samuel explained that as a girl of 8, Rachel's father had suddenly and unexpectedly died in a car accident. He left that morning to go to work, and never returned home. Grief stricken, her mother thought the best way to comfort the child was to ignore and even deny the reality of what had happened as much as possible. Rachel was kept in the dark, not permitted to go to the funeral and was never told the truth about events that had happened. In her mind, her father had simply vanished forever, without any explanation. Not able to fully understand or grieve for the traumatic death of her father, his disappearance was lodged in Rachel's subconscious as the loss of something that could never be returned.

Samuel continued with an explanation of Rachel's determining life mission and personality features chosen for this lifetime, and the events that occurred had been agreed upon by the Souls of Rachel, her father and her mother, prior to Rachel's birth. In effect, the father's sudden departure in death, and the mother's denial were both meant to create the conditions that would assist Rachel to complete her Soul's life mission as an adult.

Samuel continued. Rachel's mission in this lifetime was to learn how to be "discriminating" with respect to what is of benefit to her in life and what is not. When her mission is experienced through the positive polarity, she is easily able to always determine what she needs in life to function successfully. By being discriminating, she is able to set aside and discard anything that holds her back.

When however, she experiences her life mission from the negative polarity, she is unable to decide what she wants in her life from what she does not. She becomes stuck with the challenge of not being able to be discriminating. As she is no longer able to decide what she wants in life from what she does not, things begin to pile-up around her, until she becomes, quite literally in this case, buried under excess caused by her inability to pick and choose.

Samuel gave a side note here, just in case we were interested in the reason Rachel's Soul picked this particular life mission in the first place. As it turns out, the life lesson was intended as a counter balance to a reincarnation connected to her, where she was a wealthy landowner in England in the mid 1700's who was also a notorious glutton and sadist.

In that lifetime, her reincarnated-self publicly professed to follow the newly resurrected philosophies of the Greek sage, Epicurus, whose philosophies were interpreted at that time to mean that happiness in life can only be achieved through the pursuit of pleasure. The more exuberant and excessive, the happier one would be. That lifetime indulged accordingly, and his excesses were also the cause of his death in that life at a young age. Interestingly enough, Epicureans also discounted and denied the importance of death by shunning the act of mourning or any remembrance of a life when it was lost.

So far, so good. We were following, and it all made sense. But here, Samuel's explanation of Rachel's issues from her Soul's perspective took a turn.

In conjunction with her life mission, and in order to make the lessons more exacting, since there is a karmic component to it, Rachel's Soul also chose a specific personality feature for this lifetime. Her Soul chose for her to learn lessons around the fear of not having what she needs to make life work for her. Samuel described this as lessons around "holding on".

In the positive pole of this personality trait, she is able to find contentment, feel satisfied and have the sense that she would always have enough of whatever she needs to make life successful. But experienced through the negative polarity, this feature means that she holds onto things desperately, haunted by the fear that she will not have enough of what she needs to make life a success. As she holds onto things, including feelings, they accumulate around her until she is literally buried by them. Her hoarding was a direct reflection of this feature in the extreme negative pole.

Samuel reiterated that Rachel's condition was complicated by the fact that she was locked in the combined negative polarity of both her personality feature and her life mission. Essentially, the sudden death and disappearance of her father at an early age without closure, had pushed her into the negative pole of her personality feature, so that she held on tightly to things, fearing that they would not be there if she let go and everything would leave her, much as her father did without explanation.

The negative polarity of that feature then, was creating a vibrational frequency sent into the world that made her unable to be "discriminating" or distinguish what she wanted to have in her life from what she did not need, which would pile up around her and hold her back, literally. Thus, she was somehow captive of a negative vibrational frequency loop, if you will, where she was holding onto everything she could find in an effort to negate the fear that she would not have enough of what she needed, thereby creating the impossibility to decipher what she needed from what she did not.

In other words, she was experiencing her life lesson in the extreme negative polarity, inspired by the fear of not having enough, which caused her not to be able to discern what she actually needed in life to be happy. The current situation was the accumulation from years of being in this loop.

Naturally, the greatest part of this originated with the death and then denial of the departure of her father, which had never been rectified or dealt with consciously, but decisively helped form the parameters of her personality feature and life lesson. The subconscious fear that event generated in her caused her to emit a vibrational pattern that attracted physical reality in a way that ultimately became her great challenge. From her Soul's perspective, she was certainly learning her life lesson, but she was learning it in a negative way that was difficult and not compatible with the standards of modern life, which is never the Soul's concern.

Karen had no knowledge of the death of Rachel's father, and even under hypnosis, Rachel did not mention it to the point she thought Rachel had been abandoned as a baby, if a father had been present at all. Samuel went on to make several suggestions as to how Karen could assist Rachel to break this negative polarity loop that she had spiraled into, including specific hypnotic suggestions as well as how to use certain Jungian symbols that held relevance for her subconscious. He added to this a few other means to help break the chain of fear by calming the Ego, which guarded this information so thoroughly that even in trance, it was barely accessible unless you knew exactly where to look, which Karen had not.

Samuel's suggestions were intended to transform Rachel's conscious and subconscious vibrational energy patterns, pushing them into a positive vibrational frequency. In this way, the thought and energy patterns she was sending out to the Universe would help her attract life from the positive, rather than the far more challenging negative, pole.

After mentioning these things however, Samuel offered one additional suggestion that they said would definitively open Rachel's subconscious so that she was ready to work successfully with Karen. They reiterated that an upcoming event would serve as a major turning point to help break Rachel's energy cycle, while also blocking, once and for all, the obsessive-compulsive captivity she had experienced until then.

"In the rear of the closet of the entity's family home," Samuel said, "There is a small package, forgotten since the death of the entity's father. We suggest you tell the entity of this package, and ask that she go to the mother's house, and look on the shelf in the back of the bedroom closet, under the many other items that have hidden this package for so many years."

Samuel confirmed, in definite and concrete terms, "It is here that this entity will begin her journey towards release and healing."

Karen and I looked at each other.

"What is that about?" I asked in a 'this-is-hard-to-believe' way.

She looked at me and smiled.

"I don't know what it means either," she responded, "But it's pretty specific information, so I think I should find a way to suggest it to Rachel."

With that we ended our evening, amazed once again at the information we had received.

Early the next afternoon, Karen called me at the office. She sounded shocked, as if in disbelief.

She said she had called Rachel that morning, and told her that a psychic whom she felt was legitimate, had mentioned Rachel by name and told Karen to tell her that there was a package for her at the rear of her mother's closet that had been long forgotten. She told Rachel it could just be a mistake, but the psychic told her she should look for it, so she casually recommended that Rachel do so the next time she was visiting her mother's house across the bridge from Manhattan, in Queens.

A few hours later, Karen said that Rachel called from her mother's house sobbing almost inconsolably. Rachel said that after she spoke with Karen, she couldn't wait to go to her mother's house, and felt like something was tugging at her heart after getting Karen's call.

She raced to the house she grew up in, carried a step ladder upstairs to her mother's bedroom, and began rummaging through the old shoe boxes and items on the upper shelf at the back of the closet. Under one of the old shoeboxes, she found a small, flat, dusty gift-wrapped package that was addressed to her in her father's handwriting.

She opened it and found several beautiful ribbons, similar to the ones she used to wear in her hair as a little girl. There was a small plain white card lying on top of the ribbons inside the box. Rachel read the card.

"My dearest Rachel. Wear these ribbons and think of me. That way I can be near you even when we're not together. Love, Daddy."

He had wrapped the gift before leaving the house that day, and hidden it in the closet, intending to give it to Rachel when he returned home that evening. His plan was interrupted when he died unexpectedly later that morning. A few months afterwards, when her mother came across the gift, she pushed it as far back in the closet as possible and forgot about it completely, as part of the effort to erase their painful tragedy.

Rachel had never received it.

7. Land Mine

Almost immediately afterwards, Karen asked if I could assist her to look into some of the difficult challenges she had with other clients. I could see no real objection, and for me it was the revelation that this was even possible that was amazing. We proceeded as we had for Rachel, working nights, often with remarkable insights and success.

A few weeks later, Karen attended a Conference for Jungian Therapists in Princeton, New Jersey. She was excited about what she was uncovering in our work, and, without any real disclosure, began telling her colleagues at the Conference about the extraordinary information that was coming through, as well as the fast routes to addressing healing that seemed to be taking place in these clients. She detailed Rachel and a few other stories, and had written up some case studies based on our work, presenting them unofficially at the conference to get feedback and see if perhaps there was any interest in what she was doing.

The examples circulated in her professional community like wildfire. By the end of the Conference, Karen had become to most sought-after Therapists attending, and as soon as she returned home, she began getting calls. Jungian and other Therapists from all over the country, and a few from Europe, wanted to know if they could offer their assistance in this work, or if they could speak with me as well about their more challenging clients in order to provide her with additional material and case studies for publication.

I was uneasy at first. As a serious corporate executive, I had re-mained completely closeted about the whole thing at my day job. My personal relationship with Daniel didn't help matters either. I finally agreed to Karen's request, and now I was speak-ing daily with Therapists, who called me by appointment, all evening long from around the country and the world.

On the phone, they would provide the first name only of their client, and I would relate to them what I was told concerning their client's life mission, personality features and related pa-rameters, as well as what had caused any blockages or impasses and what they could expect coming up on the timeline for this person. The feedback, coming back through Karen, was as in-credible as it was personally fulfilling.

The volume of calls now coming from Therapists, Metaphysi-cians, Religious Leaders, Social Workers and even Gurus, all through word of mouth, increased exponentially and was be-coming overwhelming. I offered my participation in all this completely gratis.

In retrospect, I realized I was honing these skills throughout this period, but at the time I was quickly becoming exhausted, work-ing all day in a busy corporate environment and then spending half the night exploring the metaphysical world, and the life of the Soul, with Therapists from all over the place.

I was definitely changing as well, and I could feel my energy shifting with every day. I became completely apathetic and un-interested in anything other than the spiritual work I was doing evenings, sometimes until well after midnight. As that contin-ued, so did my opening, sensitivity and accuracy. It was easier than ever to tune into someone or see things. At the same time, by switching back and forth day and night, I was gaining complete control over turning it on and off, so it was not an out-of-control distraction.

Yet, the more I became obsessed with what I considered a new direction, highlighted by new intuitive gifts, the more my old life was becoming obsolete. I made the effort and continued working in the same environment, where I was still earning a lucrative living, without letting on to what was really happening, but clearly, my serious corporate life was suffering. I had not yet reached the point where I was actively providing my genre of Briefings to clients, so I was still somewhat stifled and only using my intuitive abilities secretly, to identify where to go and what to do next as far as it concerned the division under my direction.

But things were changing dramatically there as well. First of all, I noticed right away that I was now having trouble keeping things to myself and not expressing what I knew to be true, even without having any concrete "real" evidence. In fact, this has always been a major stumbling block for me, personally, since even though I know the information to be true, it cannot be truly substantiated until it takes place.

People will inevitably ask for "real" and concrete proof of what you see, which it is not possible to provide. This had also been imprinted on me like a tattoo, and beginning in childhood my mother would warn me never to make things up or say things that couldn't be proven using concrete reality, for fear of my father's wrath. I struggled, going back and forth between denial and confirmation of the esoteric insights I received. It was my own personal Cassandra experience, being exorcised from within me.

It was quickly getting to the point where I was having trouble not speaking what I knew to be true, even if I didn't have concrete evidence or any proof backed-up by reality. The fact remained that the information I received in an intuitive manner did not come from any statistical analysis.

My information came from the ether, in a manner of speaking. In meeting after meeting, after a corporate executive or two would extoll all the reasons they felt a certain strategy or plan of action should be adopted by the company, I would verbally object now, saying, "It won't turn out the way you expect."

But when asked to explain why I was saying that, I could only muster, "Because it won't". That response alone was always enough to make my insight discountable.

What reasoning or explanation could I give them? Could I say in a meeting of several serious corporate officers that I saw it in a dream or had some extrasensory vision? They would have laughed me out the door. There was no way I was ready to provide how or where I was getting my insights, but the inability to push these truths back inside me was quickly becoming impossible.

Things took a rather substantial turn when the President and Board of Directors announced to a small group of Executives that they were signing an Agreement for the acquisition of a large conglomerate that manufactured some of the most historic and famous brands in America. I felt a wave wash over me.

That evening, I took a closer look at the information around such an acquisition. Since companies and groups, including countries, cultures and all manner of other organizations have life missions and specific trait parameters formed around them, much as we had discovered people do, I was privy to the life mission of both the company acquiring this conglomerate and the company being acquired.

It was a disastrous match, and I saw all manner of incompatibilities, challenges and negative future conflicts. In fact, on the timeline, I could see a decade into the future that it would cause the ultimate demise and closure of our company acquiring the conglomerate, the eventual break-up and sale of all the company's acquired and stable brands, the closure of factories and laying-off of thousands of people and, surprisingly, the legal prosecution and eventual jailing of the Chairman of the Board for Insider Trading.

The future of this event, when remote-viewed on the timeline, was a complete mess. Now, here I was, a member of the Executive Marketing Team in charge of the company's In-House agency, knowing where this was all going, but completely unable to speak the truth. If ever there was a Cassandra experience, this was it.

To make matters worse, as Head of "Communications", a real irony considering the recent exploration of my mediumship talents, I was the one expected to serve as gatekeeper for public communications concerning the acquisition. How was I going to do that?

I tried anyway, but it wasn't long before disaster struck in the form of all things, a "Land Mine". Once the news about the acquisition was out, I received a call from a Journalist at the Atlanta Journal-Constitution, since a good many of the company's factories being acquired, which employed upwards of 10,000 people, were located in that paper's readership.

The reporter was polite enough, but efficacious and noncommittal, as most good journalists tend to be. After a long chat, concerning the details of the acquisition, she asked a simple and straightforward question to sum-up our conversation.

"How does management feel about the acquisition of some of America's finest old brands and manufacturing operations," she said, almost as if she was throwing a softball question, pleased with the information I had shared thus far.

"They feel it's going to be a *real Land Mine*," I said forcefully and confidently, without realizing what I had just uttered.

"A *Land Mine*!!!???" she questioned surprised, feeling like she had stumbled onto something.

"Is that a Freudian slip, or do you know something you're not saying?"

"Oh, I'm so sorry," I stammered back, "I meant to say *Gold Mine*."

It was too late. What I knew from remote viewing the timeline had slipped out, and she wasn't about to let it go. Suddenly, her line of questioning turned, and I found myself playing defense and forced to invent falsehoods about what a great future the company and these brands had, even though I knew quite the opposite was going to be true.

After that, I could clearly see the writing on the wall with respect to continuing in my current high-paying corporate executive persona. When the article came out, it was mixed and sounded suspect, as if the acquiring company was planning on closing down the factories and spinning off the brands.

The article was based primarily on the negative sentiments of the executives and personnel of the company being acquired, which I already knew from having looked at the situation on the timeline remotely. I also knew that I was the one that had planted that seed in her thought process.

The article was circulated widely inter office, especially the part that read, "Executives on both sides of the acquisition have expressed a mixed reaction to it, with one stating '…It could be a Gold Mine, a Land Mine or both'."

It wasn't an accurate quote by any means, but it served the article's purpose and the damage was done. The reporter ended her story by determining that this was anything but an ideal situation for either company. In a way, she had intuitively uncovered the truth as well.

Despite that, the acquisition was finalized. Even so, I had already made my decision to start to look for positions elsewhere. I couldn't continue to extoll the benefits of this knowing where it was headed, and I was being undermined now by my inner knowledge as well as my subconscious.

In any case, in ten years or less, I knew the company would only be a remnant of itself, which turned out to happen almost exactly as I had seen. That included the Insider Trading allegations and jail time for the Chairman of the Board. I started to put out feelers.

A few weeks later, as I had also seen, a new President was brought in to consolidate the acquisition. Since he had his own team of Executives he liked to work with, a group of twelve of us were brought into the Conference Room and simultaneously terminated.

Luckily, seeing where this was all going, just prior to the acquisition I had negotiated a new employment agreement with a severance package that provided me a year's salary in the event I was laid off without cause. I had quietly pushed others in the team to do the same, so the blow was not as significant for some of us as it might have been had we not done so.

This entire time, I was still working with Karen and the many Therapists calling me nightly. Now, even though I was somewhat actively involved in a corporate job search, I could do the metaphysical work we were doing days as well.

But the fact that I was overly "friendly" with Karen, seeing her almost every day and evening, didn't sit well at home with Daniel. I finally had to confess to him about the extracurricular activities Karen and I were doing. He detested the fact, and it would later become a major bone of contention.

"That stuff, again!?" was his response.

Since I had always been the primary breadwinner in the household, which allowed him to feel as if he could dabble in his work even when he was becoming successful, he felt threatened. He told me he wouldn't be happy until I found a new corporate position and forgot all about doing "that stuff", as he called it. I reluctantly went along and agreed that that was probably the best thing for the both of us.

But to be honest, had I felt any opening I would have told him I had other things in mind. Anyway, something else soon came up.

I received a phone call one evening from my father. He had heard what was happening, and wanted to know if I could help him with something he was working on. As the years went by, since my return from school many years before, we had developed a fairly stable, if somewhat occasionally tense, relationship. I was no longer the child that had taught himself to disappear while being abused, and now both of us could deal cordially with each other, at least most of the time.

Hearing I was free after leaving my position, he asked if I would go to Paris with him for a week to investigate a hotel he was planning to buy with a group of his investor friends. It sounded more like a quick vacation than work, and I thought to myself that this was just what I needed to get a fresh perspective. He was excited about the project and even offered to pay me for my time, which was flattering and generous on his part.

That evening, I took a remote view of his hotel deal, just for my own edification. It was another disaster waiting to happen, with long-term karmic implications for him and his friends.

Unfortunately, I saw that they would all lose time and substantial amounts of money on the investment. I tried to soft-talk him out of it the following day, but he was adamant that it was the best deal they had ever been invited into. Once he fixated on something, that was that, so I decided I might as well make the best of it and take the week being offered, with pay, in Paris.

A few days later, the two of us were on our way to Paris flying Business Class on Air France from JFK. Somehow without realizing it, when we checked in for the flight our seat assignments had gotten screwed up.

We boarded the plane and I was seated 4 rows in front of my father. We were both used to overseas flights, and in the scheme of things a red eye trip over the pond was not that long, especially compared to trips to the Middle East or Asia. Rather than argue with the attendants or cause a fuss, and because we both planned to be asleep for most of the flight, we just went with it and agreed to the seats we had received at check-in.

As I sat down, there was a man already seated at the window in my row. He looked to be in his mid to late-forties, was handsome, tan and stylishly well dressed, in an LA kind of way. His sharp, angular features, with dark hair and eyes that gave an intense stare, got your attention and made you feel like this was someone exceedingly interesting. He was reading a book and had glasses on, but he took them off whenever he would look up.

We said Hello briefly as I installed myself, after dealing with my briefcase in the overhead bin. Within minutes, the stewardess came by with her checklist, confirmed my name, and then asked if I wanted anything before taking off. I responded No.

Then she turned to the man seated next to me and, as if she had seen him many times before said, "Welcome back, Mr. Steller. Can I get you something to drink before we leave?"

The name was familiar, but it didn't really register. From the greeting given to him by the Stewardess, I supposed he might be a celebrity of some kind, especially since his striking features and soft-spoken, polite manner certainly had all the qualities of one.

"Sounds like you take this flight often," I said, trying to make small talk.

"I do," he said.

"Levi Steller," he continued, reaching out his hand.

I introduced myself.

"I know who you are," he said, responding with a smile.

"You do?" I questioned, "How is that?"

"The stewardess just said your name, of course. How did you think I knew?"

It seemed a rhetorical question, but somehow, I had the impression something strange was happening. He had a commanding way about him, and his voice had a rhythm and tone that pulled you into it. Was he kidding around, or did he actually know me?

"Really," he said with a laugh, "She just said your name. Glad to meet you."

We shook hands, and then he added the strangest comment.

"There aren't that many of us in the world you know, and I'm being told that this is not just a chance meeting on a plane."

"Told..." I said, more as a confirmation that I was hearing him correctly.

"Told..." he confirmed.

No one understood the concept of "told", which he was somehow indirectly talking to me about now, more than I did. When I received guidance, it was always as if I was being "told". I sometimes even referred to it this way in discussions with Karen or others who were privy to our work. I never imagined that someone else could have, or would understand, that same experience.

"I have been this way from birth," he continued, "But it wasn't until my awakening when I was hiking in the Sinai that my true calling began, and I became aware I was being "told" things others didn't know. I'm sure it was similar for you."

He proceeded to tell me details of his life, and especially his awakening as a young adult hiking on Mount Sinai. He called it his Moses experience, and the story was fascinating. It included a burning bush, darkening skies and the appearance of a giant UFO over the mountain where he was hiking alone.

He was "told" then that if he chose, he could use his extraordinary psychic and psychokinetic powers for the benefit of mankind, in ways that would be talked about the world over. I was enthralled. There were similarities, but also many differences, and his story rolled off his tongue for hours into the flight.

I shared my experiences as well, albeit in a more subdued manner. My true metaphysical journey was just beginning, and I was still reluctant to completely own who I was.

I told him pieces of the story with Karen and how I was now being contacted by Therapists from all over to help decipher their most challenging clients. I also told him stories about my experiences viewing future events as well as seeing spirits and feeling presences, which I had had since childhood.

But I was reluctant to share everything. I didn't know who he was really, or if I could trust him completely. Besides that, my father was sitting a few rows behind me, and even as an adult, I guess I still suffered from the childhood mandate my mother had always given me not to say anything about the strange things I experienced when he was around.

Once we were done sharing our stories, we embarked on our views of Universal structure and world events, according to our higher guidance. He seemed fascinated by my experiences viewing the timeline, but was most preoccupied with the viewpoint he expressed concerning extraterrestrial influences, which he said were now occurring on Earth.

He mentioned something about a "Black Box", extraterrestrial technology found somewhere in the Middle East that was now in the hands of Western Intelligence Agencies and could be used to look at the future. He also said that, like a cosmic key, it opened Dimensional Portals that existed there, allowing inter-dimensional travel to be possible. None of it was something I knew anything about at the time.

This would change for me later on, after I discovered for myself the connections he described, as well as when I became aware of formal agreements made between various world governments and certain extraterrestrial groups. For now, however, he simply introduced the existence of that topic, and I could only trust he was imparting it based on hidden or secret knowledge he had experience with.

We continued to talk most of the flight, before nodding off for an hour or two. When the lights came back on and we were preparing to land, he took out a small brass medallion with a Menorah on it.

"Have **they** contacted you yet?" he asked matter-of-factly, "I have no doubt they will."

Then somewhat sullenly he added, as if talking to himself,

"Most people have no idea what I really do. The world thinks I do party tricks for a living, but that's just the celebrity cover they invented for me in New York and LA."

Then coming back to himself, he handed me the medallion and said, "Keep this close to you to remember our conversation. It's for good luck in the future."

I thanked him, and was grateful, but at the same time I felt a cold chill go through me. All I could think about was why this meeting had occurred, who exactly "*they*" were, and why he had no doubt "*they*" would be contacting me. I was vaguely familiar with his celebrity status, now that we had spoken about his appearances on television, but I wondered what it all meant?

My tongue froze in my mouth, and we were landing now, so announcements were being made and it was difficult to talk. After we landed, as soon as the seat belt sign went off and everyone stood, I felt the need to use the restroom, so I walked a few rows up to quickly use the toilet.

When I returned to my seat moments later to collect my things and say Goodbye, he was gone. I could see my father standing at his seat waiting for me four rows back, and we disembarked together after almost everyone else had already deplaned.

"How was the flight for you," my father asked.

"Good," I said. Then I added, "I was sitting next to Levi Steller. Have you ever heard of him?"

"I think I have," my father answered hesitatingly. Then, with a bit of non-believer disdain, he added, "Isn't he a psychic, or magician or something like that. I think I may have seen him on Johnny Carson a few years back."

I was still mesmerized by our night-long discussion, but bewildered by Steller's reference to "*they*" at the end of our conversation. I had an inner sense of what he meant, but wasn't sure until later on when "*they*" did actually contact me. My sense about him was never fully confirmed, except that I heard years later about a whistleblower who claimed to have worked with Steller as part of a special Psychic Intelligence Program for the US Army.

To this day, tucked away in my wallet, I still carry the small medallion he gave me on that extraordinary flight from New York to Paris.

8. Café Les Deux Magots

That trip to Paris, among dozens from the past, turned out to be one of the most fateful I ever had. I realized afterwards it was another one of those unintended gifts from my father.

Despite his difficult personality traits and all my childhood experiences, his Paris invitation was as important and intentional as something can get, if you looked at it from a Soul-level perspective. This was another one of those things meant to happen at some point in life that was probably planned by our Souls prior to birth, and meant to assist me in exploring and using my emerging intuitive and psychic abilities.

If the Levi Steller encounter wasn't enough, the same trip brought me a second fateful event as well. The deal my father was working on wasn't going well, as I expected, and there was little I could do to help, so I called an old friend who I knew was living in Paris with her husband at the time. We decided to meet at Café Les Deux Magots in Saint Germain des Pres for coffee like we used to as University students, to catch up.

Brigette was half American, half German, raised in New York City until her family moved to Long Beach, California. Like my friend Lisa, who had returned by then to the States, she was an exchange student, and although we met just as I was about to graduate and leave to return to the States, we became fast friends.

She had a similar temperament to Lisa, so I felt comfortable telling her about my own intuitive and metaphysical experiences from the very beginning. I wasn't shy about sharing my new experiences with her now. Even though she never quite understood these things the way Lisa did, metaphysics fascinated her. Brigette was all about potential and future benefit. At times, I felt like her real interest was not so much me personally, as how my hidden talents could be used as a potential ticket to success.

After she finished University in Paris, Brigette got a job in LA and then met and married a quiet, talented man whose parents were first generation Chinese. He was a young award-winning architect, and the two moved back to Paris when her husband took a job with an older cousin, who's globally known design firm had offices in New York, Paris, and Hong Kong. That firm specialized in upscale restaurant designs, interior decoration and outfitting, and it was very successful in Europe and particularly Asia.

Leo, her husband, now ran the Paris design studio, where they lived, but the two traveled frequently back and forth between New York, LA, Paris and Hong Kong. We were in touch and saw each other occasionally, but I hadn't seen her for a few years.

At the Deux Magots, Brigette brought me up to date on her life, and I did the same. I was honest with her, since she already knew about me, and I told her about leaving my corporate position as well as the new energetic shift that was happening as a result of my experiences with Karen. She marveled at the stories, as well as the Levi Steller encounter, whom she recognized right away, since, as she informed me, he had a large following in LA and Paris.

As we talked, I could hear myself debating with her what I should do next. I had plenty of global marketing experience, and enjoyed that work since I was good at it, but now something else had emerged that was far more fulfilling, but much less profitable. I was frank, and told her I could never consider only doing that as any kind of career.

"We're getting older," I heard myself say out loud.

I shook my head to brush the notion away, and then continued my thought.

"So, now the question I have to ask myself is how do you keep doing what you're good at and can make a worthwhile living doing, but also do something that keeps you true to who you have become, so you can accomplish a higher purpose in life and do something fulfilling, even if it isn't really as lucrative?"

Without skipping a beat, Brigette responded, "You combine them!"

To be honest, I had to think for a minute about what she meant. How did the two things I was doing jive? If I blatantly admitted my talents and what I was doing in the corporate world, I would be laughed out of town and probably shunned. If I only did what I was doing helping Therapists, Gurus and Guidance Counselors understand and heal their clients, I wouldn't be able to make a living.

For Brigette, it was an easy answer, based mostly on her subtle understanding of Asian sensitivities, Buddhist and Hindu views of the world and New Age philosophies. She responded.

"In Hong Kong, no one builds or designs anything without consulting their Feng Shui expert or their Chinese horoscope," she said.

"It's the same in India, and other places worldwide," she continued. "Think of it. Nearly every corporate headquarters in China has somehow been vetted and indirectly designed by a 'consultant', who gets called in by the Board of Directors and lets them know if what they are doing has potential, or will be successful or fail based solely on its metaphysical attributes."

She smiled broadly.

"And it's understood by everyone, but no one talks about it. There's an army of Astrologers, Sooth Sayers, Feng Shui experts and Gurus who are hidden consultants, handsomely paid. They're a secret commodity. Trust me, I know. Leo works with dozens of them all the time."

"Sure, but how does that apply to me?" I asked naively.

"Okay," she went on, "So, maybe what you do is a little different, but maybe not. Why don't you become an independent International Corporate Marketing Consultant, but with a twist? You can do what you've done for years, if that's all the client wants, but as an added bonus, you invent some kind of 'Precognition Analysis', or something that offers a higher perspective on what they can expect in their future business, and the specific reasons why. Tell them their successes and their failures in advance, and forecast their business futures in concrete terms they can understand. Kind of like a modern-day corporate seer or adviser. A modern-day Merlin. It would be completely unique."

She added more.

"No one needs to know exactly where your visionary information comes from. You don't need to say, 'Oh, by the way, this comes from a higher plane of reality'," she joked.

"They get it or they don't, but odds are, they'll get it, not say a word to anyone, and then pay you for it as a 'Marketing' Consultant or Strategic Planner, or something like that."

It was as if lightning had struck. I was flabbergasted, and Brigette had hit the nail on the head. By the time we were done with our second café au lait, she had helped me map out an entire strategy for doing it. Win, win.

Then it got even better.

"Listen," she said, "Let me talk to Leo, and see what he thinks. I wouldn't be surprised if he wants to hire you himself, and maybe we could even meet up in Hong Kong or Singapore in a few weeks. We'll be moving there in a little while, and Leo is going to head up the Hong Kong office starting in a few months."

I left the Café floating on air. I knew it wouldn't be an easy transition, but since it had elements of what was familiar to me, combined with what I really wanted to do without outing myself, it wasn't frightening either.

In a way, it felt as if combining my professional expertise with my innate intuitive and precognition gifts was the only way forward if I wanted all my goals to be met successfully. I was completely right about that, until I was also wrong, as I would one day discover.

Perhaps I should have thought more about Levi Steller's sullen mood and final thoughts when he let the downside of his work slip out. But I was still blissfully ignorant about what he had meant.

As soon as I got back to New York however, it was time to face some harsh realities. If I was going to do this, things would have to change. Because we had purchased the 18th Century farmhouse in the Pennsylvania countryside only a year earlier, and were in the midst of the slow process of completely renovating the three-acre property, it wasn't going to be possible to carry two expensive homes long-term.

Selling the country house unrenovated would come at a giant loss, and when I crunched the numbers our expenses could be cut by more than half if we just gave up the apartment in Manhattan and moved to the country permanently. Commuting in and out of New York and Philadelphia to pursue the Marketing Communications and Briefing projects Brigette and I had discussed would work out fine, and at far less expense. But how would Daniel take it?

The answer to that was, not very well, and the announcement went over like a lead balloon. Still, he tried to be flexible and initially talked himself into the whole thing as a new life experience. Within weeks, we had moved out of our Manhattan apartment, and into the house in the country.

We were barely settled in when Brigette e-mailed me. She had spoken to Leo, and they had some ideas. He had several good clients that they told about my work, even the details in terms Brigette had imagined, and they were so sure it would work out, they were willing to pay all my travel expenses, provide a place for me to stay free of charge and also give me a daily stipend to come to Hong Kong and meet with some people.

It wasn't all a favor either, which I appreciated actually. It was a business transaction, and in exchange for their efforts, any potential projects would be run through their company in the US, to facilitate payments, and they would take 30 percent.

I jumped at the opportunity, and we were off and running. They wanted me to come out as soon as possible, and stay a minimum of a month, to start, in order to see if we could drum up business together. I immediately hit Reply, and excitedly accepted Brigette's kind offer. I told her I would look into travel arrangements right away, and could probably be in Hong Kong within two weeks, to minimize the cost of airfare. I probably would have flown out the next day, if it hadn't been for that.

I have to admit I was so excited about the possibilities, I really didn't fully consider Daniel. As far as I was concerned, I was being given a gift, and this would provide us both with the means to move forward. I knew it wouldn't be easy, but I thought he would understand and we would push through it as best we could together.

Daniel was stone cold when I told him the news. He immediately called his best friend Eve, a Real Estate Agent at the same company as he, and arranged to stay with her in her apartment on 57th Street in New York while I was gone. Eve's family were wealthy Jewish owners of a Shipping Line from Rotterdam, Netherlands from the 1920's to the 1940's, and her father, mother and she were among the last Jews out of Holland right after Hitler's invasion of that country. Her father was a prominent businessman and outspoken critic of Hitler, and the family would have been first on the Nazis' hit list.

Because of that, she understood what it meant to be a citizen of the world, and although Eve was a child when she and her parents left Rotterdam, and she was in her 60's now, she especially keyed into doing what you need to survive, even if it literally meant getting out of Dodge on the last train. She understood my reasoning, and softened the blow for Daniel by telling him he could stay with her as long as he needed.

Her role in smoothing things out and making it possible for me to leave can never be underestimated, especially seen from a higher viewpoint, in terms of what I would eventually do. Daniel moved in with her a few days before I left for Hong Kong, and I was invited to stay there as well the day before my flight to Asia out of JFK.

On the surface, Hong Kong was not really 100 percent Chinese, at least not then. I was immediately taken everywhere by Brigette and Leo, and introduced to a way of doing business that was overtly Western, but intrinsically and covertly Chinese underneath. That meant all the precepts of international modernism, including extraordinary corporate edifices and structures, luxury hotels, chic restaurants and on-trend night clubs on the exterior, but Asian politeness, sophistication and wholly Chinese sensibilities firmly operating in business and pleasure for those in the know.

I remember as if yesterday my first meeting with a high profile, wealthy Hong Kong entrepreneur who wanted some "insights" into his South East Asia holdings asking me where I went to school. When I answered University in Paris, he had a response, which, to me, epitomized the Chinese business philosophy and global approach I was witnessing.

In fluent English with an impeccable British accent, while nodding and thinking about it philosophically, he said, "Ah yes, Paris…Wonderful place, but they really should knock down a few of those old buildings and construct a more modern city, don't you think?"

In Asia, you smile and agree, simply because it is the thing you do. There's always a time and place to make your views known later.

I adapted quickly and well. It was something I had known how to do for years. Brigette, Leo and I made quite a team, and clients were as intrigued as they were impressed. For clients, we were a unique, one-stop-shop that could look into the metaphysical parameters present in a business or any deal, provide future predictions based on the esoteric and spiritual information being received, and then design and implement a comprehensive program that fit the future predictions perfectly. Some even asked us afterwards if we were "predicting" the future, or creating it.

Just as Brigette originally said, there was no need to say exactly where the information came from, and no one really ever asked. It was understood, and the information itself was its own credentials. Almost all of our clients were pleased to see it as insight and guidance coming from a higher source, and, in this case, that insight was being managed by American executives who also had global expertise dealing with the information that was being provided. Once proven accurate and trustworthy, we were almost always invited into the inner sanctums, which in business in China is no small feat and usually a profound complement.

Inevitably, it took time to develop such relationships, and I found myself staying in Hong Kong and traveling throughout Asia, longer and longer periods of time. I would return to New York, going through LA or flying around the world, through Amsterdam, Frankfurt or London, then go straight out to the house in the country for ten or fifteen days, and then back again. Each time, I would pick up Daniel, who was still staying in New York City with Eve, and we'd go to the country house whenever I returned.

Our relationship however, was suffering. I tried keeping up with daily emails and a call at least once a week, but things were becoming more and more strained, and I could feel the distance, even though he insisted everything was the same. There was good money coming in now, so in order to try to make it worthwhile for him, I offered to set him up in an import-export business, and even fund a small home furnishing's shop called "Homestead" in New Hope, Pennsylvania.

The items were anything other than American, but the retail markups were substantial. Daniel threw himself into running the store, while in my spare time using my new Asian contacts, I would shop Asian home goods markets, filling up twenty and forty-foot shipping containers with home furnishings items that I would send back for him to sell at the store. It bought our relationship time.

In Hong Kong, as our reputation grew, Leo, Brigette and I were soon being referred to friends of our clients in Singapore, Jakarta, Bali and Malaysia, as well as Mainland China. Some required a small gratis look at what would take place in the near future, and as soon as something witnessed on the timeline, or a hidden aspect of the company or its owners that no one knew was revealed, the pace would pick up substantially and we'd be hired.

Practicing small idiosyncrasies and following unspoken cues that most Americans, and even Europeans, consider idiotic, like subtle hand gestures at a meeting, facial expressions, how to present yourself in an auspicious way and when to speak or not, certainly didn't hurt us either. The subconscious importance of these cultural sensitivities, which should never be discounted in life, had been ingrained in us early on, living as we all did with an array of global cultures attending international schools as youngsters.

The formula worked exceedingly well for a year or more. But on one of my last trips home, Daniel would not come to the phone. Eve spoke to me, and said he had asked her to speak on his behalf. Through her, he expressed that he was happy to remain business partners, if I wanted, but he had met someone else and was no longer interested in a life together. He said I could have the house in the country, everything in it and the cars, which I had mostly purchased anyway, but wanted the shop and the business, which was just beginning to turn a profit.

I can't say I didn't see it coming, but it was anguishing just the same. Of course, I agreed, and later found out he had moved in with someone I had introduced him to years before.

I was okay with letting go of the business, even though it was becoming lucrative, since I knew it would fail in a few years, which it did. After we finalized things, we didn't speak again until after Daniel, and the business, declared bankruptcy. To be honest, I felt a little sorry for him.

Meanwhile, as well as things were going in Asia, I could sense that I was reaching the end of that trek as well, and after Daniel's departure, I was worried about losing contact with any future life in the States. In addition, Brigette and I talked and she asked me to take a look at something for her. I was forced to let her know that I could see that Leo was seeing someone else, and they would probably not last out the year.

The two of us decided that it was time to return to our roots, wherever that was. All said and done however, we calculated that we could continue doing, and even expand what we were doing, in LA and New York, with each of us working a coast and commuting between the cities. As exciting and interesting as living abroad can be, after a while, if you stay too long overseas, it becomes impossible to return to the States.

Brigette left Leo after finding him with someone else in their home, and what I had seen was confirmed. The two of us flew back to the States together. My landing back in the States seemed easier than hers, and Brigette moved back to Europe soon afterwards. There, she met an older Italian man, and they were married a year later.

I was very sad to hear it, since I knew that this would not go well. She was a free spirit constantly testing the boundaries, and her new husband's life mission was related to learning lessons about control and domination. When his lessons were being experienced through the negative polarity, he would become domineering, punishing and try to control everyone around him. The personality traits developed in childhood also instilled a tendency towards violence, with serious OCD issues that caused him to be unable to stop once he started.

The two of them were drawn together karmically, having agreed prior to the lifetime to meet up at this point so she could assist him with learning his life lesson by testing his issues of control. That was the easy part for her, being the free spirit that she had always been.

I tried to warn her about what I saw coming, but she didn't want to hear it, or know anything about what was in store. It was as if she was possessed by her subconscious Soul agreement to assist him to learn his lesson.

The last time we spoke, she called me alternating between whimpering and sobbing because he had beaten her so badly. I explained as simply as I could that his lessons around control were being dealt with through the negative polarity, and it would be in her nature to always trigger this in him. She had no choice but to leave, I told her.

But she literally was drawn to him because of his life lesson, and the desire to help him "conquer" himself and get over his issues, which I could see was going to be a losing proposition. A life lesson is a life-long experience, not something you get over and then move on from after experiencing it once or twice. From the Soul's perspective, this lifetime is created for the specific purpose of understanding every facet of the life lesson, so it will always rear its head throughout physical life in various forms, different ways and with many people.

Learning to recognize the lesson, and push it into the positive experience, is what raises consciousness, and ultimately, the quality of your vibrational resonance. It never ceases to amaze me how people can repeat the same events over and over again in so many different ways, and never really understand what is happening to them. But the Soul knows, and, in a manner of speaking, the lesson is being ingrained in them for the purpose of mastering every aspect of it.

Somehow, based on Brigette's interpretation of what I told her about her new husband, she convinced herself that it would be her mission to help him manage his control issues. But she never did. She didn't call me much afterwards, and we lost contact after that. I think it was mainly because she was embarrassed that she didn't, or wouldn't, listen to my warnings. Karma and Karmic balancing will do that to you.

Landing back in the States wasn't easy for me, considering that now I was alone, but things happened quickly. Knowing full well what I had been doing in Asia, Lisa, who lived in Philadelphia now, introduced me to the owner of an established and successful marketing and communications firm there, and once again we were off to the races. The President of that company was especially tuned into metaphysics, or at least prided herself on being "enlightened," if you can call it that.

In reality, she had only a superficial grasp of these things. Having always wanted however, to offer trend reporting to clients nationally based on a remote viewer approach, she now envisioned a way to do that. She had a strange competition going in her head with other national trend agencies, and dreamed of out-Faith-Popcorning, trend-reporter Faith Popcorn. After speaking with me, she thought she had discovered a completely novel way to do that using my skills.

Her motives didn't concern me, since I was still acting independently and doing exactly what I had been doing globally since my first meeting with Brigette at the Deux Magots. But this woman had an array of upscale clients and could make substantial introductions, mostly through a brother-in-law who had the dubious claim of being one of the richest men in America.

In a short time, I was creating secret "Briefings", as I still called them, for companies, executives and celebrities from Boston to D.C. and LA to Hong Kong. Since I had rekindled my relationship with Karen in New York, I was also taking occasional calls again from her Jungian colleagues from around the world as well.

I was in the midst of working on a new project for a Producer at NPR who had just produced a show launched on Public Radio from WGBH. She wanted a professional consultation as to whether or not the show would be successful and how to improve it in a way that was compatible with its mission and future direction, from a higher viewpoint. It was an interesting project, but also an extremely difficult one because of what I saw transpiring behind the scenes.

When I took a look at it, she had gotten the production because her live-in boyfriend was having an affair with an older high-level, married and closeted male executive at NPR. She had no idea her boyfriend was bisexual, and both he and the older executive were acting on the down-low.

The executive had recommended her for the position, and then pushed for her to get the show as a cover for his affair with her boyfriend, so they could use it as an excuse for the three of them to become closer, since business would necessitate it. His plan was to have a permanent cover for seeing her boyfriend whenever he wanted, so there would be no suspicion about their affair.

This was going to be a difficult Briefing to write. The good news was the show would be a tremendous success, and she would go on to do many more and become one of the best Producers at Public Radio. The bad news was, she was about to find out that not only was her boyfriend bisexual, he was cheating on her with her Boss, who was married. It would have been hard not to tell her the truth, and I have to imagine she already had her suspicions.

I did hear from her briefly a year later to thank me. She had decided not to challenge or out anyone right away, but quietly broke it off with her boyfriend without telling him why once she discovered hard evidence it was all true. The show went on to have a great and long-lasting success, just like I had seen, and even today she is an important and well-known Producer for Public Radio.

It was when I completed the NPR Producer Brief, that I got the call from the friend of a friend of Leo and Brigette in Hong Kong, asking me to return to Asia for a special "project". I was ecstatic to get away and return, so I didn't question the details, and just went with it, picking up the tickets she sent to me at the airport. I agreed to leave immediately.

The friend of a friend, who I had met in passing once or twice in the past, collected me at the airport when I arrived and took me to her luxury high-rise apartment suite overlooking the harbor in Kowloon. The first thing I wondered was how this seemingly unattached, young woman could afford this spectacular apartment.

In any case though, once there, we relaxed and she explained the project to me, while also impressing on me the absolute importance of discretion and secrecy. She had organized this on behalf of her contacts in the Macau administrating government, and almost as if a warning, she assured me that it would never be traced back to anyone but herself. That by itself was odd.

The project turned out to be a new direction for me. The next day we were on the high-speed ferry to Macau to meet high-ranking government officials and discuss what I remote viewed on the timeline that would take place after the official Portuguese handover of Macau to the Chinese took place.

Leo joined us at the government offices, but both he and the close "friend" were excluded from the actual meetings, which were meant to be completely private. They were asked to wait outside while I was brought into a large conference room to discuss the near term and long-term implications of the territorial handover.

Their main interest was seeing these events from a higher metaphysical perspective, and what effects, if any, could be remote viewed on the future timeline. The official in charge headed every meeting, and I noticed that nearly everyone deferred to him. For his part, he wasn't at all shy about sharing with me its mystical purpose and intent from the get go.

He was Portuguese, of course, but spoke perfect English. Looking to be only slightly older than me, he was handsome, charming and polite, with grey beginning at the temples and a closely cropped beard. At times I got the impression he was flirting, but European men, especially those from the South, have the tendency to act that way, when in fact they are just trying to charm you, so I acted reserved.

He listened patiently and attentively, as I looked into various situations and worked to remote view questions that others, who walked in and out the room at random intervals, would put in front of him. Sometimes they would stay longer, sit down and take notes without speaking. Others would sit and listen to segments related to their questions only, then rush out as soon as the question was answered.

This was a new experience for me considering that I was not alone writing a Briefing for later consumption, but was answering questions spontaneously on the spot. To be honest, it takes time to remote view a situation, and there can be a dizzying array of vibrational information that you access that needs to be translated carefully.

Information viewed this way tends to flood your head all at once through various senses and images, or combinations of impressions, and it can take time to decipher with accuracy what you are seeing, as it moves dynamically on the timeline or energetically attaches to a specific question or situation. This was a very complex amount of information that was being condensed and relayed by me, and it had vast fields of energy attached to it with major implications. I made my best effort doing so with an audience present, despite needing the time to tune in and dissect what was useful from what was not, but they didn't seem to mind.

After the first day, we were all invited out later for drinks and dinner by the official who had headed the meeting. We relaxed together and even won some money playing old slot machines at the Hotel Casino where we were staying. Although nothing came of it, since this was very much a business situation, the official actually was flirting after all.

This went on for a day and a half, and as I left Macau I was reminded again of the secrecy surrounding the information that had been imparted. A good deal of it concerned Chinese and European relations carried forward on the timeline well into the future, things relevant even now to the Pacific in the coming World War.

Secrecy isn't a problem for me. Usually, I don't fully remember the information anyway, since much of it is obtained in a semi-trance state, and when people ask for further information at another time I usually have to go through the process all over again.

When that happens, information generally reappears the way it previously did, unless there has been a subtle change on the timeline, which happens, albeit infrequently, because of free will or some other mass consciousness dynamic. Timeline events can shift their position on the timeline because it is dynamic and constantly evolving, but the variables such as archetypal Soul expression, life lessons, Soul missions and personality features do not change. The backdrop might change, but the reactions and opportunities generated off of the events on the timeline tend to be consistent and particular to the subject.

Sometimes, things that transpire in the negative polarity can look vastly different from things that take place in the positive polarity, and vice versa. And things will always tend to revolve back and forth between the two polarities, sometimes for a short duration, but sometimes for an entire lifetime. Nothing remains static for long unless it is consciously monitored and, in a way, pushed into this or that polarity using consciousness, awareness and free will.

You can see something on the trajectory happening from the positive pole, and it can look dramatically different from what would happen in the negative pole. Yet the lesson learned is, nonetheless, consistent. It just is not recognizable as such at times. This can sometimes be the reason people will say a particular prediction was "wrong" or inaccurate. In reality, the basis is the same, but the event has shifted polarity, and the experience of it in the eyes of the beholder seems different from what was originally seen on the timeline.

Add to this that in personal matters, sometimes you can even have a case where the person's Soul has moved on, leaving the Ego in full control of the lifetime at some later point in life, or where another Soul has "walked-in" to take over the physical body and lifetime for their own Soul purpose. The person's psyche and Ego, as well as their personality parameters, remain intact, so no demonstrable change on the outside is usually evident, but the life mission can shift dramatically in accordance with the temporary mission of the new Soul, who is a temporary resident in that physical life.

This is rarely the case though, and when it happens, it is not only infrequent, but usually also noticeable to those close to the person. Inevitably, friends or family members will marvel that he or she is like a completely "new" person, with a complete change of heart. That's because they are, through the change of a Soul and a new habitant of the existing body.

Such arrangements between Souls only take place by full agreement with the departing Soul's energy. Usually, as an example, this takes place through some life event, such as major illness or trauma, and the new Soul will inhabit the body simultaneous to the departure of the existing Soul. The new Soul inhabitant of the body then goes on to fulfill some minor growth objective that does not require a full lifetime to accomplish.

Both Souls achieve expedited growth as a result. What is sometimes referred to as a mid-life crisis can be the result of simple middle-age boredom and questioning as to the meaning of life, or it can actually be the departure of one Soul that has accomplished its life mission without the experience of physical death, as a new Soul walks into the existing lifetime with a new purpose, preferences and direction. The bottom line is how many variables there are that need consideration by the intuitive or remote viewer, when looking at all these factors from a higher perspective.

After Macau, we returned to Hong Kong to celebrate the project's success. I stayed in Hong Kong a few more days, then flew out to Bali to visit with friends at my favorite boutique hotel, secluded in a terraced rice paddy in the mountains, just outside Ubud. It was exactly the break I needed after the intense subject matter I was being asked to look into. Two weeks later, I returned to LA flying from Denpasar, and then went on directly to New York.

Immediately after my return from Asia, following a one day stay with family in New York City, I made my way home to the peace and quiet of the 1750 stone house I had, at this point, finished bringing back to life in the Pennsylvania countryside. But it didn't stay peaceful or quiet for very long.

I hadn't even unpacked when, within a day or so of my return, I received the mysterious call from someone named Colonel McCormick. Two days later, I was walking into that strange empty house in a deserted suburban neighborhood on the Main Line. It was my visit with the Colonel there that brought me the recognition that "*they*" had finally materialized and were now ready to make themselves known, having prepared an in-house position for me at Quantrolics, Inc.

9. What You Can Find in a Pennsylvania Dutch Cornfield

As I hung up on the Investigative Journalist from the Boston Globe, who said she was writing the story on front companies for Alphabet Agencies running black budgets to avoid Congressional oversight, my head started to ache. It was getting late, and I had jetlag.

I wondered for a moment if maybe her call was a test by the Colonel to see how I would respond, or if my discretion could be depended upon. But inside I knew the truth. It was a legitimate call, and hers was a real investigation.

In any case, a decision would have to be made, and I knew it would affect every aspect of my future. I was pretty sure now who "*they*" were. Even if I didn't have complete details yet or a confirmation on exactly which agency we were talking about, it was clear this was the same "*they*" that Levi Steller had referred to sullenly. It was the same "*they*" that knew about the things Anthony and I had unwittingly done as teens for Steve Moreau decades ago. And it was the same "*they*" that already had an inch-thick file on me, knew the details of my very private recent trip to Hong Kong and Macau, and even had my exact arrival dates home.

It didn't frighten me or turn me off. Mainly, I was curious. If they knew who I was and what I actually did, they certainly weren't letting on up front. Instead, they seemed to be dishing it out in small morsels.

But just how could they know all about me, but not know how I really worked, especially considering the details they had on the project I just finished in Macau? How could they not know about my hidden skills, yet know about the Precog Briefings I prepared for companies, organizations, individuals and, now, government officials? Were they toying with me, or was this the way it was done, with everything hidden between the lines and nothing ever said out loud or actually acknowledged?

I decided that must be it, and this is how business is done in this field of endeavor. Remarkably, their approach looked to be about the same as mine – no need to speak the obvious, just keep it camouflaged and hidden under cover of a perfectly reasonable and understandable business function, without offering any explanations and without confirming what is actually happening. A front in front of a front, with plausible deniability inherent at every level.

At some point, I was well aware that Karmic balancing would kick in. Somehow, we always wind up experiencing what we do to others, and I was experiencing that now. That's just how the laws of Karma work.

But there is a caveat, even with Karma. Karma can be minimized or negated, when others are informed of what is intended beforehand, even in some indirect way. Movie plots, fictitious stories, opinion articles, corporate press releases, diplomatic communiqués, news reports and even political messages that communicate in advance what someone or some group is intending to do can curtail or even completely negate Karma for the perpetrator.

If the recipient of the advance warnings of someone's willful intention chooses not to object or rebuke what they have been informed about, or actively work to not permit the injustice in some way, then they have signaled to the Universe that they accept what is happening using their own free will. In that way, the Karma that one would expect to be generated on the part of the perpetrator is almost always absolved. Perhaps absorbed is the better term.

This is a universal precept within a consciousness and planetary system based on free will, which ours happens to be. Karmic balancing is simply the result of universal structure trying to correct itself and reach homeostasis when energy becomes lopsided. But if there is conscious acceptance, or absorption of the excess energy on the part of the recipient beforehand, then there is no energy pushed out of balance. Hence, no Karma is generated.

I debated what I knew about Karma in my head for hours, trying to find an out for myself, or at least a better awareness of what "*they*" wanted and what was happening to me. Several times I was given the famous quote that, from a karmic perspective anyway, "...the only thing necessary for the triumph of evil, is for good men to do nothing".

This was to become a real test of Karmic law for me, as well as a test as to whether or not I truly trusted the information I received from my higher source. But I was not given precise information concerning why the test would occur, since that would eliminate the learning experience for me personally, which my Guides would not wish to do. I would need to muddle through this one just like anyone else, since it involved my own personal Soul growth.

I knew for a fact that self-doubt, like fear, lowers your vibrational integrity and can attract choices from the negative polarity, sometimes with detrimental effect. Maintaining conscious faith in your Soul and the ways of the Universe is always the answer to conquering fear.

On the other hand, however, hadn't Samuel impressed upon me the fact that good, bad, right and wrong are not universal standards, but subjective standards created by men. What is good, bad, right or wrong changes and evolves constantly.

Who was to say "*they*" were intending something nefarious or evil? For that matter, who could say whether or not the lucrative position "*they*" were now offering at Quantrolics was any better or worse than what someone else offered me? From a Karmic perspective, I asked myself over and over if I was prepared to consciously object to whatever "they" were planning for me now?

Truthfully, without emersion in the actual reality or experience of it, the answer was, "No". I started to understand how my clients felt when they received a Briefing, and even considered that regardless of what I told them, they would need to experience their future in order to learn from it. It was the same thing Brigette was going through, knowing full well what was in store for her with her new husband, but inexplicably drawn to the experience anyway, as a learning experience her Soul needed her to complete.

Still, in keeping with the universal Karma model I had been instructed about, the bottom line was that by hinting at what was happening to me, even without complete disclosure, the Colonel, Quantrolics and whomever else comprised the collective "*they*" in this affair, were all likely absolved from any Karma generated with me personally going forward. I would be subject to my fate, at least until my experience was such that my consciousness rose to the point where I mastered my reluctance and objected to them. That is, as long as I didn't meet a physical demise first, somewhere along the way.

This was the future I saw peering at me every time I looked at the situation. I kept trying to look deeper, but eventually it reached the point where I was told, "No further help can be allotted." I had only heard this response one other time years earlier. I was asked to look into the sad and difficult terminal illness of a young woman in her twenties, asked by an enlightened but exasperated medical professional who wanted to know if there was a way he could help her.

The message the doctor received wasn't out of cruelty or indifference; it was because her illness and imminent death were specific to her entire life purpose at a Soul level. Death, in this manner and from this illness, was something she would need to experience that could not be altered or changed. Although it was difficult to share that answer in the past, I knew from it that for myself now, there was a higher purpose in play. I was on my own.

Based on everything that had happened, and still having the words of the Boston Globe Reporter etched in my brain, when I called the phone number the following day that the Colonel had given me, and asked to speak with Ron Mallick, I was noncommittal. I left my name and number with his secretary in a perfunctory manner, and simply asked that he return my call.

I neglected to mention specifically that I had been referred by Colonel McCormick, and assumed that if it were important to them, someone would take note. After I hung up, I asked myself if maybe I was looking for an out, or being coy.

But I didn't receive any call back. After a day, I thought they had either lost interest in me or Mallick was out of the office. Whatever the reason, it didn't matter, and I refrained from calling back. As an excuse, based on personal experience managing an in-house division, I told myself that there was nothing worse than a nudge looking to be hired that kept calling back incessantly.

By the fourth day, towards the end of the week, I put it out of my mind almost completely and got back into my routine at home. It was when I was coming back from a follow-up meeting with an old client in Philadelphia and thinking about my next possible gig, that I suddenly remembered I hadn't heard back from Quantrolics.

Even though I was already well into telling myself, "it-doesn't-really-matter", I decided I'd try one more time, if only as a courtesy to the Colonel. This time, I left a message that specifically included the fact I had been referred by him, in case he spoke with them or asked about me.

The return call came within ten minutes. Clearly, mentioning McCormick's name held weight.

"Mr. Mallick would be very pleased to meet with you," his Secretary said, after introducing herself and saying she was calling back on his behalf. "Can you come by our offices tomorrow at 11:00 AM?"

"Certainly," I said, fairly impressed with the speed of getting a meeting this time, "Let me just confirm that address with you again."

"Yes, that's it," she responded. "See you tomorrow at 11:00 then."

The address was correct. Just as I thought, it was located some-where in that cornfield.

The morning of our meeting it rained. In fact, it poured up until about a half hour before my arrival. It was still overcast and foggy when I pulled up to the gatehouse, which appeared out of nowhere after you turned off the main road and drove another 100 feet or so. If you weren't actively searching for the place, with address in hand, sharp eyes and plenty of patience, you'd never see the tiny sign at the junction of that country lane and the small private road that notified you this was the en-trance to Quantrolics, Inc.

I stopped at the gate, and a uniformed guard wearing a dark rain slicker quickly came out and stood at the car window.

"E.M. Nicolay to see Ron Mallick," I said, in a business-like way.

Holding a Clipboard in front of him, the guard looked through his list of visitors by running his finger down the page slowly, and then, stopping three fourths of the way down, shook his head in acknowledgment.

"It's Building Three, to the left of the parking lot as you drive straight ahead," he offered.

Then walking back into his small post, the rail in front of me lifted magically, and I drove past him.

It was gloomy, and the weather wasn't helping. As I drove through the lifting fog, past the high shrubs and new corn that was grow-ing but was not quite high enough to totally camouflage the buildings yet, I emerged into an enormous paved parking lot.

The lot was in the center of three buildings that flanked it, almost like a town square. I remembered that the Colonel had told me how the company was divided into three divisions run by an executive management team of three executives who reported to the physicist owner, and suddenly wondered if everything at the company was built around the number three.

All the buildings were single story and had an exceptionally low profile. In truth, they looked more like a series of giant warehouses than a corporate world headquarters. The building facades were a mix of brick and metal siding that were a blend of browns, tans and beiges, the color of dead vegetation in the winter. Everything melded together to look like the drab shade of dry corn stalks, which must have made the buildings completely disappear from early Fall through Spring.

Other than those features, with smaller than usual main entrance doors and high little windows dotted around the upper portions of the structures to allow for light, but not allow anyone to look in or out, the buildings were completely non-descript and basic. They sat like abandoned airport hangers huddled around the massive parking lot.

What impressed me most was that the parking lot was gigantic, and almost entirely full. With so many cars, the first thing I asked myself was where all the people were. The second thing that went through my head, as I found an empty "guest" space and parked, was how in the world they fit the number of people that must go with these cars into these three smallish looking warehouse buildings.

My mind flashed to the first impressions I had entering the

Colonel's office, at the empty house in that abandoned suburb on the Main Line. Something just didn't make sense.

It was almost 11 when I exited my car, and began the short walk up to the single main door of the building I was about to enter. As I walked, I had the same sense I had back on the Main Line just prior to entering that odd house to see the Colonel, as if someone or something was looking at me from over my shoulder.

The feeling grew so intense; I paused for a moment and looked up. There were cameras everywhere. There was one on every street lamp, on the corner of every building, and even on posts positioned between the buildings. Everyone who came here was being closely monitored.

My suspicions were confirmed when I was within a foot of the drab solid main door to Building Three, which appeared to be locked and alarmed. Before I could even reach out my hand to test it, I heard the door click loudly and snap ajar, as if someone had just buzzed it open. I obediently pulled at it, and walked through, expecting to find a large receptionist desk where I could announce my arrival.

Instead, standing about 10 feet from the door I had just walked through was a tall woman older than me who was elegantly dressed in business attire and high heels. She was thin and attractive, with curled blond hair that fell to her shoulders, and she smiled warmly at me as I looked up at her.

I immediately felt that she seemed out of place here, almost too good or too sophisticated to be holed up in this warehouse-like building, especially one that was out in a country cornfield with a team of eccentric engineers and physicists. She held out her hand, and smiled again.

"Mr. Nicolay, welcome to Quantrolics," she said.

"I'm Sarah Kennedy, Mr. Mallick's secretary. We spoke yesterday on the phone. Mr. Mallick is looking forward to meeting you."

I smiled back, and shook her hand, feeling more at ease in her presence than I had a moment before.

"It's a pleasure to meet you Sarah," I said, adding, "And thanks in advance for all your assistance."

"Of course," Sarah said, "I'm glad we could get you in so quickly."

"I was expecting to announce myself at a reception desk, but this is a much nicer greeting," I told her, looking for something pleasant to help break the ice.

"The guard at the gate let us know you had arrived," she said, "There are no receptionists in any of the buildings here due to the security doors, so we meet and accompany visitors around here."

Then she added whimsically with another smile, "Just so no one gets lost."

With that Sarah motioned for me to follow her. I did my best to look around, but frankly, there wasn't much to see. The area we walked through was large enough, but there didn't seem to be anything else there. I knew from looking at it outside that it was a single-story building. But on the inside, it was a large, empty hall, almost like a reception hall or auditorium. There were no offices or anything else, from what I could see.

In fact, it reminded me of American public schools or commercial buildings from the early 1960's. Painted concrete block and metal or sheetrock everywhere, resting on terrazzo-like floors wherever you looked. The hall even reminded me of an elementary school gymnasium or auditorium, where public life was always focused for school children in the day.

We walked through the auditorium-like hall and quickly approached what appeared to be the back wall of the building. It struck me as odd, once again, that the building on the outside was one story and seemed so much larger than what I was currently seeing now. Was she going to lead me through an invisible passageway, into some vast expanse behind the wall of office cubicles? Was that where everyone belonging to all those cars was currently working?

Sarah stopped in front of what looked like part of the wall, but at closer inspection, since it was the same color as the wall, turned out to be the outline of a steel elevator door. It was unlike any I had ever seen before, except possibly in Europe where ordinary doors were sometimes used for small elevators. Except for the fact that this one was on a much grander scale, larger and more camouflaged.

Before I could make out completely what she was doing, she waved the ID card from around her neck in front of the glass panel on the left of the frame. Instantaneously, the door seemed to double in size and slide open, and she led me into an oversized elevator that you could have driven a car from the parking lot into.

There were no buttons or controls inside the elevator, so I hesitated for a moment. Then I heard Sarah say clearly, to no one in particular, "Sublevel One". Immediately, the wall-door closed, and we were descending.

Now I get it, I said to myself, it's all below ground, just like the Colonel's office was. As we descended, Sarah explained briefly that Quantrolics technology was being used in the elevator, even though neither the audio-command nor the glass panel technology, which she called Li-fi, a term no one had ever heard of at that point in time, were widely in use anywhere but at Quantrolics.

Proudly, she continued to point out that many of the company's futuristic audio-visual and photon technological advances were incorporated throughout the complex. She also added that all three buildings were primarily underground to "preserve the environment", just as the Colonel had explained. I would have rolled my eyes then and there, except for the fact that I wanted to make a good first impression.

We didn't have far to go, and the doors opened spontaneously once we arrived at Sublevel One. I was never claustrophobic, and actually preferred smaller spaces, which were an essential feature of the 18th Century stone home I had just restored, but I was beginning to become concerned about being trapped in this space. As the doors of the elevator opened, that thought was dispelled by the new expansive view in front of me.

Almost as far as I could see, there were cubicles in the center built around large offices with floor to ceiling glass that went around the entire perimeter of the building. The ceiling height was at least 12 to 15 feet, and the space was modern, efficient and very well lit. The air even seemed fresher than outside, and I wondered if maybe they were pumping something extra in with it that relaxed you, since my concerns vanished the deeper we got into the complex.

When we had gone as far as we could go, I was led into a large, corner office. It was the only office I had seen so far that did not have floor to ceiling glass, and instead had a solid wall that offered privacy and a measure of uniqueness to the space. Inside, there was a large desk to the side, and another attractive younger woman sitting at a desk opposite that larger one. A closed door sat on the far wall, in between the desks.

"If you'll wait here for a moment, I'll let Mr. Mallick know you've arrived," Sarah said.

I stood in the center of the space as she disappeared through the far door, closing it behind her. Suddenly, I had a paranormal sense that there was the presence of a much older woman standing next to me.

She had a kind and concerned energy, looked to be in her late 70's and was wearing an elegant dress from a few decades earlier. I could make out highly coiffed bluish grey hair and a well-powdered face, but most of all; I could see she was there to tell me something.

Truthfully, I hadn't had this kind of spontaneous experience with disembodied spirits since those first experiences with Karen. I quickly learned how to separate those out from reality and only tune in when needed or required, but now, here she was.

"He will die as a result of it," the kindly older woman said firmly, but calmly. "Please tell my son not to be afraid, I will be waiting for him when it happens."

Sure. Just the kind of thing you want to say to someone who may have your fate in their hands that you've never met! Was there anyway in Heaven I was going to be able to walk in there and say, "Your mother wants you to know you're going to die but, don't worry, she'll be there to meet you."

All I could do was shake my head and smile. As I looked over at her, the younger woman who had been watching me smiled back. I think she thought I was smiling at her, or, at the least, smiling about my situation, as I stood there between the two desks in the center of the antechamber of Mallick's office.

Before I could go on about it in my head, Sarah reappeared, and with the door held wide open for me, she said, "Mr. Mallick will see you now."

Still smiling, I briskly walked passed her through the door, into his office.

The office was modern and appealing, with a fresh, clean clutter-free appearance. Several awards and photographs hung framed on the walls, and although not as numerous or recognizable as the Colonel's collection, you got the immediate impression this was someone well known and respected.

"Ron Mallick," he said standing behind his desk.

I walked up, and reached out my hand.

"EM Nicolay," I responded.

"E - M…" he said, thoughtfully. "Is that a given name, or does it stand for something? What do you like people to call you?"

I laughed, mostly because it sounded like he knew the answer already, but was looking for something to open the conversation.

"Everyone calls me by my initials," I answered. "They have since Boarding School. It stands for Eugenio-Michel, but I gave up on getting people to understand that name early on. So, now it's just E.M."

"Then E.M. it is," he agreed. "Italian?"

"French-Italian, actually," I corrected, as I usually do. "My ancestors were members of a fairly well-known family from France that fled the French Revolution to wait out the results in Italy, since a relative was well connected at the Court of the Kingdom of Naples at the time. Half the family returned to France afterwards and regained their titles, while the other half remained in Italy as successful magistrates. But I guess they never completely lost touch with their Franco-side, shall we say."

He listened attentively, and seemed interested, so I added, "In 1905, my father's father was sent to be educated in America when his father, an important Italian Magistrate at the time, received death threats against his family for passing down prison sentences on the sons of a local Mafia leader. He became naturalized before World War I and never returned home."

"Fascinating," Mallick said, adding, "Family history is unbelievably rich, and extremely telling, if one knows where to look."

Ron Mallick was tall, elegant, soft spoken and poised. He was the kind of man everyone wanted for a father, sympathetic, acknowledging, calm and inquisitive, but also commanding and decisive. He towered above everyone height-wise, and had to be 6'5", at least.

Combined with the deference I noticed people giving him, he had the air of a famous retired sports celebrity. He looked like he had been through it all, and was now ready to impart the wisdom he had learned over the course of what looked to be seventy-some-odd years.

I wondered if I would ever find an opening in the future to tell him about my experience with his mother's spirit, and then thought that if I ever found one, I would find a way to oblige her. Sitting down in the chair in front of his desk, I was distracted from that thought when I noticed that sitting at the center of his desk, right in front of him, was the one-inch file with my name emblazoned on it. It appeared to be the same file the Colonel had, or some duplicate.

"So, let's get down to brass tacks," he said, moving forward.

"I spoke with Colonel McCormick, and he told me he explained pretty much everything to you, so the rest we can make up as we go. There are a few odds and ends you need to clear up with Human Resources, and also a kind of personality test we like to give people around here. HR can administer that now, if you have time, and it only takes about 40 minutes to complete. There are also a few people I'd like you to meet a bit later. When can you start work?"

This was moving fast, much faster than I had ever expected.

"I'm sorry," I said, almost stammering, with my eyebrow buckling.

"I didn't realize a decision had been made, and just assumed I had several more interviews and steps to go through first."

Mallick looked at me sympathetically and slightly amused.

"You'll find that Colonel McCormick is very thorough, and

around here, what he says generally goes. The job is yours if you want it. We're past the interviewing stage now. But to be clear, we're creating this position for you, so it will be to our mutual benefit to feel our way together, since there is no hard and fast job description or duties you need to be aware of just yet. The only given right now is the fact that you'll be working in our International Division, and you will report directly to me. You'll need to take it from there, and fill-in the position, rather than the other way around. When we ask you for a "report", drop everything and do that. Otherwise, do what you feel is appropriate and needed."

I was silent. How could there be no job description, and no duties I needed to be aware of? Was this a joke? Then he added some additional thoughts.

"If there is a report about a country, a region, a population, a group or a global market that you think we should be aware of, please take the initiative and send it to me. Secondarily, if from time to time you feel like we could use a new brochure or two, here and there, something you think would work better for getting local projects in global markets, go ahead and take care of it."

He paused momentarily, and then continued what he was saying.

"Stick to your budget on those things, and we'll be just fine. But keep me apprised, and try not to bring too much attention to the international division. We need just enough to have credibility, but not so much we bring attention to ourselves. You'll understand this better as we go."

I kept wondering what this all meant. I had no trouble investigating what was needed or complying with a Briefing when asked from time to time, which is what I assumed he meant. And I had no issues keeping him informed of everything I was doing or sticking to any budgets.

But isn't the whole objective of marketing and communications to bring attention to the company? What about expanding global sales of Quantrolics technology? Doesn't that require wide spread market recognition and penetration?

In particular, what did he mean by "just enough to be credible, but not so much we bring attention to ourselves"? Wasn't that the point of all this in the first place? The whole thing sounded amazing on the surface, until you realized it didn't make one bit of sense underneath.

"You'll find me to be a very relaxed Manager, and I won't be needing cajoling, flattery, endless requests or constant contact from you," he said following a short silence. "And don't expect that from me either."

Then his tone changed as he said, in a more somber way, "Even so, you shouldn't get the wrong idea. I will *always* know where you are and what you're doing, so rest assured, if you don't hear from me, it's because what you're doing has my approval."

In a way, that was comforting to know. I had been an independent contractor for years now, so being under someone's thumb or needing to constantly get approvals would not have gone down well with me. He was basically saying I was going to be an in-house, independent contractor. At least that's how I interpreted it.

Yet, something was also disconcerting. What did he mean, he would *always* know where I was and *what* I was doing? Despite all the questions I was asking myself, I nodded in understanding and appreciation anyway.

"I prefer my direct reports to be autonomous and independent, under one condition," he said rather sternly.

"Always remember, **you** report directly to **me**, and no one else. Should anyone try to inform you otherwise, or get you to do something for them that you have doubts about, let me know about it first, and ignore them until I tell you it's something we want you to do. Hopefully, that's clear, and I dare say, this will all become much clearer as we work together. So, when do you think you can start?"

I quickly shuffled current obligations I had in my head, looking for a response.

"I guess I need about two weeks to finish up some things and tell old clients I am going in-house somewhere," I answered.

I was thinking mostly of the woman in Philadelphia who was trying to out-Faith Popcorn, Faith Popcorn. She wasn't going to be thrilled with this news, but I knew from the start working with her wouldn't last.

"Would two weeks work for you?" I asked.

"Great," Ron said happily. "Let's make it official then."

With that, he shook my hand again, and his demeanor lightened.

"So, if you still have some time today, why don't we do this," he said, as if he had come up with a worthwhile idea.

"Go take care of whatever paperwork you need to with HR, and ask to take the "Test" they've prepared for you that everyone here takes prior to joining us. After that, it should be about lunchtime, and, if you like, you can join me for lunch at my Country Club. It's not very far."

There was nothing about this man someone wouldn't instinctively like. He was disarming and hospitable. But I reserved my final opinion, feeling something was still hidden, if only remembering what the spirit of his mother had suggested with her statement just a little while before.

In short order, I agreed to his plan, and he rose saying, "Good, let me introduce you to someone you'll be working with closely, and let's see if she can help take you down to HR's offices on Sublevel Two." With that he led me down the hall a short distance, waving and nodding to people behind the glass office walls, or in their cubicles as we went. Most acted surprised to see him out and about, and I wondered if he ever walked anyone down the hall, or if this was his way of signaling to certain people his approval of me.

We stopped in front of one office where an attractive young woman was sitting at the desk working on her computer. She was Chinese and wore a traditional navy-blue silk dress with a 1930's-style Mandarin collar that had been altered to please more modern, western tastes.

To carry through on the theme, her dark black hair was cut in a style that also looked like images I had seen of sophisticated cosmopolitan Chinese woman from the mid 1920's in Shanghai. On her, the look was uniquely sleek and modern, even now. I immediately felt some kind of connection to her, as Ron walked me into her office.

"Hui-Lin Jang, this is E.M. Nicolay," Ron said, introducing us. "E.M is going to be working with us in International Marketing, Communications and Strategic Planning in a role yet to be fully fleshed out."

"Lin works in International Sales and Installation, and she is our Asia expert," he continued.

Then he qualified something.

"She doesn't report directly to me, since she works in global sales, engineering and installation, but much of what you do will go hand in hand with what she is doing, and I'd go as far as to say that the two of you will be tied at the hip, and touring the world together rather extensively."

Then, almost to cement our association, he added, "Lin is an accomplished Engineer in her own right, and one of the most brilliant and capable people we have working here at Quantrolics."

Most people would have been turned off by such an introduction, or at least felt slightly intimated. But I was intrigued. I didn't speak Chinese, other than a few words and short phrases I had picked up over time, but I vaguely recalled that Hui-Lin, as a woman's surname, meant "wise brilliant one". The name alone resonated with me, and made me feel a higher connection to her.

Names often echo a person's spiritual awareness, consciousness or life path. I discovered this accidentally working with Jungian Therapists from around the world in the past, who only needed to mention someone's first name in order for me to tune into their Essence and Life Path information. Inevitably, even though tens of thousands of people might have the same name, a person's first name, and at times its combination with their last name, holds a unique vibrational signature that you can ride upon as a Remote Viewer when connecting to their Soul's information.

I often used that very technique to arrive at higher spiritual information about a specific person. I would listen to their first name, find their vibrational energy and follow that distinctive energetic signature to the Akashic Records, which is a depository of light energy imprinted as information on every person and event. The Akashic are housed in the Eighth Universal Dimension.

Among many other things, the Akashic is the energetic storehouse of a Soul's plan and all of a person's actions for the lifetime, as well as all its reincarnations, existing on that dimensional timeline. In fact, if it weren't for the Akashic, seeing the reincarnations linked to each other by virtue of their Soul would most likely not be possible.

The Akashic then, becomes a repository of Soul awareness and progress for every dimension, and each Universal Dimension has an "Eighth" dimensional sublevel, where the Akashic for that timeline is linked and stored. It is a dynamic depot that is always evolving, so one has to be careful to distinguish what is permanent and meant to happen from what is in a state of flux and changing. This is also similar to the way in which the dimensional timeline evolves, changing reality constantly and moving events backwards and forward on the timeline as well.

Hui-Lin, or Lin as she was known, was friendly and charming. She had been in the country since the age of 10, when her father, a well-respected engineer and metropolitan planner in Taiwan, and her mother, a descendant of Chinese nobility that had fled to Taiwan during the Cultural Revolution, had immigrated to the US in the early 1970's. Her English was flawless, as was her Mandarin, and like me, she had been educated and had traveled abroad extensively.

"Lin," Ron asked politely, "Would you be so kind as to show E.M. to Human Resources, and have them accompany him back to my office as soon as they're done with him?"

"See you in a few," he said to me, as he pivoted and walked out of the office.

By the time Lin and I made it to Human Resources on Sublevel Two of the building, we were fast friends. It felt like my first meeting with Anthony at Boarding School, and we seemed to think alike from the very start. She was easy to talk to, and most of all I appreciated the philosophic depth she had that few people I met these days, especially Americans, seemed to have. I could also tell she was a gifted intuitive, but her talents were as yet untapped, so they weren't prominent, even though she intuitively understood the concepts we talked about briefly in passing.

Lin explained that she lived nearby, which meant she also lived fairly close to me, and, together with her husband and young daughter, she had just finish restoring an 18th Century stone farmhouse not unlike my own. We compared home contracting nightmares, and laughed that we were ever able to make it through them to finally enjoy the results. It might have been her Buddhist upbringing and outlook on things that I found most appealing, but no matter what happened at Quantrolics, I was certain we were going to be close.

We spent the last moments together exchanging mobile numbers. I had been thinking about the possibility of planning an impromptu outdoor cocktail party at my farm to celebrate the upcoming Summer Solstice since getting back into town early in the week. Solstice fell on a Saturday this year, so it seemed a natural idea.

In addition, I hadn't had friends over since Daniel's departure, or completion of the house renovation. It seemed like high time I get back into the swing of things and on the spot; I decided to make it official. I wrote down my street address on the back of my business card, and handed it to Lin.

"If you're not doing anything on Saturday the 21st, please stop by my place between 5 and 9. I'm going to have some people over to celebrate the Summer Solstice."

Lin didn't commit, but took the paper from me and thanked me for the invitation.

The paperwork and "Test" at Human Resources sped by. It included some kind of government Security Clearance applications that, for the most part, had been filled out for me and said 'Pending'. Oddly, they seemed to have everything prepared and just waiting for signatures. All I needed to do was read over some things, answer a few questions, provide some identifying information, take the Test, and sign what I submitted.

The Test was administered in a tiny private room that was more like an interrogation cell than an actual office. What was strange about it was that they asked me to put a small skullcap on with electrodes attached that were connected to what appeared to be a brain wave measurement device.

I was told this was to monitor my brain's electrical activity in conjunction with the responses I made in real time. A harness was also placed around my chest, and I got the impression I was being given a lie detector test at the same time. I was assured this was all standard practice and perfectly normal.

Since it seemed more silly than invasive, I let it happen, and began answering the questions when they said "Start" through a speaker. The questions were mostly inane, about what you would do in this or that situation, in an attempt, I imagined, to elicit brain waves and emotional reflexes. There was a series of questions about my life, and how I "felt" about certain world topics, as well as questions related to various life, religious and cultural philosophies.

I'm usually reluctant to provide answers to questions like that because they only represent a snapshot in time. The responses seemed inherently subjective, since they were constantly evolving, and I didn't think they were a true indication of life purpose or one's true outlook, at least not at a Soul perspective.

Of course, I knew that there was some sort of deeper psychological and other testing going on, but nevertheless I was satisfied to answer the questions as quickly and truthfully as I could. I wasn't overly concerned with the results. They were what they were.

Afterwards, I was promptly brought back up to Ron Mallick's office by a young Human Resource professional who looked and acted more like a military recruit, complete with buzz cut, than a corporate professional. In fact, I was amazed that nearly everyone in HR, women included, had a kind of Defense Department or Hospital Facility-like edge attached to them.

Ron already had a light raincoat on and was waiting for me, when I was deposited back in the antechamber where Sarah and her assistant had their desks.

"Shall we go," he said, adding, "Why don't you follow me in your car, since I won't be coming back to the office after lunch."

I had heard about the Overbrook Country Club, particularly how private it was, but had never actually been inside. I followed Ron in his car, and after we pulled into the main entrance, noticed as he motioned to the Clubhouse Gate guard that the person in the car behind was with him. They waved me on obligingly.

I drove up with Ron to the Clubhouse, parking behind him on the turn-about right in front of the main portico. It was about 1:20 PM, and there was no one anywhere outside. Ron signaled for me to follow him in, giving me a brief history of the club as we walked into the Lobby and headed back towards the large dining room.

Once there, I saw Ron nod in an odd way to the Maître D, who also responded with a silent nod. Fully expecting him to seat us somewhere in the larger room that looked out on the award-winning Golf Course, the Maître D steered us into a small, private dining room off to the side of the restaurant.

"Hope you don't mind," Ron said, "I prefer some privacy so we can talk and get to know each other a little better."

It sounded reasonable enough, except for one thing. Other than staff, there was no one sitting in the main dining room. Most people would have considered the entire restaurant to be "private" at that point.

I didn't say anything, and followed his lead into the small dining room where we sat directly opposite each other at a small table.

We hadn't received menus, and when the waiter came in, Ron said, "It's a limited menu at this hour. Are you OK with a cheeseburger and fries?"

Then without waiting for a reply, he said, "How do you like your burger?"

"Medium-rare," I responded. He said softly to the waiter, "Two of the same," and the waiter exited almost as stealthily as he had entered.

Suddenly, I noticed a change in his tone. His voice became soft and melodic, almost hypnotic in rhythm. Something stirred inside of me, and I heard that familiar voice loudly telling me, "He's going to try to hypnotize you."

I remained silent, and just stared in front of me. What Ron didn't seem to know was that I was well acquainted with hypnotic suggestion and trance, having worked with Karen and so many Jungian Therapists in the past. I knew almost all the NLP and other hypnotherapy relaxation techniques, and understood exactly what he was doing and what was happening now. I also had a pretty good handle on how to block those manipulations.

He began using a technique I had seen employed before by Therapists and Hypnotists where he slowly started to tell a story that was like a childhood fable. The story always meandered and was meant to lull the listener into deeper relaxation so they would become entranced and could be easily entrained.

I kept telling myself what was happening, and used every ounce of conscious intention to fight what he was doing. I went as far as to sing songs in my head, and at one point imagined my fingers in my ears, hearing myself saying silently, "NA, NA, NA, NA", just to keep from listening to what he was saying.

I don't remember the story exactly, since I was successful at blocking most of it out. It had something to do with wolves and sheep, how wolves need to guard the sheep to keep them safe and from running amuck. By the time he was giving me the hypnotic entrainment, I was so busy singing the words to every song I could remember in my head, I could hardly make out anything he was saying.

The last thing I understood clearly that he said was, "You will use your talents to benefit us, to help the wolves protect the sheep in our care..."

It was ominous. But truth be told, I wanted to laugh because it also sounded comical and childish. I played along anyway, acting as if I was listening intently when in reality I was now singing every verse I knew from Fleetwood Mac's Gypsy album, with Stevie Nicks' voice blaring over and over in my head – "... Lightning strikes, maybe once, maybe twice; It lights up the night, and you see your Gypsy...da da da da..."

I was saved by a cheeseburger with fries, as the waiter walked in and placed the plates in front of us. Then I realized that even the no-choice cheeseburger meal was calculated by Ron, since grounding is important to cement what the hypnotist has just done, and there is nothing heavier, and therefore more grounding, than eating meat.

True psychics almost always turn to meat, sex, exercise or some other compulsion for grounding after a long session, since the work they do can be so disembodying. It's also the reason so many Psychics have weight issues, because they spend most of their time trying to come back down to Earth, and excess weight is the body's unconscious and misguided means of doing that.

Sensitive and intuitive people also regularly have high blood sugar levels, and usually have weight issues their entire lives. For these people, this can be the true cause of Insulin Resistance, which becomes the body's hormonal fight to "turn-up the volume", so to speak, and pack the cells with grounding, at least until the cells can no longer respond to the insulin impetus.

Ron seemed pleased with himself, even a little smug, but I wasn't amused. Did he honestly think I would fall for this? Did he do this with every new direct report? I didn't know whether to laugh or to run.

Lunch was over almost before it began, and we were out of there within 50 minutes. As we got to the entrance of the Clubhouse, he stopped and stepped aside to take a call on his mobile. Ron listened intently, and then pressed the red button that said End on his phone.

"Good news," he said. "You passed the HR Tests."

I snickered politely as he moved closer to me.

"Your answers were truthful, and you scored off the charts on Creativity and Perception. You also seemed to be able to trigger Theta Brain Waves at will, which indicates you're the real McCoy," he mused.

"But they had one issue," he said. "The Tests demonstrated you have *no* real concept of time."

"Yeah," I said with a laugh, "I do tend to be late for things."

"*No*," Ron corrected. "They meant you don't seem to be solidly fixed in this dimension. The testing suggests your perception of time transcends this reality."

I smiled again and shrugged. It made perfect sense to me.

10. The Handler

I was still smarting from Ron's attempt to hypnotize me, but wasn't sure it was a deal breaker since I was able to fend it off. It bothered me that someone so charming and accommodating would make such a blatant attempt to gain outright control of my autonomy. I added it to all the other things that were clandestine and worrisome about Quantrolics, but decided not to let it over-influence the direction I was headed in now. I was venturing into new territory, and needed my wits about me.

Cleaning up odds and ends before joining the organization wasn't hard, and as I anticipated, the roughest part of it was informing the woman who was building a business around my Intuitive Briefings and Reports that I would no longer be available to advise her clients. After the initial shock and expressions of sadness, she became icy when she realized her dreams of advancing her own unique precognition business consulting agency were being dashed, and soon afterwards refused to speak with me any further. It was exactly what I expected to happen, and in truth, she wasn't going to be missed by me.

As I planned my upcoming Solstice gathering, there was still an important question unanswered. That old, one-inch thick file that I had seen at the Colonel's office, and a second time sitting on Ron Mallick's desk, was weighing on me. I decided to do a little research, and see what I could uncover to confirm my suspicions about the origins of the file, as well as shed some more light on my connection to Anthony's brother, Steve Moreau.

It was harder than I thought it would be. I knew it wouldn't be possible to ask Anthony, who still seemed overly affected by his deceased brother, so I began by searching for his brother's name as best I could. Finding anything would have been fine, but the pickings were slim since at the time web information wasn't as easy to find, as it would later become. Google only existed in Beta at the time, and I had to wade through a variety of odd search engines used by different Browsers, including AOL, Yahoo and Netscape.

Nothing much came up other than a short mention of an oil transport transaction in the Financial Times. I couldn't even find an obituary. Then, about half a page down in one of the Search Engines, an out of print book popped up with a sentence that contained the name Steve Moreau.

Without clicking on it, I looked at the short line that appeared under his name highlighted as a hyperlink in blue. The line read: "Steve Moreau was well known in the wild world of international espionage beginning in the late 1960's…"

I read it again, and then a third time. It had to be him. Was this the connection I was looking for?

When I clicked on it, it took me to a website with Open Source digitized excerpts from a book written in the mid 1990's. The book had gone out of print almost immediately, for no exact reason, and it turned out to be an unknown author's pick of the 12 individuals he described as the world's leading "secret agents" of the past several decades. According to the Index, there was an entire chapter on Steve Moreau.

I read through a few excerpts quickly with my mouth open. It was riveting and the gist was all too clear. Steve Moreau was a highly successful special agent for American and British Intelligence masquerading as a successful international business man, financier and movie producer based in Switzerland beginning sometime in the mid to late '60's.

The bulk of his money, which was a carefully crafted cover, came from the fact that he was the supposed owner of several large oil tankers that were leased to the Royal Dutch Shell Company. No one knew his exact origins, but he was believed to be of Jewish decent, fluent in Russian, English, French, Italian, Spanish, Hebrew and Malay.

He was also thought to secretly oversee a wide range of agent and asset operations, including important networks in Eastern Europe, Continental Europe, England, India, Indonesia and Malaysia. The book was unclear, but he either disappeared or died under mysterious circumstances just prior to its publishing.

Rather than read the excerpts again, my first thought was to get my hands on that book. I began a search of the title, and could only find one small out of print book seller in Maine who had a copy of the title listed online. I called, and despite the hefty $75 price tag for a fairly recent out of print book, not to mention a steep $22 shipping and handling fee, I gave my credit card information and address over the phone to the seller.

A few days later, the book arrived by UPS. I couldn't wait to open the package and read the chapter, feeling I now had proof in my hands that Steve was connected to the CIA and M16. If he was somehow a "colleague" of the Colonel, as the Colonel said, then it was probably a good bet that the Colonel, and most everything else associated with Quantrolics, was also connected with one or both of those agencies.

As soon as I ripped open the package, I started thumbing through the book. Then I felt my stomach sink to my knees as I got to the middle. There was a Chapter Nine, and there was a Chapter 11. But where the chapter on Steve Moreau should have been, Chapter 10, all I could see were jagged edges sticking out from the spine of the book's interior. The chapter had been ripped out of the book.

I don't know if I was furious or shocked. I went straight to my computer and looked for the digitized archive of the book that I had found online a few days earlier. It was gone. I hit the bookmark where I had found it in the Browser five times. Each time, a blank white page appeared on the screen with the message: 404-Page Not Found.

To keep from becoming overwhelmed, I had to put the whole thing aside. It didn't matter anyway. I now had seen confirmation with my own eyes that these connections were real, and what I saw happening, was really happening. The Colonel and Quantrolics definitely represented the "*they*" Levi Steller had referred to, and it also must be one of the front companies for the CIA that the Boston Globe Journalist was investigating.

What I found most remarkable was that I had confirmation I probably was groomed for this by Steve Moreau, not to mention his associates, since arriving at Boarding School in Switzerland in the mid 1970's. Movie scripts about terror plots written by teenagers?!? Luxury automobiles run between Geneva and Monaco, and other exotic places, with explicit instructions not to open the boot!?! Sure!

Maybe they even knew about me before that. I suddenly recalled how my father came home and said he had met a man at the Breakers Beach Club in Palm Beach, who appeared at precisely the right time to "suggest" the exact Boarding School in Switzerland where I should be sent.

Having come from money, most of the time my father was easily swayed by elitist suggestions. This was no different. Within weeks of their meeting, with the new stranger's offer to help through his personal contacts, everything was arranged, including immediate acceptance of my school application and transcripts. I was packed-up and on a plane headed to Geneva within a month.

The only thing I still wondered was what exactly Quantrolics wanted from me and what their mission was in all this. I could have remote viewed it and picked-up something, but I was reluctant in case I found things I wasn't comfortable with, especially since my intuition was telling me to be on guard. There was time enough for me to do that later, in case I felt the need.

I knew what I could do, and I knew they knew what I could do, but no one had asked me for anything yet. To appease my desire to stay morally correct, I convinced myself I was joining the good guys, and, with this kind of backing, I could really expand my talents and use them productively. Together, I thought, we'd be able to remote view and identify things on the timeline that would help make the world a better place, or at least lessen the impact of the nefarious.

How could that be wrong? It seemed an exciting prospect, if naïve in retrospect. Besides that, I felt sure I was up to the challenge, and went with the flow.

The Solstice event I was putting together in record time was the first party I had ever thrown at my newly renovated house. I had helped coordinate dozens of events before, so organizing things wasn't particularly difficult, but this would be one of the first parties I ever hosted by myself. There wasn't time to mail invitations, but I called a few friends locally, then added some from New York and Philadelphia. They called their friends, and the list grew exponentially just by word of mouth. Before I knew it, I was expecting about 70 people coming from far and wide.

It would be a late Spring, outdoor garden party for the most part, and because I had a full five acres over which the old farmstead was spread, including a large 19th Century bank barn that could be opened up and used in case of rain, I wasn't worried about space, mess or weather. Once I had ordered two Porta-Potties to ease the burden on the private septic system, engaged a string band to play in the background, and hired a caterer from a nearby town to oversee food and drink, there was no turning back.

Lisa was living in the New Hope area, about an hour from me, with her new husband. He was an internationally famous, glass sculpture artist collected by some major institutions and modern art museums worldwide, including MOMA, and I was happy that they had found each other and were in the process of settling down. She offered to help by bringing a whole goat she would marinate and prepare, and local history reenactors agreed to roast it on an open spit and tend to it.

Meanwhile, her husband, a bit of a pyromaniac who had channeled his Soul-chosen personality obsession for this lifetime into a positive polarity, becoming an expert at glass blowing, offered to create and supervise a large bonfire in the middle of the garden. He was the perfect example of taking a personality feature from your Soul and living it through the positive polarity, and subsequent constructive circumstances. The alternative polarity of that expression could have been a real challenge for him.

I knew this was going to be quite a party when a friend from a neighboring farm called up with an unusual request. She was an herbalist healer who was also a member of a local Wiccan Coven, and having heard that the party was to honor the Solstice, she asked if they could stop by and conduct a Solstice Ritual and Blessing for anyone who wanted to join in. I was more than happy to invite them.

The party went off without a hitch. Even Lin from Quantrolics showed up, which was a surprise. I was busy, but able to spend a few more minutes chatting with her before being dragged off by another guest. It confirmed how much I liked her, seeing her now outside of that strange corporate environment.

As parties go, everyone that night was in an exuberant mood, and the whole thing was looking as successful as it was spontaneous. What I couldn't realize at the time was what a major impact the party would have on me in the future. I began to feel things coming together in a way that would intertwine with my fate permanently.

That realization increased shortly after Lisa and her husband arrived. Lisa had invited several of her friends from Philadelphia, and among them was a famous forensic sculptor, artist and renowned psychic named Louis Lidner. Louis was an extraor-
~~~~ ~l, whose artistic talents were eclipsed only by
~chic abilities.

~ked with detectives and police depart-
~ld to psychically sculpt and reconstruct
~ f crime victims based only on their bones

and the few scant remains found years after their deaths. Countless victims were finally identified as a result, and each case he worked on was well documented and publicized.

Not only was Louis a preeminent sculptor and psychic, he was a kind and animated individual who helped bring closure to families and justice for every manner of victim, reconstructing what they looked like so they could finally be identified. He also helped psychically point to how they were killed, the murder weapons used and, at times, the perpetrator's identity as well. Louis was a popular subject of conversation in police homicide divisions all over the country, and he was talked about by criminal investigators, detectives and sleuth clubs, as well as art professionals, from the FBI to Interpol, and from the Philadelphia Museum of Art to LACMA.

I met him for the first time that evening, when he arrived with Lisa and her husband to attend the Solstice event. Naturally, I knew him by reputation, having heard Lisa speak about him often, and I had also seen a segment on the local News channel about his most recent murder reconstruction case. Lisa was more excited than I had seen her in some time when she introduced us.

"I want you to meet Louis," she said with glee, stepping aside so I could shake his hand. "Louis, this is my best friend, the person I told you about."

Louis stared at me intently. His eyes seemed to glisten, and I recognized right away the wheels in his head that were turning in that place that only a few of us had the talent to access.

"There's someone you need to meet," he said.

It was an odd first thing to say to someone you had just met.

"Really, there's someone I need to introduce you to as soon as possible. It's your destiny!"

"It's great to meet you," I said, wondering what he was talking about.

There were 50 plus people walking around my place, and more than half of them I had never seen before. I was still uncomfortable with crowds, so this whole event was a real effort for me as I tried to curtail the barrage of intuitive information and feelings that normally overwhelm me in group situations. Meeting someone new, who wasn't there now, was the last thing on my mind.

"Anytime," I added. "Just let me know when and where."

Things were getting busy, and the Wiccans had arrived. I wanted to talk to Louis a little more about his work, but I had to stay present, so for the time being I walked away.

In short order, the Wiccan Solstice Blessing began, and to my surprise everyone in attendance participated. Each person wrote on a piece of paper what they wished to leave behind. On another, they wrote down what they expected to see come into their life in the next growth cycle.

On my paper, I wrote "…let go of doubts around joining Quantrolics". On the other, I wrote the words, "…a lasting relationship".

Lisa's husband then lite the enormous pile of wood he had constructed for the bonfire. As flames shot 15 feet into the night sky, people crumpled up their pieces of paper and threw them into the flames one at a time, delivering them via the rising smoke as prayers to the Universe. After that, the group feasted on the goat Lisa prepared, which the reenactors had roasted to perfection on their outdoor spit. The whole evening was magical.

I bumped into Louis two more times as I walked around the gardens talking to people after dinner. Each time he would stop me, and in the most serious tone he could muster, tell me how important it was that I meet this person in Philadelphia he wanted to introduce me to. I didn't know if he was making a spontaneous psychic connection and prediction, or if he had arrived at the house with that in mind, but something in me knew this was another turning point. Regardless of not knowing exactly what he meant, every time I met up with him I would nod in agreement, and then quickly excuse myself.

The day after the party, Lisa telephoned several times. Louis was calling her incessantly and said he wouldn't stop until I agreed to come into town to meet the person he had mentioned. She told me he was obsessed, and insisted this was something meant to be. Then she apologetically asked if I would please come down to Center City to meet up, if only to get Louis off her back.

I couldn't think of a reason not to go. The Quantrolics job hadn't started yet, and there didn't seem any harm in an evening downtown early in the week. Lisa and I decided we would all meet for drinks somewhere, Louis Lidner could ask whomever he wanted to join us, and as soon as we finished cocktails, I would be on my way. It was a solid plan.

It was another beautiful early summer evening that night. The only change in our plans was that Lisa, her husband and I met nearby first, and together we joined Louis for drinks at the home of the person he wanted to introduce me to.

We made our way to a stately townhouse on Delancey Street that was in the middle of the block of one of Philly's most exclusive neighborhoods. It was an extraordinary mid-19th Century Dutch Colonial, with large picture windows looking out on the street, and beautiful antique lead-lined Stained glass framing a massive entranceway.

Lisa's husband turned the dial on the vintage manual bell that protruded from the center of the door, and a loud, distinctive old-fashioned jingling sound rang out. Almost immediately, a man who looked about my age opened the door. Louis stood behind him, and as we all stepped into the large foyer he began a round of introductions.

When he got to me, Louis said, "E.M. Nicolay, this is Dean S. Martin, the person I wanted you to meet."

Before I had time to reach out my hand, I laughed out loud.

"Dean Martin?" I chuckled. "Like the crooner?"

He rolled his eyes, as if he'd heard that one a million times before.

"My mother was a huge fan. Since our family name was Martin, she thought naming the first son Dean was a great idea. Can't make this stuff up. That's why I always include my middle initial - S."

"I get it," I said sympathetically, with both of us laughing at the same time.

It immediately broke the ice, and I could feel a connection. Suddenly, something unexpected was happening. My face turned bright red, and I realized I was the last one to understand. It was a set up! This was some kind of a blind date.

I didn't know if it was Louis, or Lisa, or both of them, but I didn't really care, other than to be embarrassed by the fact that I hadn't anticipated it. I half thought Louis wanted to introduce me to someone who had skills like us, or who had some common interest and was inquisitive about what each of us did. I really didn't think, as adults in our late 30's, that they might be attempting to make a romantic match, and hadn't even thought about the possibility.

Maybe because of that, I also had absolutely no expectations or investment in the meeting, other than to enjoy getting to know someone new. Even so, my mind flashed to the wade of paper I had crumpled up and disposed of in the bonfire at the Solstice party.

This seemed the perfect way to meet someone new, with no real intentions or expectations. It made the meeting spontaneous and natural, and it dawned on me that maybe sometimes knowing what the future holds is not the best thing, especially when it comes to affairs of the heart

Dean had an air of class and poise about him that few people could match. A distinctive Y-shaped clef in his chin dominated a rugged, handsome face that was softened by inquisitive hazel eyes and short layered, sun-streaked golden-brown hair. His hair color seemed almost too good to be natural, and I wondered if he used some kind of sun-kissed hair coloring to achieve those perfect blondish streaks.

Paralleling his inviting personality, his physical appearance was also too good to be true. He was dressed in expensive, tailored gabardine trousers that cascaded neatly over shiny, wine-colored alligator loafers. The baby blue short-sleeve Brooks Brothers dress shirt he was wearing had initials embroidered on the breastplate, and the sleeves had been tailored and shortened to accentuate his biceps.

I was immediately reminded of pictures I had seen of my father in his twenty's or thirty's, out at some club looking impeccably groomed and dashing. Those pictures all looked like the shots of debonair young Hollywood celebrities from in the day, sailing through a sea of fame, success and money.

Inevitably, in those photos my father would be sitting at a table of beautiful women and handsome men, looking like life was an effortless journey from one cocktail party to the next. I often wondered where my mother was hiding, since she never seemed to be in many of the pictures. Was she the one taking them?

My father had the same gift for disarming people that Dean displayed, and both of them had the innate power to make anyone think they were now speaking with the most educated, charming and important person they had ever met. Not many people suspected the cold that often ran through my father's veins, particularly when alone with close family, and I wondered now if Dean had that icy trait hidden under his friendly, warm and inviting exterior.

I would soon find out how much Dean truly resembled my father. But for now, seeing him standing in his enormous living room, opening a bottle of champagne with a loud pop and pouring for the group was exhilarating. He looked like the most alluring and handsome person I had ever seen, and as far as I was concerned, Louis wasn't kidding when he said he knew someone I **had** to meet.

After one round of drinks, the group quietly split into two. Lisa, her husband and Louis broke off to talk amongst themselves, and Dean and I quickly fell into a long, deep tête-à-tête about who we were, or considered ourselves to be, publicly as well as privately.

He told me he was an attorney, licensed in D.C., Maryland, Pennsylvania and, of all places, Montana. He boasted proudly that he was a partner on track to become a Shareholder of a law firm in Philadelphia. Surprisingly, the firm was presented as an underdog, founded in the 1920's by Jewish lawyers unable to break into Gentile firms, and Dean joked that not only was he the only Gentile attorney at the firm, he was also the only Gay lawyer there as well.

The question of Montana led to discussions about his family, who moved to the State from West Germany in the early 60's when his father, a tough and seasoned Air Force Captain and Pilot, was transferred to Malmstrom Air Force Base, just outside Great Falls. Dean grew up there, and after a short stint attempting to follow in the footsteps of his father at Military Academy, left and went the MSU, getting his law degree there in the late 1970's. He said he gave up on a military career when he realized that being Gay in the US military, in Montana, in the 1970's, was tantamount to trying to drive across North America using a map with nothing but dead-end streets listed.

He frowned when he spoke about his family, and gave examples of life growing up that sounded exceedingly rough. As children, boys were not allowed to use tissues because it was effeminate, shoes were to be worn with socks and inside at all times, and walking to and from school in heavy snow or minus 10-degree cold was fairly common.

They lived on a ranch outside the base, and chores were dictated with military precision, as well as mandatory, even with a raging fever, or despite breaking out in blisters all over your body from severe allergies to hay. He must be faking it, Dean's father would tell his mother, since boys don't have allergies, only girls do.

That escalated when, at the age of five, Dean developed tachycardia, a condition that causes the heart to speed up dramatically because of a disturbance in the electrical system of the organ. His parents were convinced he was making it up, until he passed out and was discovered by EMT's to have a pulse over 100 beats per minute, so fast the heart couldn't pump blood and he was literally at death's door.

I listened attentively, but the entire time I was reading him, and analyzing what I was being told about his life mission and the reasons he had chosen, prior to the current lifetime, to grow up in such an environment. It got fairly complicated, but it included the fact that we were personally karmically linked as well.

Dean's life lesson was to learn issues around acceptance. When lived in the positive polarity, he would be accepted for whom he was, would be appreciated and would accept himself for who he was. When his life experiences were channeled through the negative polarity, he would experience rejection and demise, and in turn would come to reject and loathe himself. What tempered his experience were the personality traits that had been instilled in him by his early family life.

Those lessons revolved around issues of pride, being proud of who you are versus having vast insecurities and feelings you are never good enough. Whenever he was satisfied that he was good enough, he would create a vibrational frequency that moved into the world to attract acceptance for who he truly was. But when he was insecure, and acting out through the negative polarity, he would learn his lessons through insecurity, fake pride and, ultimately, rejection.

I was told that the connection we had, tied into a past life that also was the origin of the reason his Soul had chosen this particular life mission. We were known to each other in the 13th Century in Central Italy, where he was a young Prince of a small principality. His father died when he was young, and his throne was usurped by a devious Uncle who stole the crown, everything that went with it, and exiled the young Prince. Distraught at what he had lost, and having lost all sense of pride in himself or his future possibilities, he died by his own hands at the young age of 14.

Sadly, I was his mother in that lifetime, and my agreement was to look after him and help him look beyond the position and riches he had lost, so that once he had given up any attachment to superficial "trappings" he would win back his crown later in life. Unfortunately, despite trying, I had failed as his mother to prevent an early demise at his own hands, and that had generated energetic karma between us that would now need balancing in this lifetime.

Not knowing him well yet, I matched up his story with what I was being told from a higher perspective. Soon it became clear that Dean had a strange and almost unnatural attachment to his belongings -- the house, the furnishings, the artwork, even the shoes -- not to mention an odd obsession with position and one's place in the world.

I could tell from what he said about his family that he struggled with feeling rejected and out of place as a child growing up. Although his lot had improved greatly, through his own talents and resources, he still suffered from a sense of isolation, discrimination and rejection in his life and career.

I felt for him. Although it wasn't my issue, I knew better than anyone what rejection from a father could feel like. It became the departure point for our new connection, and we went on from there.

The evening flew by. At some point, Lisa said she was hungry, and we were surprised to see that it was already 9PM. We left the house with Dean noting that we had downed 4 bottles of good Champagne, and slipped around the corner to a quiet neighborhood restaurant where we sat down for a quick meal.

Once again, we broke into groups with Dean sitting opposite me, and in no time the two of us were a million miles away in conversation, even though there were other people sitting right next to us at the table. Truthfully, I don't remember anyone else being there.

At some point, it was time to leave, and I still had more than an hour's drive ahead of me. I said goodnight at the restaurant, and Dean and I exchanged numbers. Suddenly, Louis dove into our conversation headfirst.

"So, isn't it great that you two might be working together," he said, slightly inebriated.

"What do you mean by that, Louis?" I asked, turning my head towards Dean.

"Louis said you might be working at Quantrolics," Dean offered, and then added quickly, "They're a client of our firm. We handle all their legal work..."

I looked at him surprised, wondering why he didn't think that was something to tell me upfront.

"...But I don't handle that client, so we wouldn't be working together, really," he said, dismissing the professional connection and brushing away any possible misunderstanding.

It was odd, but I was glad to hear him distance himself from the company, and that was enough to satisfy me. I wasn't going to let a small detail like that derail what had been a great evening. I didn't give it another thought.

Early the next morning, Dean called. He said he really enjoyed talking to me, and was thinking of taking tomorrow off to go into New York and visit a friend from England who was passing through the city. He wondered if I'd like to join him.

Coincidentally, I had an errand on the Upper East Side that I was thinking of running in the city before joining Quantrolics, so it seemed opportune. Besides, it was another chance to spend some time with Dean.

"That sounds really nice," I said.

"Great," he responded enthusiastically. "I could come up today after work, and then we could drive to New York early the following morning. Does that sound alright to you?"

I knew exactly what he was asking, and smiled to myself at how coyly he had asked to spend the night.

"Sounds like a plan," I answered.

That evening, Dean arrived around 6PM. He was driving a rented Ford Ranger pick-up truck, and when I heard him park in front of the barn, I came outside thinking someone was lost. A pick-up truck didn't quite go together with the alligator shoes and preppy look from yesterday, but okay.

Dean was newly transformed and sporting high-end, casual weekend wear. I couldn't quite tell if he felt a little out of place in the country, or if he actually was out of place. He looked for a sidewalk where there wasn't one, and I led him laughing across the lawn, which needed a trim, between the house and the barn. I was happy to see him, and we picked up where we left off the night before.

After he explained that the car rental company only had a small pick-up truck left to rent, which we laughed about, we had a light super and retired. It was new and exciting, as well as comfortable and pleasant, exactly as I expected.

The next morning, we got up early. Somehow, I felt like we had done this a dozen times before, and it seemed like we were settling into a natural and easy groove together. Since my car was much more comfortable for a long trip into the city, I offered to drive, and he accepted gladly.

"Great idea," he confirmed, happy with the idea, "That means I can have a few extra cocktails when we see George in the city."

He didn't explain who George was exactly, other than to say he was an old friend he met when he lived in Washington D.C. who had fallen in love with a Scottish Lord. I got an insider's view of the married, and otherwise, "haute-homosexuel" population in D.C., which sounded like a pretty exclusive and connected, albeit unofficial, club. Apparently, George, a wealthy "society" member, moved to Scotland a year or two earlier to live with his newfound Lord in a 15th Century Castle outside Glasgow, towers and moat included.

It sounded like Dean traveled through various elite milieus with ease. We laughed comparing how stately homes that have stood for barely a hundred years in America are considered exceedingly old and prized, when nobility in England and Europe were still living in dwellings built over 800 years ago.

Our day together was exceptional. Dean was attentive and charming, and being with him was effortless and comfortable. I felt wooed and flattered. It had been years since I had that feeling with anyone. On and off, I thought to myself that this was someone I could be with for a long time. The thought elated me.

For the most part, we spent the day on the Upper East Side, since that's where my errands were centered and George was staying at the Lowell Hotel, just off Madison on 63rd Street. As a matter of convenience for us all, I made reservations at six for dinner at a charming French Bistro and Bar, directly across the street from the hotel. The owner was a friend of my mother and father, whose townhouse was down the street off Park Avenue, and they had encouraged him when he first started out and opened his small café in the mid 1980's.

Dean and I arrived somewhat early, and the owner greeted us warmly. He sat us down while asking me how my family was doing. It was a nice recognition, and I could see Dean was impressed as he immediately sent over a round of cocktails on him.

I was never much of a drinker, for no particular reason other than the grounding issues that I knew I had difficulty with sometimes. Drinking alcohol or using drugs was not a very good idea for someone whose head was frequently entering and exiting other dimensional realities.

The cocktails were strong, and I got the impression the bartender had been told to be extra generous. By the time I finished one, Dean had had three, and was ordering his fourth.

George arrived, and you would have thought the prodigal son had returned, judging from the alcohol-induced exuberance coming from Dean. We ordered dinner, and had a fairly nice conversation about living in Great Britain. Dean appeared slightly over-served, and for the most part, drank rather than ate.

He held his liquor well, and although somewhat loud, he wasn't falling-down drunk, at least not yet. After dinner, since George was feeling jet-lagged, we decided to cross the street for a quick nightcap at the bar in his hotel before heading home.

At the hotel bar, Dean quickly downed a Bourbon and Soda, followed by another double shot of Bourbon, neat. I had to help steady him walking out of the hotel after saying goodnight to George, and we made our way slowly down to the Parking garage on Lexington. I didn't mind really, he was cute enough and things like this happen in life.

Maybe he was nervous, introducing someone new to old friends. In any case, I was a forgiving person if nothing else, knowing full well that everything happens for a reason. In my world of higher perspectives there were no accidents, or any coincidences for that matter.

Once in the car and on the road, Dean was showing the full effects of someone so drunk they were stammering and having trouble keeping their eyes open. I told him he should take a nap if he felt like it, and I was fine with driving home since I had done it so many times in the past.

For some reason, telling him it was okay if he napped riled him. He became animated the way alcoholics can become agitated for no apparent reason, and he suddenly lashed out with a ferocity that was unexpected. I wondered if he was a mean drunk, or if this was just an anomaly.

"Don't tell me what to do!" he demanded, slurring his words. "It's bad enough I have to watch over you!"

I ignored him.

"You're drunk," I said, annoyed.

"Yeah, what do you expect, when your whole life's being hijacked."

He was becoming belligerent now, not to mention incoherent.

"What's it going to be like, tied to you?" he mumbled.

I continued to excuse him, telling myself it was the alcohol talking. What he was saying didn't make much sense anyway. I answered without expecting a reply, unconcerned we were having a real conversation and certain he wouldn't remember any of it tomorrow. But, I could feel myself becoming agitated.

"Sorry, Dean," I said in an icy tone. "We just met. You don't have to spend any more time with me. We can call it a day whenever you want."

There was a long silence.

"You…have…no idea…who you're dealing with…do you?" he said menacingly, sounding as if he had marbles in his mouth.

"Is that a threat?" I asked, trying to figure out if he was talking about himself or something else.

"You'll be the end of me!" he mumbled again, shaking his head.

It all sounded ridiculous. Was this some form of irony, like when someone tells you they feel so strongly about you they're worried you're going to run them over emotionally?

"How did I get into this?" he whined. "What the Hell do *they* want from me anyway?"

"*They*!?" I questioned, becoming more agitated.

Did he mean the illusive "*they*" that no one ever seemed to identify? Levi Steller's "*they*"? The Steve Moreau, Colonel McCormick and Quantrolics "*they*"?

He turned to me and murmured, "This is *your* fault. If you hadn't shown up, no one would have asked me to *handle* your situation!"

I looked at Dean and saw his eyes drooping. He was as close as anyone can get to losing consciousness.

"What the Hell do you mean, '*handle*'?" I demanded.

He closed his eyes and groaned one last time, annoyed by the question. Slowly, he spelled out an answer before drifting off.

"Handle, as in…H - A - N - D - L - E - R…"

After he passed out, I drove the next 60 miles in silence feeling completely alone.

11. The Borg

We got to my place around one in the morning. Dean was snoring in the passenger seat and I was still reeling from his drunken outburst, so I decided to leave him asleep in the car, parked in front of the barn. I was having my doubts, for sure, but I didn't think he was dangerous. My sympathetic-side kicked in as I walked into the house, and I left the door unlocked in case he woke up and needed to come inside during the night.

Despite being tired the next morning, I was up at 6 and headed into the shower when I heard someone downstairs come into the house. After a few minutes I could smell coffee brewing, and, having fully processed everything from last night, I was, more or less, ready to leave behind what he had said in his inebriated state. It wasn't ideal, I knew that, but now I was pretty clear on what had really brought us together.

Louis Lidner didn't have all those FBI, Interpol and police connections for nothing. He had played his part very well. I assumed Lisa was innocent in all this, and was sure she had no idea she had been duped into being complicit.

Truthfully, before long I started to feel like, so what? Lots of people get together for strange reasons at the beginning. Why should this be any different? What was important was I was learning to recognize exactly how "*they*" worked, not to mention the lengths to which they were willing to go. Still, I wasn't afraid of them, and didn't have anything to hide, so why should it matter?

I was also enamored with the idea of what Dean and I could potentially become together, even if wishful projections like that can badly cloud your inner vision. Maybe it was a good thing he knew all about me, including what I did. Now, I also knew where he was coming from.

He certainly didn't seem to care about what I did, so why should I care about what he was doing. I started thinking it might not be so terrible to have him around in the future to monitor what was happening. If that meant he was going to "handle" me, more power to him.

Besides, I knew we were linked karmically, and that karma would have to be met before we would be released from each other's hold. I suddenly found myself standing in Brigette's shoes, understanding fully how, even when you know exactly what is going on under the surface, the universe will still steer you to the edge of a cliff sometimes to ensure success of the Soul growth it has planned.

As I showered, the door of the master bathroom pushed open slowly. The next thing I knew, Dean was standing there naked, and walked into the small shower with me. He smelled masculine and rugged, like Oak and aged Bourbon, and put his arms around my neck. It was as if nothing had been said the night before.

While we were having coffee and toast afterwards, I asked him if he remembered the evening at all, telling him he was pretty drunk towards the end. He blushed and held his head, which must have still been spinning.

"Truthfully," he said awkwardly, "The last thing I remember was crossing the street to George's hotel. After that, it's pretty much a blur."

Then he added, "I hope I wasn't obnoxious, and didn't say anything embarrassing. Good thing you were there to *handle* me."

"Not to worry," I answered, looking into his eyes. "I can handle *you*. The question is, are you handling *me?*"

He didn't react, but at that moment, it was as if we had come to an arrangement. Once again, nothing was said outright, but everything was implied. Maybe he was telling the truth and didn't remember anything. Then again, maybe he remembered, and this was how the universe had intervened to provide us both with a mutual understanding, so we could fulfill our karmic bargain without resentment.

After coffee, we said a quick goodbye, and Dean made his way out to the rented pick-up and drove off. I was still semi-cautious, but I liked him, and this wasn't a dead stop for me. I decided to let things run their course.

There was other business to think about anyway. In a few short days, I'd be starting at Quantrolics. God only knew where that would lead, especially considering everything I now understood, which technically I wasn't supposed to know, at least not consciously.

Dean called a few times, trying to ingratiate himself and being overly apologetic about the previous night. I expected it to be him for the third time when I picked up the phone again, but it turned out to be someone from Quantrolics calling.

"Mr. Nicolay," a woman's voice said on the phone. "This is Mr. Spivak's secretary calling from Quantrolics. Mr. Spivak was wondering if you could meet with him in the next day or so, before you officially join the company."

"Mr. Spivak, the owner of Quantrolics?" I questioned surprised, wondering why the illusive older physicist would want to meet me.

"Oh, excuse me," she said, "I meant to say my boss, Aaron Spivak, Jr., the Chairman's son."

I really didn't know there was a son, but it was intriguing, since I was constantly told this was a privately held company.

"Do you think you can come by tomorrow around 3PM to meet with him?" she asked.

"Yes," I said, "That's fine, "Which building are you in?"

"Center building, Sublevel One," she said, "Your name will be at the gate and I'll meet you at the door.

"Very good, see you at 3," I told her.

Hanging up, what Ron Mallick said about always remembering whom I reported to flashed across my mind. I couldn't help but wonder if I was getting dragged into some corporate power play, even before officially starting the job. Things were definitely moving fast.

When I got to Quantrolics the next day, I went through the

same routine I had gone through a week before when I met Ron Mallick for the first time.

The only difference was that when Aaron Spivak's secretary met me in the lobby, she handed me an envelope and said, "HR asked me to give this to you. It has all your credentials and copies of your paperwork."

"That Security Clearance card will get you access to the three buildings here, as well as any areas you're authorized to be in."

"Sounds serious," I said. "So, you mean there are areas inside each building that are off limits?"

"Yes, indeed," she responded, "But for the most part, your clearance is pretty high, so you'll have access to anyplace you need to be. This is an Interim Security Clearance for now, since the full clearance investigation can take months."

"Need to know basis," I said, half joking.

"You get used to it around here," she added with a wink, as if we were sharing an inside joke.

I was somewhat surprised when I looked at the vertical-shaped laminated card, and saw that it looked like an official US government security clearance with the Quantrolics name and logo printed at the top. Under the picture and fingerprint, which were floating over a waving American flag, were the words 'Interim Clearance Application: Active-TS/SCI'.

"What's TS/SCI?" I asked innocently.

"Top Secret, Sensitive Compartmented Information," she responded without a second thought, as if I would know what it meant.

I didn't really, so I clammed up. Instead of asking anything else, I placed the lanyard with the card attached around my neck, and wondered why I was getting a clearance package from her and not from Ron's assistant Sarah or someone in his office.

Immediately, I got the distinct message I was to be "shared" between Mallick and Spivak. Ron Mallick had simply gotten to me first, in an effort to implant himself as the dominant player, but now Spivak was going to attempt to brand me as well.

As we walked through the entrance hall of Building Two, I saw Lin come out of the elevator.

She stopped, and said, "Thanks again for Saturday. You're going down to see Aaron, right? I was just there."

I shook my head, and she looked at me intently.

"He's not as bad as he seems," she mused, rolling her eyes.

I was confused. Was she being serious, or joking with me about him. I didn't even know he existed up until yesterday. As I looked over at his secretary, she seemed to be smiling and nodding in agreement.

"You'll see what I mean. It's all good," Lin said, before saying goodbye.

We made our way to Sublevel One of Building Two. Everything was nearly identical to the building next door, which I was in a week before, except in this building Aaron Spivak Jr.'s office was located on the opposite side of the building. Other than that, you would have thought you were in the same place. I wondered if Building One had that same layout.

"You must be the one everyone's talking about!" a voice boomed as it came towards me, before I was through the door.

"Aaron Spivak," he said, shaking my hand vigorously.

"E.M.," I said, responding.

Aaron Spivak, Jr. was about my age or slightly younger, with an offbeat smile. The first thing he said to me, which came immediately on the heels of stating his name, was that he was an Engineer with a Ph.D. from Stanford. He added the date he got his Ph.D. at Stanford as part of identifying himself, which I found really amusing.

You'd never guess his credentials from his dark brown hair, which was cut in a way that made it stick straight up in spikey waves on his head. The look gave him the appearance of someone that had put his finger in a light socket, but lived to tell the tale.

I immediately understood what Lin was talking about. He seemed to gush and act overly enthusiastic, even eccentric about everything. I could see where he might turn a lot of people off with his directness, and, more than that, the strange awkwardness of his movements that personified him.

Regardless, I don't know why, but I liked him. Maybe it was because unlike Ron Mallick, who was a thousand times more charming and sophisticated, Aaron would never have spent half our first meeting together trying to entrain me with hypnotic suggestions. I just couldn't imagine that in his repertoire. He wasn't subtle, considerate or mesmerizing by any means, but he was upfront and outspoken. It was somewhat refreshing, especially after experiencing firsthand the evasive tactics I saw being employed all over Quantrolics.

As I spoke to him, it quickly became apparent that he was intellectually brilliant, but socially inept. Anyone would have just thought he was quirky and awkward, but I was also being told by my Guides that he had chosen to experience personality traits in this lifetime that made him seem aloof and disinterested to almost everyone.

It didn't bother me in the least, and knowing it made it easy to cut through the noise and enjoy his overtly intelligent but stilted nature, even if he did have a hard time looking me in the eye or expressing recognizable emotions. God knows I was always considered "quirky" myself, and if I hadn't learned what was actually happening to me, or figured out how to relegate the invisible things I saw to their proper compartment, I might have been treated exactly the same way he may have been treated at times.

I think he liked me from the start, but one couldn't be sure, mostly because of the way he remained emotionless and noncommittal. Still, I got the impression he felt comfortable, and maybe that was because he was aware, based on what he knew about me, that I was aware of his hidden personality traits. That may have made it easier for him to talk to me.

The conversation went all over the map, which I found fun. He wasn't afraid to tell me how much he wanted to work with me and hear what I had to offer, and was particularly interested in hearing my "analysis" of the global issues he felt we faced.

Aaron explained that his main area of interest had always been the international arena, and he said he would follow my initiatives and reports very carefully. He also told me outright that it was important that we "keep up a good front". So, almost as an afterthought, he asked me to put together good global marketing materials whenever I got the chance. It didn't seem pressing to him, but he explained that his reasoning stemmed from a desire to make sure the company would always be selected to install its control systems in major building projects around the world.

He also seemed incredibly proud of the company, as well as his father, who he referred to as Mr. Spivak, Senior. Aaron became clumsily animated talking about the fact that the company's technology was used in national banks, embassies, government buildings and corporate headquarters around the world. He even let it slip that by continuing to place Quantrolics products in important building projects, through the company's constant wooing of architects, developers, designers and end-users, the extraordinary service being rendered to the free world would continue.

It was an odd take on the company and its products, unless, as I suspected, they were being used for a purpose other than the one intended. Little did I know at that point where my suspicions would one day lead.

Luckily for me, Aaron did almost all the talking and I only had to agree from time to time. Even then, he didn't really listen, but would go off on some tangent about the importance of a strong façade, and especially, the contribution Quantrolics was making to national and global security, which was equally strange.

I hadn't met Spivak, Sr. yet, but as I watched, I identified with someone whose father was more of a competitor than a parent. I felt sympathetic, and decided that if possible I would try to help him.

I was told his life mission was to learn lessons around pride, and because of that I knew he would always look for ways to boost his standing at Quantrolics. He needed to cement himself into the company's future based on his own merit in ways that went beyond nepotism. Choosing the father that he did for this lifetime, it would always take triple the effort to prove his self-worth.

Our conversation was far less formal than any meeting I had had so far at Quantrolics. It was when I was most relaxed that he came up with the real reason, at least from what I could tell, that he had called the meeting.

It turned out that Aaron wanted one of my "Briefings". This was the first real request from anyone at the company, and I was pleased to get it.

The Briefing he was looking for would be two-fold, so essentially two different reports. First, it was to analyze the future goals of China. He asked for details that would explain how I felt about the Chinese government and "market" in general, particularly what they might be planning in the future. It was a pretty broad topic, considering.

I wasn't put off by it however, since coming on the heels of my work with the Portuguese Mission in Macau on the future of Hong Kong and Macau after turnover to the Chinese, some of the information had been glimpsed by me already. I had only to relook at things, and then make a few additional comments to create a new report that would answer Aaron's question.

Secondarily, he wanted me to take a look at the Middle East, and in particular the Islamic world. This would require more work and much more time. I had some basic experience at certain levels. I had numerous friends at school that came from Iran, Kuwait and Saudi Arabia, had spent periods living in Indonesia when working in Asia and had visited Turkey, Lebanon, Tunisia and Morocco in the past. But that was pretty much the extent of it.

I had never been asked to remote view these areas however, or look at Islam as a whole and what was highlighted around that on the timeline. It would be difficult to do a thorough job, I thought to myself, but I was excited about the challenge. I was also intrigued by what we would find out by remote viewing events in that part of the world on the current timeline trajectory.

"Good luck, and see you soon," Aaron said without any real emotion, looking down and already moving on to another project.

I went straight home after our meeting, determined to begin work on the Briefings immediately. As expected, when I tuned-in, the information I uncovered was striking. There was so much flooding forward as I looked, my biggest dilemma was what not to include in the Brief, not to mention how to express it all without seeming overly dramatic or alarmist.

I wanted my first Briefing to be a thorough and objective example of what I could do, including what I saw on the timeline. But I also wanted to reveal a higher perspective on what would occur far into the future and why things would happen this way, demonstrating how future events I saw on the timeline were integrated into a higher, albeit hidden, universal purpose and destiny.

First up was the China Briefing. My report began by stating that outwardly, there would be no apparent change in China's strategy towards the outside world between 2000 and 2015. The Briefing for that period described China's domestic and foreign policy as a unique long-term strategy of "assimilation."

I emphasized that the Chinese had no time limit allotted to this, and did not have any intention of aggressively taking over anything. For now, they were content to very slowly "assimilate" the Pacific, if not eventually, the world.

China's ability to hold US debt was not only part of a plan to ensure markets for its cheaper goods, but needed to be seen as part of a greater global strategy of dominance through this strategy of assimilation. In addition to influence in the US, there was also a plan in place to finance large-scale modernization projects that would serve to ingratiate China in the Third World, particularly South America and Africa. This was also an important phase of its world "assimilation" program as seen on the timeline through approximately 2025, and even slightly beyond.

At that point on the timeline however, China's assimilation policies looked to become far more aggressive, taking advantage of coinciding world events, particularly extraordinary turmoil that would take hold in the United States after 2020. I made a specific reference to a fabricated global biologic event that would grip the world in the late 2010's, as well as extreme events that would emerge in the Middle East less than a decade after that, which I would detail in my Middle East Briefing.

The Briefing suggested those dramatic Middle East events would emerge out of a CIA-fabricated war on terrorism that would begin earlier, after the year 2000. It would smolder for decades and ultimately be the basis for World War III, especially when it was seen to spill out from Iraq and Syria, where it had been contained, into Palestine, Lebanon and then Israel, years later.

This resulting conflict would culminate in limited nuclear exchange in the Middle East, and would bankrupt the United States, as well as the West in general. That failure would lead to an opening for Chinese and Russia in their quest for world dominance beginning after the mid 2020's.

I touched on the fact that after what would become known as World War III, following the long and devastating upheaval that would begin in Eurasia and spread quickly through the region and into the Middle East, a path would be paved towards a future cultural renaissance centered there, as well as in parts of the Pacific. Once begun, this artistic and cultural renaissance would spread worldwide and be a prevalent force globally through the second half of the 21st Century.

Often, when viewing the timeline in this way, you can see events strung together that would seem to be independent and have no real connection, but are actually closely interlocked as the same event. These appear this way either because they are karmically linked, or because they are a direct result of mass consciousness and the events are being used as a background against which Souls experience opportunities for growth in the prevailing time period.

An example of linked global events would be viewing World War I, World War II and World War III as separate events, as they are expressed in history due to large gaps of time between them. They appear as one unified, consistent event when remote viewed on the dimensional timeline.

Unfortunately, what I remote viewed after 2000 on the timeline did not bode well for North America, especially the United States. I could see clearly that the great experiment that was the United States would falter sometime between 2025 and 2030, leading to the eventual breakup of the US into regional powers. Former US States appeared on the timeline to band together following this disintegration, caused as a result of war, bankruptcy and extreme partisan internal bickering and chaos that would lead to the demise of the US Federal Government.

Those former regions of the US that banded together successfully would navigate the difficult times in North America of the 2030's through 2050's. This was especially true of regions such as the Pacific Union, the New England Alliance, the Michigan-Illinois-Minnesota-Wisconsin Territories, the Republic of Texas and the Florida Union.

Hawaii would fare the best, becoming wealthy as the new "Monaco" of the Pacific. It would become used by future international elites, especially from China and Russia, as a financial safe haven and money-laundering center.

Alaska, on the other hand, would encounter invasion by Russia sometime in the first half of the 21st Century. Called a "reclamation" project by Russia, fierce Alaskan militia resistance would last years, but eventually drive out the Russian attempt, leading to the formation of an independent Alaska after 2050.

It appeared that those areas of the former US that exhibited the most intense bickering and backsliding beginning in the mid

2020's, especially those States in the middle and south of the current country, would erupt into chaos. These areas would be fought over by warlords, gangs, religious factions and anyone with a following, enough money or standing militia, creating City-States similar to those in history of the Dark Ages.

These conflicts would appear to the outside world as a Second US Civil War. Population's still living in these regions would suffer immensely, and it appeared their fate was a karmic balancing of events from the first US Civil War of the 1860's.

Incursions of militias and marauding bandits into areas controlled by newly formed regional States, would cause successful former US States, in conjunction with Mexico and Canada, to request the assistance of China and Russia in policing these areas. This would fulfill prophecies of Russia and Chinese joining to invade North America, while also fulfilling the Karmic balancing needed as a result of years of American interference and "policing" of other world regions, where in the past the US government and military had instigated revolution, crime and chaos in distant parts of the world using the excuse of national security.

To drive the concept of Chinese assimilation home, I likened the Chinese to the "Borg" from the sci-fi TV series, "Star Trek". The efforts of that fictional extraterrestrial group of transhumanistic cyborgs to infiltrate parts of the universe, was as close as I could get to describing the Chinese strategy of assimilation, which I saw being implemented on the dimension timeline. I thought the analogy would be widely understood, since it was a relatively new and well-known subject depicted in the well-liked Star Trek series, but as I would discover, I was wrong.

In any case, what I was trying to impress upon the reader essentially was that, at the time, China was not interested in the conquest or take-over of anything. However, it was in fact, obsessed with the idea of "assimilating" everyone and everything into a Chinese sphere of influence. There was a subtle difference. As an example, I stated Hong Kong and Macau would simply be assimilated, and, over time, every aspect of Mainland China would be introduced, as these city-states became the first territorial gains made by China through the process of assimilation. That process would be applied down the line, as it were.

Describing this concept in the near term was easy, as it applied to the coming 20 to 30-year period after the year 2000. After 2020 however, things on the timeline seemed to shift dramatically and China appeared to become a much more aggressive player in world affairs. By 2050, China would be a major force to be reckoned with, called upon, together with its future ally Russia, to become the world's police state, in ways similar to how America served in that same role globally after World War II.

My Briefing explained this by detailing a shift coming in energetic flows that travel around the world from East to West over the course of given periods on the dimensional timeline. These winds of change result in various world regions, civilizations and cultures becoming highlighted and energized at those times, and the process can be seen metaphorically as a kind of energy "weather" pattern that traverses the planet in conjunction with the dimensional timeline.

The current Ascension period, the evolutionary process that all Galaxies, Planetary Bodies, Universal Dimensions and Souls go through, which would be at full throttle by the mid 21st Century, coincided with this shift in energetic spheres of influence. These influential energies would pass from North America to

Asia, in much the same way the same shift occurred from Europe to North America in the 17th Century, and before that, from Eurasia to Europe at the time of the Roman Empire, from Mesopotamia to Eurasia (and Egypt) before that, and, even earlier, from Asia (India) to Mesopotamia.

I saw the spiral timeline coming full circle again. The shift of energetic power was making its way back to Asia and would play an important part in future events beginning after 2030, and particularly after 2050. Its impact would alter not only China's role in the world, but its view of itself forever as well.

I finished the Brief by stating that China had made covert agreements with an off-world civilization, which had secretly shown them the same information I was remote viewing now. I refrained from providing everything I saw. Some of it was so shocking and removed from the norm that I worried I would be laughed at. Sadly, as part of their alliance with this extraterrestrial group, the Chinese were provided with technology that would help it increase its military and technological prowess in ways the US could not even fathom.

In addition, the extraterrestrials were providing secret factions of the Chinese government with transhumanistic bio-technologies that would alter human and Earth biology forever. What the Chinese were unaware of was the fact that they were being used to alter human physiology in ways that would allow extraterrestrials Souls to easily incarnate in human physical form in the near future, thereby allowing extraterrestrial Soul dominance on Earth over the coming 250 years.

I was afraid of not being taken seriously if I related too much of this information, so I left large parts of it out, even though it was truthfully what I saw on the timeline as an important aspect of the coming global age of bio-terrorism. That included sanctioned 21st Century global initiatives that would shunt Human Beings innate Soul connections and guidance, as well as alter human, animal and plant biology in detrimental ways after 2015.

As these threats became clearer on the timeline, I tried to include more of them in my future Briefings whenever it was applicable. Yet, I always remained reticent about sharing these insights.

I never received any comments on those aspects of the Briefings anyway. At times, I wondered if this was because those behind the people I reported to also had their own extraterrestrial connections, similar to the ones I described the Chinese as having.

That was something I could also see on the timeline, and it may have also explained why there was never any comment on these parts of the Briefs, as well as why I continued to be reticent about providing that information. Perhaps they just didn't take that subject seriously, but more than likely, since they never disputed or ridiculed anything either, it may have been because it was true.

What I found most interesting, and somewhat important personally, was that as this information emerged more and more often in my own remote viewing sessions, my understanding of Levi Steller's concern and fascination with the subject also grew clearer. Extraterrestrial involvement, under secret agreement and treaty with various world governments, including the US, Russia and China, among others, was a truth that most would scoff at. It was an involvement I could now plainly see that confirmed the predictions Levi Steller had mentioned to me during that fateful plane ride to Paris years earlier.

Whereas the China Briefing was a story about opportunism, with a government willing to take advantage of global opportunities, wherever and whenever they presented themselves on the dimensional timeline, the Middle East and Islam Report was another matter entirely. I was unsure how to approach this one, since when I looked at it there were so many consequential tangents, connections, twists and turns. It seemed almost unfathomable.

Whenever I see this kind of complexity come up on the timeline, I know these are not random, opportunistic happenings based on the Free Will of individuals, nations or groups. These events are the stuff of destiny. They appear on the timeline as things that are meant to be, with little to no alteration other than the actual time period, which shifts backwards and forward on a timeline that is dynamic and changing constantly. These are the events that shape the mass consciousness of the world and the environment against which Souls incarnate, for decades, if not centuries.

There was a bit of overlap with the China Report, but this Brief would have far reaching impact, from what I could tell. I decided to give some background, so I began with an explanation of the symbolic importance of world locations, as they relate to the electromagnetic grid system of planet Earth.

The electromagnetic grid system of Earth is essentially the Chakra system of the planet. It is the heart and main access field of vibrational communication between dimensions, as well as between dimensional sublevels. In addition, and perhaps most importantly, it is also the central unifying means by which a Soul energetically connects with the physical Beings it incarnates on Earth at any given time on the dimensional timeline. Soul energy is channeled through the electromagnetic grid of Earth.

Through this system, higher guidance is communicated to each of us through the physical body's Chakra system. This messaging is communicated through an individual's DNA and Pineal gland, and, as a two-way street, the Pineal and DNA energetically message back through the same vibrational system, informing the Soul of our daily status in physical reality.

It this way, the Soul is in constant communication with us, providing guidance and instruction via the glandular structure of the body, the Chakras and the DNA, as well as other related physical and energetic systems. In turn, each of us is also vibrationally communicating our status and progress back to our Soul, albeit subconsciously.

Cellular memory and genetic, or DNA, activation connects through the grid in this way as well. In other words, unique vibrational messaging coming from the Soul is relayed interdimensionally and picked up electromagnetically through a person's energy body, or energy system.

Once interpreted by the person's DNA, as informed by their glandular and genetic structure, as well as their overall cellular makeup, Soul purpose is achieved. The same vibrational messaging happens in reverse, from a physical living Being back to their Soul. In understanding this, it becomes clear how vital Earth's Chakra system, or electromagnetic grid, is to everyone incarnated on the planet. And precisely because of this, a high degree of symbolism can be seen contained within it.

I decided to begin the Brief there. First of all, I explained that every age, or period of civilization, has three symbolic focal points that represent the era's energetic expression. These three focal points symbolize an historic era, or civilization's Heart, Mind and Soul.

For the current civilization, the symbolic focal points seen on the dimensional timeline were 1) the Bamiyan Buddhas in Afghanistan, representing the heart chakra of the culture; 2) the World Trade Towers in New York City, representing the mind chakra; and 3) the Cathedral of Notre Dame in Paris, representing the Soul chakra of the Age itself.

Because of their symbolic importance related to the modern age, each of these "temples" were highlighted on the timeline as targets that would be marked for destruction. Their destruction would symbolically signal subconsciously to each and every Soul incarnated on the planet that the current Age and civilization was coming to an end.

I explained how "terrorists" would appear to be the perpetrators each time. This was the point at which there seemed to be a connection to Islam. But this was not entirely correct, and since it was a complicated scenario, with many twists and turns, a complete explanation was imperative. These events would not only change the geopolitical face of the world over the coming 3 to 5 decades, it would lead directly to what would eventually be designated World War III.

The Report connected the coming events to the past, in particular to World War II. I went as far as to mention a strange tie-in I saw with Kamikaze attacks used in a new way that would shock the world. I mentioned that those perpetrating these upcoming events were actually trained in the West, and they would use the cover of religious zealot, although they were actually proficient military personnel trained by Western Intelligence, particularly covert US agencies.

Ironically, these individuals were seen on the timeline as reincarnations of Japanese who had lost their lives when American pilots dropped the first atomic bombs on Japan. I went as far as to state that the American and other victims of the coming attack on one of these focal centers would be the reincarnations of individuals who were either connected to the development of those bombs, or were in some way connected to its deployment.

Thus, I could see individual karmic balancing taking place on an individual Soul level. In addition, karmic balancing could be seen happening on a larger scale as a result of devastating war atrocities that had taken place during World War II, with the atomic bombings of Hiroshima and Nagasaki.

As a result of the destruction of at least one of these focal point grid "temples" in the near future, the Brief stated that an all-out effort would be made to "punish" the perpetrators, who would be identified as terrorists associated following a new interpretation and fundamentalist approach to Islam. However, as is often the case, which I felt the readers of the Brief would resonate with, designation of these groups as terrorists, formed part of a carefully crafted "front" for another group entirely.

In reality, the groups initiating these terrors were being financed and trained by the West itself. On the timeline, it appeared that covert factions of Western military intelligence, reaching back to the Soviet conflict in Afghanistan, would implement a plan to turn public sentiment in the West against Islam, thereby permitting military intervention in the Middle East over the course of decades.

Once implemented, following the destruction of the symbolic focal point, Western military intervention, which, among other things was intended to reorganize the geo-political makeup of the Middle East and prolong use of the US Petrodollar as the global currency of trade, would readily disrupt governments regionally and internationally, eventually leading to a massive World War that would be used to alter the geopolitical structure and face of the modern world.

These conflicts would seem somewhat contained for decades, but eventually violence would spill into Syria, in one form or another. Tensions there would escalate and various international coalitions would become involved.

The conflict would bubble over and spill into Israel and Lebanon at a much later date. This marker would be the primary signal that World War III had actually begun. Despite the fact that the conflicts would appear to be unrelated, in truth they had been orchestrated to develop in just this way over the course of decades.

I did not go into the final outcome of all this in the Briefing, since I saw it would be devastating for the West, and I wasn't certain those at Quantrolics were ready to hear it. It hadn't been part of Aaron's original question anyway.

However, I clearly saw that this war seen on the timeline, decades in the future at that moment, would lead to limited nuclear use in the Middle East after 2025. After that, it would also include the revenge use of suitcase nukes by underground terrorists planted for decades in European cities, including Rome and Paris. There was even a limited or curtailed event seen on the timeline in the late 2020's in the US.

This same vision saw alliances form between a newly empowered but faltering Russia and a calculating China, while simultaneously, turmoil from inside itself would lead to the disintegration of the US Federal government. In time, partisan turmoil, combined with the bankrupting of the US, and what appeared to be a rebellion causing Congress to hold-up in the Capital Building in Washington, D.C., would begin an inevitable chain of events that would lead to the complete breakup up of the United States by the 2030's.

After completing the Briefings based on Aaron Spivak's questions for Quantrolics, I was exhausted. I proofed the work several times, removing anything that might sound too astonishing or overly extreme, and wrote an email to Aaron, copying Ron Mallick. Then I relaxed, expecting to start my new position on Monday.

Meanwhile, Dean called and asked if I wanted to get together for the weekend. He thought he would come up to see me in order to save me a drive into the city, and said he would try out one of the bus services to find out what they were like. It was a good idea to try different methods of seeing each other if we were going to spend time together, since we were still living an hour away. I also realized, based on my New York experience with him, that drinking without the need to drive home might be a real consideration.

I picked him up Friday evening at the small bus terminal in Reading, and we had a nice weekend together, getting to know each other better and enjoying all the aspects of finding out about someone new that you like. The unwritten agreement we had seemed to be holding, and I had no objection to being with him, although I decided I would never mention anything I was doing for Quantrolics, particularly items like the Reports I had just accomplished a day earlier. Dean never asked about my work, even indirectly, so it was a perfect arrangement.

I dropped him off at the bus terminal early in the evening that Sunday, and went home to spend a quiet night getting ready to start at Quantrolics the next day. When I got home, there was a message on my home answering machine. It was from Aaron Spivak.

"E.M., Aaron Spivak here. Great Reports," he said flatly.

"So, there's a change of plans and Ron's in full agreement with me on this. We'd like you to take a trip globally for us, and look over some of our foreign operations and offices. Get to know the places and people in those offices, if you see what I mean."

It sounded exactly like something I would tell myself to do, if I were them. His message continued.

"It will probably take you about 30 days to complete, but we'd like you to leave immediately. Instead of coming into the office tomorrow as planned, why don't you do whatever you need to prepare to be away for a while, and we'll have our agency send you over an itinerary to leave the day after tomorrow."

Was he joking, I wondered. They don't want me to bother coming over to an office ten minutes away, and instead they'd like to send me around the world first? I was mystified, but in a way, excited. I got the distinct impression I was being accepted by them, and the Briefings I created had somehow either intrigued them or cemented my abilities in their eyes. Whatever it was, the one thing I knew how to do was travel. You might even say it was my forte, other skills aside.

After getting the message, I decided I'd better take a look at my emails as well. When I checked, I already had an email from the company's in-house travel agency. The email asked me to provide them with a list of travel particulars, as well as any details I wanted them to know about airlines, frequent flyer information, hotels and other preferences.

Next up on the list, I saw that Ron had responded to my Briefs as well.

Ron's email read: "Thanks for forwarding these very interesting Reports. Aaron will be speaking with you, and I concur with the decision. One question – What is the "Borg?""

I laughed. Of all the things in those Reports, this was his question? In a way, I got the feeling that by not asking for any further explanations, but agreeing with Aaron on the decision to immediately send me around the world, he was tacitly confirming the validity of the Briefs. At least that was my hope.

I smiled to myself, and at the same time decided I wouldn't respond to him about the "Borg". If he were really interested in understanding what I meant, he would need to find out for himself.

12. Around the World in 30 Days

By nine o'clock the next morning, a messenger had arrived at my house with an around-the-world business class ticket in hand. At least I wouldn't be roughing it.

The package also included an itinerary with cities, dates and hotels, as well as a typed-up company directory, with office locations, contact names and phone numbers. The in-house agency provided a sheet of travel arrangements and directions, and a 24/7 phone number and email address, in case of necessary changes or problems.

There were also a few simplistic Quantrolics brochures included in the envelope, all using the same layouts and rendered in various languages. Essentially, they were all the same brochure, with images of building system control panels, transistors and related undistinguishable high- tech equipment with text translated into Chinese, Japanese, Spanish, French, Italian, German or Arabic, depending on what country the brochure happened to be used in.

The images were static, stale and old fashioned, and I could tell that the brochures had been designed by some engineer who had no clue what he was doing, and probably didn't care. From the two I could read, one in French and one in Italian, I could see they were awful, literal translations, practically incomprehensible when translated from the original English.

I immediately thought of the classic American branding gaffe, where Chevrolet spent a small fortune introducing their new car, the "Nova", to South American markets. None of the arrogant American brand managers sitting in Detroit had thought to consider that in Spanish, "No-va" means "doesn't go". The Quantrolics brochures seemed equally laughable and ineffective. I would need to fix that as soon as I could.

When I checked my email again, Ron had copied Aaron and I on emails he sent to most of the contact names on the list, introducing me and asking for their full cooperation in showing me around and introducing me to Quantrolics' overseas operations. He described me as the company's new International Marketing and Communications Director, and I was impressed with the efficiency of it all. Clearly, they had done this before.

With so much planned travel, I was determined not to bring too much, so I packed my favorite international carry-on bag that amply held a suit and whatever I needed to make it through at least 7 to 10 days at a time. It was summer, so I didn't need any cold weather items, and I had never been afraid to use hotel laundries, like some people are.

Judging from the upscale nature of the hotels I was booked at, sending things out wouldn't be any problem. One good carry-on and a large, flexible leather brief case that could hold some files, my laptop and a book, was all I really needed. It wasn't going to be a fashion show.

After I had put my things together, I took another look at the tickets and had an idea. I would be flying from Philadelphia to Hong Kong, via San Francisco the next day, so why not spend the night at Dean's place in Center City, and then just take a taxi to the airport, which wasn't far from there.

I called Dean to let him know what was happening, since I really hadn't had time to tell him the news after finding out myself late yesterday evening. It was a good opportunity to test the waters and see how he felt about the possibility of not seeing me for the coming month, and I wondered if we could sustain what we were building, considering how new it all was.

When I reached him and told him, there was a complete lack of surprise in his voice that was noticeable. Maybe it's because he's at the office and someone is listening, I reasoned.

"That's very interesting," he said, matter-of-factly. Then he added, "You know, I've been thinking about taking a few days off sometime this month. When will you be in Europe?"

I looked again at the itinerary and read the destinations out loud. They had me going to Hong Kong first, where I would meet local company representatives, then on to Mainland China, going to Beijing and Shanghai. That was possible since I already had a multiple entry business visa for Mainland China from my previous life with Leo and Brigette. After China, I continued on to South Korea, and then Tokyo. From Tokyo, I went to Taiwan, then on to Singapore, and then to Jakarta.

I knew Java pretty well, so I entertained the idea of a personal side trip to Borobudur in Yogyakarta, or Bali, two of my favorite mystical places on the planet. I imagined I'd check into that possibility when I was there, depending on how busy I was.

After the Asia and South East Asia legs of the trip, I would fly from Jakarta to Amsterdam, then from there to Hamburg in Germany, then on to Geneva, Paris and London. From London, I would fly back to Philadelphia. Around the world in 30 days.

"Paris," Dean said calmly, "That sounds like the ticket."

"How about I plan to meet you for a weekend in Paris as your trip is winding down." Then he added, "You can catch me up on everything I missed."

It was an odd statement to make, and I remembered again the drunken discourse in the car coming back from New York that night.

"Sounds good," I said, without missing a beat.

"Oh, and one other thing," I said hesitatingly, not wanting to sound too pushy. "Would you mind having some company tonight? Instead of going to the airport directly from here to-morrow, I can have the car service bring me down to your place early this evening, and then I'll just take a taxi to the airport in the morning. I'm scheduled to leave from Philadelphia on United at around 11."

I was relieved when he responded that he thought it was a per-fect idea. As soon as we hung up, I called the in-house travel agency to change the car service pick-up for later that day, going to Center City, Philadelphia, instead of the airport. Then I fin-ished getting ready for my trip.

Dean and I had a quiet evening. Our relationship was becoming familiar and comfortable now. I left my carry-on bag downstairs since I had the few things I needed for one night in my brief case.

We spent most of the time talking, and he asked me to email him as often as I could from wherever I was to tell him how it was going. I winced, but shook my head in the affirmative. I had always been a prolific letter writer, and even though most of it was by email now, I still corresponded with old friends, like Lisa and Brigette, on a regular basis providing them with a fairly unique blend of travel log and metaphysical observation. Keeping in touch with Dean wasn't going to be an issue. At least he wouldn't be disappointed in whatever I sent him.

We left the house at the same time the next morning, and I made my way to the airport to check-in for the flight. I was running a little late, so I went straight to the gate to wait for boarding.

Sitting there by herself reading, I saw Lin.

"What the heck?" I said smiling, as she looked up. "Are we on this flight together?"

"Didn't they tell you -- that's just like them," she answered, shaking her head back and forth. "Aaron called Sunday night and said he thought it would be a good idea if I joined you."

As we sat talking, I wondered if maybe Lin had intuitive or remote viewing skills of her own. It certainly would make sense to put us together if that was the case. Like having a fail-safe switch, relying on confirmation from both viewers to validate the information being received by either one.

We'd have to see on that, but in the meantime, I was happy about the situation. In fact, I was thrilled at the idea of having a travel companion, if not a colleague who would understand exactly where I was coming from, especially one that I really liked.

"But haven't you seen this all before?" I asked her.

"Yes, I have -- when I started with the company about a year ago I did a similar 'tour'," she said. "I've been to most of the offices in Asia, and know the people involved there. Definitely some language barriers, so that's probably why they thought it was a good idea if I went too, at least for the Asian part of the trip."

We were flying business class, but weren't sitting together. We changed planes in San Francisco, and walked on and off the flights together talking. As per most long-haul flights to Asia, the business section was relatively large, so we barely saw each other in flight once we were on that leg of the trip.

When we arrived in Hong Kong the next morning, we were weary eyed, but still somewhat rested, since flights to Asia are long enough to allow some continuous hours of sleep. Going the opposite direction, from West to East, was always a more problematic direction for me. This is because the natural flow of planetary energies travel from East to West, so flying against them is contrary to the natural flow of energy, and it can be felt within the physical nervous system.

Trips to Asia from the East, allow the body to naturally adapt to frequency and vibrational changes, whereas trips East, such as to Europe, are far more jarring on the physical body, since it doesn't have time to adjust to the electromagnetic changes that are always interfacing with it. For that reason, among other things, flights to Asia are always more enjoyable for me.

Lin and I made our way to the Grand Hyatt Hong Kong, where we were staying. Hotels in Asia are amazing in that each is a world unto itself. They are fabricated as cities within cities, constructed like forums in the ancient world, where business, commerce, entertainment and pleasure all seamlessly meet. This is true as much for locals as it is for international business and other travelers.

The concept of energy circulation, elemental influences and curing energetic anomalies, including karmic imbalances, through Feng Shui and other means, which many in the West would ridicule and call magical thinking, is never lost on good hotels or businesses in Asia. I clearly remember my first meeting with Leo and upper management of a giant hotel group in Hong Kong years earlier, and distinctly recall our discussion concerning the use of ancient energy techniques and Feng Shui throughout the company's corporate building, as well as all its hotels and other environments, in order to subtly and subconsciously entice every person into a specific state of "being" as soon as they walked through the door.

Some people, especially business people from the US and the West, are unaware how well orchestrated the invisible energy factors of these businesses can be. They assume that the feeling they get is just a matter of coincidence, good luck, force of will or some other unknowable. In fact, using subtle energies and spiritual purpose to improve the odds is a highly sought-after marker of success, and esoteric initiatives meant to achieve desired goals of this kind are grounded in metaphysics, and carefully cultivated for maximum benefit.

Sometimes, simply understanding that an influence can be derived from such things is half the battle to using it successfully. The West, thinking itself serious and modern, scoffs at such ideas to their peril, especially at a time when the winds of change energetically favor the Pacific Rim and Asia. The Grand Hyatt Hong Kong, relatively new at the time we checked in now, incorporated all these philosophies in spades, and the experience was exactly as you would expect. The place was energized from within, and stunning.

We didn't have much planned the day of our arrival, so it was mostly spent recouping from the long journey. In the hotel room, I opened my suitcase to take out a change of clothes and get my suit pressed, and lying there on top of my carefully packed clothes was a leather-framed, 5X7-photographed portrait of Dean.

It was a black and white glamour shot, professionally done, taken from above with him looking over his shoulder, chin pointed upwards. He could have been a 1930's movie hero in the shot, and I had to laugh at how posed it looked. Dean must have slipped it into my bag when it was sitting downstairs at his house the day before.

Nevertheless, it was unexpected and completely endearing. I decided once and for all that this guy was a keeper, even if he was somehow loosely connected to Quantrolics.

The next day, Lin and I hit the town moving fast. Our first stop was the Quantrolics office not far from the hotel in the Wan Chai district, off Hennessy. The office was small and cramped, as many are in older buildings in Hong Kong, but Lin was well received by the Manager there, and he gave me a warm greeting as well. The first order of business was to go over current projects.

Quantrolics was in the process of installing complete building control systems in the headquarters of one of the largest banks in Hong Kong, as well as all of its bank branches located throughout the city. It was doing the same in Shanghai, under the supervision of the Shanghai Quantrolics office, which we would be visiting in the coming week, and there was a secondary plan to do the same at offices around the world at some point in the future.

Lin and the office manager went back and forth about the project, most of which was in Chinese and completely uninteresting to me since it involved engineering discussions concerning installations, importing materials, testing and training. At one point, spreadsheets with costs were shown around. I couldn't follow the conversations in Chinese, so as they talked I looked over the spreadsheets, which clearly either came to them from the US, or were formatted in a Western manner.

I glanced at the numbers on the page, and then looked again more closely. They didn't make sense. Any high schooler could see from the spreadsheets that the entire project was being done at a tremendous loss to Quantrolics.

Thinking I was missing something, I asked Lin if I could ask the Manager a question, explaining politely at the same time that since I was very late to the game, I probably wasn't reading the numbers correctly.

"According to this," I questioned, "The entire project is being implemented at a giant loss?"

Then, just in case I was making a fool of myself, I added, "I apologize if I'm misunderstanding."

The entire room went silent. The Chinese who spoke English looked at me like I had just said the unspeakable. Lin said something in Chinese quickly, and then turned to me.

"Let's talk about that later. For now, the discussion is how to get some of the Quantrolics equipment needed for this project through customs, which Jacky is handling for us so we can move on to Phase III."

I agreed, and remained silent. After the meeting, I told Jacky, making sure I was deferring to him, how impressed I was with his work, and said I was happy to assist him and his team in any way I could.

I also promised that, per my introduction from Ron and Aaron, I would create new marketing materials for him that would impress his clients in Hong Kong, and help him ensure speedy access through customs and otherwise. I knew how important a strong "face" can be in Asia, and this would be something he could legitimately use that would resonate with him.

At the same time, although I didn't say it out loud, I was cynically thinking to myself, 'Some gloss-varnished new brochures and a few hundred bucks to a custom's official should speed things up nicely'. It was probably judgmental on my part, but having dealt extensively with business in Asia, I knew it was a normal part of doing business there, and a consideration most Chinese would make.

As soon as we left the office, I turned to Lin.

"What the Hell, Lin? I blurted out. "Quantrolics is losing its shirt on this project! Is there something I don't know?"

She looked at me in agreement.

"I've been thinking the same thing since I joined the company," she said. "Every time you ask about it, everyone just gives you a blank stare. I can only think they don't care, or they plan to use this as some kind of lost leader, to get other, bigger projects in Asia. The problem is, all the projects are big, and they're all lost leaders."

"You know, the "money-is-no-object" attitude I've seen at this company seems pretty pervasive. Am I wrong?" Then I added, "Are they making money on the other side, with add-ons, repairs or subscriptions – like when you buy the cheap printer, but the replacement ink cartridge cost more than your monthly salary?"

"I've wondered about that too," Lin said, "Not that I can see. There aren't any add-ons after the fact, and tech support for life is completely free. Repairs are nominal too. The other odd thing is that back in Pennsylvania, they don't seem to care about the expenses or the losses, and they *really* don't want to talk about it either."

"Well, I guess it's a private company, so they can do whatever they want," I said, trying to reason out the inconsistencies. "They're privately held, so they don't really have to answer to anyone, and they're not obliged to release financials if they don't want to."

Lin agreed.

"I've basically been told not to go there," she said, then added, "And I was told my job is to just oversee the sale of certain high-profile installations, keep the end-users happy and keep more projects coming."

I thought about it as we rode through Hong Kong to our next stop. We hadn't been there for 24 hours, and already I had identified something that was shouting at me for closer attention. It would be hard for me to put it down. I decided I would need to take a deeper look at the situation as soon as I had some time.

Our meeting with bank officials was mostly ceremonial. I noted to myself that everyone at the table looked like they were fresh out of Grad School, when in fact they were all fairly seasoned executives. At least that was the air they projected, which is also common in Asia. Still, I could tell they looked to the West for guidance, and they were especially enamored of anything high-tech oriented.

Lin presented them with an update, and showed the proper amount of deference, while also imparting what they considered superior knowledge about the project overall. They listened silently with stone faces, but based on what I could feel happening under the surface, they did everything but ooh and aah.

I learned at that meeting how extensive and invasive the building and office control systems that Quantrolics designed, sold and installed could be. From security to lighting, right down to heating and cooling, employee monitoring, audio-visual equipment, security fencing, safes and deposit box settings, and even window shades, Quantrolics provided a seamless high-tech approach to complete building system controls.

All control systems funneled pertinent information, as well as control, to one central source that could be monitored and maintained by a handful of personnel. I had to admit, the company's systems, which were designed and specifically tailored to meet the client's needs, big or small, were impressive.

When it came to engineering the systems, and describing them, even explaining half in Chinese and half in English, I could tell Lin knew her stuff. She dazzled our audience, and I understood why Quantrolics considered her an asset. We left the client meeting at the bank to a plethora of compliments, and excitement about the future.

When we were finished in Hong Kong, we went on to Mainland China, starting in Beijing first. To be honest, Beijing is not one of my favorite places. The strong scent of Clove cigarettes as soon as you walk out of the airport, and the thick air caused by clouds of pollution hanging over the city can be trying. They've made a valiant effort to clean things up, but in my opinion, it hasn't been very successful.

The sheer number of people also makes it a difficult place to navigate, and that factor, which is prevalent throughout Asia, causes there to be a distinct lessening of the worth of each individual's life. It's not unlike walking into a room with so many objects and things in it, nothing seems to have any great value, whereas a room with a minimum of objects strategically placed, makes each individual item seem extremely valuable and important.

I am always reminded how once, sitting in an office on the 10th floor of a corporate building looking across at a building being built there, we watched as a worker plummeted 15 stories off of the bamboo scaffolding to his death. There was no fanfare, hardly anyone watched and not even a siren sounded as the ambulance pulled up, picked up the body unceremoniously and then pulled away.

It dawned on me at the time that there are so many people in Asia, and the concept of reincarnation is so widely accepted, misconstrued though it might be, that the value of a single life is diminished substantially. Westerners have difficulty understanding this, since the value of human life in the US and Europe is pronounced, and in the absence of a concept of reincarnation, life is a one-time adventure, which gives the current physical journey great importance. The West would do well however, to understand the Chinese outlook on life, particularly as it would play out in any future great war or conflict.

Still, Beijing has significant importance as the political heart of the People's Republic of China. It's also one of those places where you can be assured that hidden behind every door, and sitting on each light post, there is some apparatus recording or analyzing your every move. As a tourist, you don't really consider it, but when conducting business there, it's practically all you think about. Doing or saying the wrong thing in Beijing is not just a frivolous gaffe, it can be detrimental, and the Chinese are well aware of that.

Our meetings in Beijing revolved around Quantrolics projects that were underway for various other building developments, including one major museum and several European Embassies and Consulates. Some of the Embassy and Consulate projects being installed in China, were actually connected to much larger international projects contracted elsewhere, including Europe, Africa and the Middle East.

It was clear to see that Quantrolics had its hands in the installation of high-tech control systems stretching from corporate to institutional and governmental projects, with links across borders worldwide. It was an extraordinary array of projects.

We didn't meet with officials representing those clients, but met with Quantrolics project representatives instead, all of who were accommodating and cordial, even if they weren't ready to volunteer much information. I explored what they thought might be most useful to them, and to a person they stated the need for marketing materials that would give them a sense of legitimacy.

Appearing to be "real" within the local market was always their greatest concern. For me, that was an easy matter to solve, having long dealt with legitimizing high-end brands in order to generate an umbrella effect that enabled the companies I had worked with in the past to sell $80 Dollar T-Shirts that cost $1.95 to manufacture. The real question was why Quantrolics hadn't done any of that already.

The idea that so many of the company's projects were being conducted at a substantial loss, combined with the fact that they were such high-profile projects that had huge financial backing, just wasn't adding up. It was clear the Quantrolics projects were being purposely low-balled to ensure procuring the contracts. The question was, why?

Our meetings in Seoul, Tokyo and Taipei flew by. Everyone in those countries was anxious to cater to us in some way. For me, modern though they may appear, Seoul was a place still stuck mentally in the 1960's, where nothing really ever finishes; Tokyo is as close as you can get to visiting a different planet, where the thought process dramatically contrasts the rest of the world; and Taipei is the slightly laid-back cousin of China. After being at the same basic meeting from Beijing to Shanghai, Seoul to Tokyo and Taiwan, I was glad when we finally got to Singapore.

It was at that point I decided it was time for a heart to heart with Lin. Whether she knew more than she was saying or not wasn't really the point for me. What I was after was someone to at least question what we were doing, so I didn't feel like we were just mindless pawns going from country to country, acting our way through some international charade.

But before I would speak bluntly with her, I needed to take a deep look for myself from a higher perspective, and I did so alone in my hotel room the night we arrived. What I saw was jarring, but there was no way it could be confirmed by me alone.

It appeared that Quantrolics was installing building control systems, just as sold and intended. However, I also saw that the same technology that controlled all the systems of a building on behalf of a client or developer, was also secretly communicating back to Quantrolics.

In fact, I saw that unique and unknown listening technology was being implanted everywhere that could record and transmit virtually anything and everything within the premises where it was installed. Suddenly, it all made sense. Embassies, government buildings, banks, hotels and corporate headquarters around the world were being sold high-tech building system controls that communicated back to an unknown source without anyone knowing. Now the question was, who was monitoring all this?

The next day, we met with the Singapore office staff in the late afternoon, and then went for an early dinner by ourselves. I decided this was the perfect time to confront Lin with a few questions based on what I had remote viewed the night before.

Lin and I walked along the River and, even with the rising heat and humidity, sat down at a location outdoors that felt private and safe. I still didn't know where she stood on any of this, what she knew or what she didn't, so I would have to approach the subject carefully. I didn't think so, but there was always the possibility she was performing double duty, which might include reporting any of my observations or actions back to Pennsylvania.

"I had a question for you, Lin, if you don't mind me asking?" I said opening slowly. "Is the technology used in Quantrolics building control systems proprietary? I mean, is it exclusive to Quantrolics, or is this tech that other companies might have?"

I was treading lightly.

"In a sense, it's proprietary," she said, "In as much as these transistors and the systems they're used in are unique compositions, and patented by the company. Others wouldn't be able to use the exact same technology. But I guess someone with the proper engineering know-how might be able to reverse engineer it somehow. Is that what you mean?"

It was just an opener, and I wasn't really interested in the answer to that question, per se.

"In a way," I responded thoughtfully. Then I decided to take it further.

"Could the technology be used not only to control the actual building systems, but also to, say, transmit information?"

I hoped I didn't sound like I was fishing too deeply, but I was trying to build up to my point.

"I suppose so," she answered, "After all that's what it does now within a loop, it transmits information on the systems involved, funnels it back to a central server, interprets it and allows the end-user access to it via the controls."

"Genius technology," I said, trying to flatter the engineer in her, as well as keep the conversation inquisitive and light. I kept going.

"I was wondering," I continued, "Do you think the equipment could have a dual purpose?" "Could it be used to transmit information, even audio-visual communication, to a third party, as an example," I asked hesitatingly.

"I don't see why not," Lin responded. "Of course, there are security measures and pretty tough firewalls are built in. Someone from the outside would have enormous difficulty hacking into these systems, if that's what you're thinking."

"Yes," I said, "I thought as much. "But hypothetically, if you were already inside the system, as an installer let's say, could you possibly incorporate an add-on that would transmit data or something like that without anyone knowing?"

Lin looked at me shocked. She was getting an inkling of what I was suggesting. I decided to back off slightly, but instead she went full speed ahead, leaning forward and talking in a whisper.

"You know, I've wondered about that myself at times," she said quietly. "There are extra components that I've noticed in a few of the systems, and I can't tell what their actual purpose is. I thought they could be redundancies or back-up systems, but they could just as easily be planted there for third party access, or some other purpose entirely. And since the information is always going in the same direction anyway, if it's built in there from the start, it could probably be arranged so that no one ever knew it was there communicating outside, without taking the entire system apart."

We were on to something now. It wasn't a true confirmation of what I had seen when tuning in, but we were closer. Suddenly, the idea of a lot of high-profile control projects installed in Embassies, Consulates, Museums, government buildings, banks, corporate headquarters, hotels, restaurants and wealthy homes around the world was stunning.

They were all being installed at a tremendous financial loss, and they all had the capability of feeding audio, visual and other data to a third party on the outside, without any need to hack or any way to trace where the data was going. It was starting to make sense.

We had covered enough territory for one evening, so I changed the subject, and we started talking about the great food choices in Singapore. One thing was clear, unless she was an extraordinary actor, Lin had the same suspicions as me, and didn't seem to be privy to anything other than installing and selling the control systems. After our conversation, Lin and I seemed to be on the same wavelength more than ever.

In Jakarta, after various other meetings, we met with a Chinese-American entrepreneur who invited us to his house that evening in a new Chinese gated development in the Kemang district of South Jakarta. I knew the place pretty well since most ex-pats in Jakarta lived in the neighborhood. There was even an American-style supermarket, selling items like Aunt Jemima pancake mix and Jiffy Peanut Butter.

The development consisted of a group of enormous 5,000 square foot houses, all with gardens, pools, ornate statues and gilt furniture everywhere. The entire complex was surrounded by walls that were so tall and thick armed guards could walk around on top of them, and they did in large numbers.

Jesse Chin was a very wealthy entrepreneur who had been born in Indonesia to a Chinese-Indonesian father and American mother, and his family had close ties with the country's leadership, especially in the military. Even after Suharto's departure, the military remained the only real power in the country.

That was true even when Suharto's family members were said to have their fingers in almost all the business pies in Jakarta. A joke among ex-pats working for multinationals in Indonesia was how representatives would show up at your office each month to collect their share of the receipts. It was clear Jesse had his fingers in a lot of the same pies.

At his house, we joked about the Suharto days, and about the fact that Jesse was forced to live in an armed encampment, albeit in the lap of luxury, because approximately every 25 to 30 years, a segment of the Indonesian populace seemed to go mad on cue, blame the Chinese for all their woes, and riot and kill as many Chinese as they could get their hands on. As part of the turmoil, they inevitably would also burn down whatever Chinese homes and businesses they could break into. There was no question in my mind that someone as connected as he was would be a real target.

According to Jesse, the real reason he had invited Lin and I to his house was to discuss the possibility of installing Quantrolics control systems at a luxury Hotel, famous for housing dignitaries and others visiting the Merdeka Palace, Indonesia's version of the White House, not far away. Then he even dangled the added possibility of installing systems there as well. He assured us that he had ties to Generals who could make the project happen, and hinted that having such control systems installed in the Palace would be of great "benefit" to America.

It was clear to me right off the bat that he had some kind of working relationship with the "they" I was now becoming familiar with, but he stopped short of saying anything else. This was definitely something Quantrolics was interested in pursuing with him though, and both Lin and I had received emails from Aaron Spivak pushing us to start negotiations for any deal we could get. Aaron even suggested he'd be willing to fly out personally.

Regardless of that, I wasn't convinced that anything he said was true, and actually was being "told" the whole thing was a set-up. After dinner, he cozied up to me and asked if I wanted to join him upstairs. I declined feigning fatigue and pointing to Lin, and told him that although it was an enticing prospect, perhaps it would be better some other time.

The truth was I realized it was a trap, and a clear effort to compromise me. Since he seemed to be very friendly to Quantrolics, I assumed maybe they were looking to get something on me. Either that, or he was working on his own with the same purpose. Both scenarios were possible.

I had no interest, and for better or worse, I felt a commitment to Dean at this point, even if he was also loosely connected to Quantrolics in some way. The photograph he had planted in my bag had done the trick though, and it wasn't a real effort to dodge the Jesse bullet.

Lin and I left the house with promises to continue discussions about possible new "control" systems projects in Jakarta, and we invited him to the US to speak with upper management further in the very near future.

As we left, I told Lin, "Let Aaron handle that one."

13. Les Pays Basque

Indonesia for only a few days and Asia for nearly three weeks was enough for me this time around. The summer heat was starting to bear down on us, and I didn't even think about the possibility of extending the trip for a side excursion to Yogyakarta or Bali. Anxious to get to Europe, I was relieved when we left Jakarta for Amsterdam, and the roughly fifteen-hour flight was exactly the break, not to mention the rest, needed.

Even though it's a beautiful, picture-perfect city in many respects, with cascading flowers and historic gable-topped buildings lining picturesque canals, I always found Amsterdam chaotic, from a metaphysical or energetic viewpoint. Granted, it's a different kind of chaos then you find in Asia, but it's chaos nonetheless.

Most likely, it's the water running through it, which can generate and magnify energy in sometimes strange and unexpected ways. Haunted by dichotomy and confusion, the city is literally a place of extraordinary psychic activity, where the veil between worlds is ultra-thin, and spirits wander aimlessly, magnetized to the extremes that bind them there. Venice has the same issue, and it's the reason people are subconsciously attracted to these two places, and places where water flows in general.

On top of that, I find the pragmatism that is quintessentially Dutch and German to be alien to an intuitive-driven nature, like my own. Yet, I understand it. My mother's family was

Dutch, so I grew up well acquainted with the shunting of feelings and deeply buried emotions that can be a genetic trait, if not a cellular memory, that Western Germanic peoples carry.

Why else would my mother, and hers before her, work so hard to deny their own inner truth, and hide the intuitive and psychic skills they possessed. Fortunately for me, although I inherited their intuitive and psychic gifts, I did not inherit their pragmatic approach to life, which can crush those same gifts as well.

Still, it was good to be on the Continent again. Lin and I made our way to the hotel for a quick overnight in town, and as the taxi drove down boulevards and streets we admired how relaxed the tall, young, handsome men and women sitting in the sidewalk Cafés looked. Lin laughed when I said they appeared so impeccably scrubbed and wholesome that they were probably all sitting there, drinking milk. I was only half kidding.

We didn't have much business to conduct in Amsterdam, and landed there mostly as a convenience because of easy connections to and from Indonesia, which was a Dutch colony until World War II. Our big meetings were the following day, after we made a short hop over to Hamburg, Germany. Quantrolics was participating at an international technology trade show at the Convention Center there, and we were scheduled to meet with the head of the company's European operations, a man named Hans Reinecker.

German-born Reinecker was based in London, and his official title was Director of European Sales and Installations. He wasn't an engineer, but Lin said he had the ear of people that really mattered at Quantrolics, whoever they were.

I looked forward to meeting him however, and thought he'd share some interesting insights into European operations, especially the large projects he seemed to easily sign-up and accomplish. My real interest at this point was finding if all his projects were being conducted at giant losses like the ones in Asia.

We met at the very small Quantrolics booth, on the floor of the Hamburg Convention Center, and within 30 seconds of meeting, I knew this guy was a hard pill to swallow. Hans was an arrogant, 60-something, died-in-the-wool, SOB. He was the kind of person you tried to avoid, and if you couldn't, he was the kind you wanted to get away from as soon as possible.

I wanted to stay open, but bristled at most everything about him. Even so, I could see where some people, especially men from a certain milieu, might be attracted to this brand of cold-war, Ian Fleming-style villain. In addition to his crotchety persona, he was also a generational misogynist, and I watched as Lin disappeared quickly to spend time elsewhere with members of his European team of engineers that she already knew. I wasn't as fortunate, and had to stick close by him.

I didn't have anything to sell him, and really didn't care who he was or what he thought of me, so I decided to just let him take the lead and do all the talking. The problem was, he only spoke in guttural quips, and obviously didn't like complete sentences or full thoughts. He was clearly an "information is power" person, so you weren't going to get anything out of him without a full, head-on approach.

After he was done berating me as if it was open season on the new guy, whom I'm sure he assumed was clueless, I decided to go for it.

"So," I said thoughtfully in a voice filled with irony, "Are the projects you're managing in Europe all being conducted at an enormous loss like the ones in Asia?"

Impact. I had gotten through and hit a nerve. He paused as if thinking, and then smirked before turning to stare me down.

"You're not as stupid as you look, are you," he said.

"Maybe not," I answered.

"Well, that's none of your business, is it? How 'bout you stick to your side of the playpen and just make us a few pretty brochures so we look legitimate," he said, getting angry.

I had received the two answers I was looking for.

First, he indirectly confirmed it was the same scenario as in Asia, where the projects were all lost leaders just to get inside the buildings. Secondly, he had no idea who I was or what I did.

To him, I was just some guy that was going to make up a few brochures to wallpaper over their front. He clearly hadn't been informed yet about my real skills, at least not the precognition role Quantrolics was looking for me to fulfill, and I immediately thought to myself, "need-to-know basis."

"No problem," I said, flippantly, and just to make sure he knew that I knew, I said, "It's in the pipeline and you should have your wallpaper in 6 to 8 weeks. No one will know what color the wall that's painted underneath actually is."

It was as if I had said something in code and it clicked. Suddenly, we understood each other. I was now a Hans insider, and he warmed up considerably, even though he still spoke in riddles. I think he liked the fact that I could converse in riddles and quips too.

Hans wasn't cocky to me after that. I'm sure he questioned if I was a visitor from the "need-to-know" class of Quantrolics. This was confirmed at dinner later that day, which we were obliged to attend with Hans and his team. At some point in the evening, he made his way over to me and took me aside.

"Your itinerary says you go to Geneva tomorrow to look in on that big project underway," he said under his breath.

"You've already met the team leader," he said, turning his glare to a young, geeky-looking guy at the other end of the table.

"Another oblivious engineer," he snickered.

Then he became dead serious.

"Maybe skip Geneva this time around. Too much attention from corporate isn't a good idea right now. It's complicated."

Hans had recently won a contract to revamp several building control systems at a major world diplomatic organization in Geneva. Outside of New York, the offices of the organization in Geneva were a major hub of global diplomatic and other activity, linking hemispheres and continents.

I knew he wasn't making a threat, because I could hear the distinctive voice of my guidance telling me he was legitimately warning me to back away. Then an image was added in my head where New York faded into the background, while Geneva, which I knew fairly well from my days at school in

Switzerland, became hyper-prominent with dark clouds hanging over it. Lightning was striking the buildings pictured beneath the clouds.

Images can be an intrinsic part of clairvoyance, and when I am not hearing or being told something, I often receive messages in the form of visuals. Somehow, I knew I was being shown something I needed to pay attention to.

"You're right," I told him, handing Hans a win and giving him a vote of confidence, "I don't need to go."

Then, to cement the deal and win more favor with the old 007-guy who was working in the trenches, I said, "If Aaron wants, I'll come back later – when *you're* ready."

Hans gave me a wink. We had just accomplished another successful round of talking between the lines, where he assumed I was someone in the know. That assumption would play an even greater role in the upcoming days.

Early the next morning, I spoke to Lin about my "talk" with Hans. We both agreed it would be a good idea to skip Geneva, and that meant going on to Paris. Lin had never intended to join me in France, since she had other obligations at home in the States and had arranged to fly back to Philadelphia. For my part, I changed my ticket and instead of going to Geneva, flew directly from Hamburg to Paris.

I had been in touch with Dean throughout the trip, and he was scheduled to join me in three days for a long weekend in Paris. Since I had already met the people from the Paris office while in

Hamburg, and because Hans seemed to be the real linchpin, there wasn't any need for me to meet up with them again. I probably would have shortened my trip and gone straight to London, had it not been for my scheduled upcoming visit with Dean.

Feeling somewhat guilty about spending an extra 3 days without focusing solely on Quantrolics business, when I got to Paris I decided I would spend some time looking through the treasure trove of miscellaneous materials I had been collecting from various sources starting in Hong Kong.

Mostly I was looking for any sexy, techy, generic marketing information I could throw together to create the needed collateral as soon as I got back. It was what I had promised nearly everyone along the way.

There were so many inconsistencies and contradictions in the background materials it was almost laughable. It was as if they were flaunting what they were really up to and thumbing their nose at the world. Then again, perhaps so many contradictory things just added to the confusion and camouflage, making it almost impossible to go down any avenue -- financial, technical or operational -- without eventually coming to a dead end.

I was quietly looking through some paperwork concerning operations on the continent, when I saw something that jumped right off the page at me. It was buried in the fine print of a list of innocuous addresses, supposedly a list of remote company locations in Europe.

"No, it's not possible," I said to myself, out loud, "No fucking way."

I recognized one of the locations listed. It was a place that Anthony and I had driven to nearly 25 years ago at the request of his brother, Steve. Number 638 Herrialdeko Errepidea, in a place called Biriatou, France, about 30 minutes from Biarritz, smack dab on the border of France and Spain.

I remembered it like it was yesterday for a whole slew of reasons. First of all, the street name became a memorable joke when we first heard it. It was such an odd name, I asked Anthony what the Hell it meant, and he told me his brother said it was Basque for "Country Road".

We laughed at that because of the song by John Denver, 'Take me Home, Country Road', which was popular around the same time. We passed that joke between us for hours, with Anthony saying, maybe it's in West Virginia, to which I would reply, maybe Mountain Mama will be there.

"It just couldn't be," I said again to myself out loud.

Although my memory of the exact location was vague because of the years that had passed, I was brought right back to the entire experience. At Steve's request, one long weekend at school in Switzerland, Anthony and I drove a brand new, bright orange Porsche 914, which was essentially a Volkswagen with a Porsche engine, from Geneva to a similar address in the Basque Country. I have no idea why, and we were never told.

It was a miserably uncomfortable 9-hour drive, and somewhere outside Toulouse when I was driving, I got stopped by a cop for speeding. To this day I don't know how I talked my way out of it, but I told the French Gendarme I was speeding because I was frightened after passing an enormous truck going up a hill on the two-lane road, explaining to him that I only sped up momentarily to pass safely. I think he just didn't want to deal with us, so he waved us on.

We laughed for an hour about the cop letting us go. That was the second memory about the trip that stood out.

Third, was the fact that when we got there after dark, we were certain we had arrived at the wrong address because the building looked derelict and abandoned. It was on an isolated country road, as per the name, and the large old farmhouse sat in the middle of nowhere, less than a foot off the road. The shudders were closed, and the place looked like no one had been there in years.

It was a surprise when we knocked on the door, and someone immediately opened it. They asked for the keys to the car, then without any explanation or questions, loaded us into the back of an old Citroen delivery truck, and dropped us at the Biarritz airport about 30 minutes away.

When we got there, the last flight had left for the day, so Anthony and I camped out at the airport, which you could do in those days, sleeping on benches until we were able to catch a flight back to Switzerland the next morning. That was another memory of that particular trip, which stuck in my head because it was so damn uncomfortable and unpleasant.

Even with all that, I couldn't believe this could actually be the same place listed on the sheet. But I couldn't stop thinking about it either. What if it was the same address? Wouldn't that mean I had found a direct link between Steve Moreau and Quantrolics, just like the Colonel had indicated.

Early the next morning, I decided I needed to know one way or the other. After all, I had three more days to kill before Dean arrived, and this was listed, albeit only in one place, as a Quantrolics office.

Didn't I have the right to check it out, as part of my new role with the company? And besides, if it wasn't the same place that Anthony and I had been to years ago for his brother, all I would lose was a day or two spent on Quantrolics business visiting a remote office with a quick trip to Basque Country. It seemed explainable.

I grabbed my briefcase and a few things for overnight just in case, but didn't check out of my hotel on the Ile St. Louis. It was the place Dean and I planned to meet, and I didn't want to take any chances that they would be booked up when I got back.

I expected I'd only be gone a day at most anyway. Then I took a taxi to Orly airport, where I was able to find a commuter trip on a small plane down to Biarritz. I bought a round trip ticket, and made a reservation to return later the following day.

After landing in Biarritz, I rented a Renault V at the airport. With my map laid out next to me, I began the drive down to the border between France and Spain, looking for "638 Country Road", at the junction of Chemin de la Forêt and Route D258, in Biriatou.

To tell the truth, I became a little discouraged when nothing outside of Biarritz looked familiar. For a moment I thought I had let my imagination run wild in a big way. But then I realized it was decades ago so things were bound to have changed. I also remembered that it had been dark when Anthony and I first drove through the area, and that revitalized me making me think it was still possible this was the same place. I'd have to find it to know.

As I drove slowly down Route D258, the road narrowed as it turned into Herrialdeko Errepidea. I started to get excited. More than two decades later, this place was still as isolated as you can get and in the middle of nowhere. Suddenly, a large, old derelict white farmhouse hung over the street. It was sitting right on the road where I had last seen it, and all the shudders were still closed. It was definitely the same place.

I sat in the car a moment, wondering what to do next, then got out and began to walk over to the door. Before I could reach it, the door opened and a tall, handsome muscular man about my age with a dark complexion, black hair and dark eyes came out to greet me. He was wearing a black T-Shirt and black Calvin Klein jeans, and I thought he looked something like a cat-burglar ready to scale a rooftop.

I was thinking the worst when he warmly took my hand and in French said, "We're so glad you could make it. Hans said we should expect you sometime late today or tomorrow. I guess you got in early."

I froze momentarily. He was expecting me? Hans told him I was coming? I certainly hadn't said anything to anyone.

"Thanks," I said responding in French, and shaking his hand. "I was with Hans in Germany yesterday."

It was the truth, after all. I decided to go with it, but knew I shouldn't lie too extensively, just in case I needed to explain whom I really was and what I was doing there.

It seemed best to just assume, even pretend to myself, that Hans had told him to expect me, but I knew within 30 seconds that wasn't what was happening. This was a case of mistaken identity.

He was expecting someone else that Hans had told him would stop in, and I just got there first.

He ushered me inside, taking my elbow. Then he shook my hand again as he closed the door and introduced himself.

"Maurice -- Mossad."

It wasn't a last name. It was an affiliation.

I stood there shocked until I heard myself say my name in Italian, "Eugenio - Quantrolics".

He laughed as if my response was odd. I think he thought I was making a joke out of it, since he had said "Mossad" as part of his identity.

"You guys are usually a lot younger," he said, "It's good to finally see an adult."

I had no idea what he meant and could only assume he was talking about whoever he was expecting. I ignored it.

In any case he quickly became fascinated with my accent. He asked me if I was French or Italian, and mused that I spoke French with either a Swiss-French or Italian-Venetian accent. That was a pretty good observation for only speaking a few sentences, and I had heard it before.

I told him that I was actually American, which surprised him, but briefly explained my family history and the fact that I went to school in Switzerland. The idea of school in Switzerland seemed to amuse him even more.

At that point we switched to speaking English, and his English was even better than his French, which was impeccable. Maurice was smart, thoughtful, knew how to think on his feet and was no flunky. He was the genuine article.

Realizing that, I started to worry about the mistaken identity thing. I really didn't want to escalate any misunderstandings. But before I could clear the air and explain, Maurice was ushering me into the inner sanctum and showing me around his kingdom.

In a way, I think he was so glad to see someone his own age from the outside world, he really didn't care who I was, and it didn't disturb him in the least if I was who he thought I was, or not. His confidence was impenetrable.

The ground floor was nothing more than a warehouse. It was large and dark, and seemed to go on forever, filled with boxes and, from the looks of it, years of junk. Maurice led me up a stairway on the side of the old building, and we emerged into a giant room upstairs, without any windows or natural light. One computer bank after the next, stretched for as far as you could see.

At each desk, mostly men sat wearing headsets staring at computer screens. The screens were split, in some cases quadruple or more, like security screens at a reception desk. There were lights flashing and beeping sounds coming from every computer.

Then I saw what summed it all up for me. Each bank of computers had an identifying sign hanging over it. There were embassies, government buildings, court houses, multi-national offices, corporate headquarters, hotels and major European banks. The names on the signs, all of which were substantial enterprises and continentally-based, went on and on.

They were all there, every Quantrolics European project I knew about and then some. Beneath each sign were one, two, three and sometimes an army of people sitting, staring at computer screens and taking notes. They were monitoring it all.

Maurice walked me around a corner, and pointed to an empty set of desks with non-working computers and dark screens. Above that section was a sign that read "Geneva-World Conference Headquarters".

Nearby, he walked me into a small office and closed the door.

"The Geneva complex monitoring station is our biggest yet," he said proudly, "It will be ready to go as soon as the project is installed. When will you start?"

"Start?" I asked. "I'm sorry, but I think there's a misunderstanding, Maurice."

"Aren't you one of the new tech officers the DIA sent?" he asked without sounding surprised, as if he already knew I wasn't.

"No, I'm not. Sorry if there was a misunderstanding."

Then I explained as best I could.

"I work at Quantrolics, but I'm not a technician. I'm more of an analyst and strategic planner, and we're working on some materials to cover the projects, and close a few more deals. Corporate sent me to get the lay of the land."

I kept talking saying whatever came into my head that I thought might smooth things over.

"I've been to all the offices and projects in Asia and on the Continent. I work for Aaron Spivak and Ron Mallick."

He looked uninterested, so I needed to convince him quickly that I could be trusted. I used the only name I was certain was an ace in the hole.

"Colonel McCormick recruited me for the job recently."

Maurice continued letting me talk. I felt like he wanted to see if he could give me enough rope to hang myself. When I finally ran out of things to say, he spoke.

"I thought as much. You don't look anything like the people they usually send us to do this job."

Then he added, "But now that you've been here, we're going to have to kill you."

He laughed loudly almost rolling around in his chair before I could react.

"Just playing with you," he said, still laughing.

It was at my expense, but we had found some common ground, and I hoped now we could begin to speak openly. But even though we had broken the ice, I had no doubt that if push ever came to shove, he wasn't joking at all.

He knew the Colonel, and of everything I said, I was fairly sure that's what put him at ease. He called him the "Old Man", and asked me to say Hello the next time I saw him.

I told Maurice no one sees him much in person these days, but

I would definitely say Hi on his behalf when I did. I realized for the first time what an important keystone the Colonel was, coordinating aspects for these government agencies, and plugging them into the privately held front companies that acted on their behalf.

Regardless of our cautious newfound trust, I could tell Maurice was finished sharing any information. We mulled over a few banalities for the next 30 minutes or so, about the country side, Biarritz and living in Pays Basque, but it was clear I wasn't going to get much more out of him.

I decided to bring it to a close by telling him I enjoyed meeting him, and offered my assistance in case he ever needed anything at Quantrolics in the US. I also mentioned for a second time that I would say hello to the Colonel, even though I knew I probably never would.

The entire car ride back, I couldn't stop thinking about what had just happened. Since this was the same location that Anthony and I had been to more than twenty years before on behalf of his brother, the realizations were coming at me left and right.

If Anthony's brother was in fact an Agent for British and American Intelligence who knew Colonel McCormick, and if Colonel McCormick was closely involved with both US Intelligence and Quantrolics, then Quantrolics was indeed a front company for the CIA, just like the Boston Globe journalist had informed me. Not only that, but Steve Moreau must have somehow been involved with Quantrolics, not to mention Colonel McCormick, from way back when.

Suddenly, the file sitting on the Colonel and Ron Mallick's desk with my name on it made all the sense in the world. It had grown to be an inch thick because they'd been watching me since the late 1970's.

Secondly, if Quantrolics was low-balling building projects just to get a foot in the door, installing high-tech control equipment at embassies, banks, hotels, government buildings and major corporate headquarters all over the world, and that equipment was being secretly modified so it could be used for surveillance, I had inadvertently uncovered their purpose. I now had confirmation that Quantrolics was actively monitoring and surveilling whatever equipment it installed.

Third and most importantly, they were likely doing it without anyone knowing, via data and audio-visual transmittal direct to secret servers, at locations just like the one I had seen here. The proof was in the signage hanging above endless banks of computers, all neatly hidden away in windowless buildings, as far from scrutiny as anyone can get.

What I had found on Country Road in that old building in Biriatou confirmed exactly what I had already remote viewed. Trying not to think about it anymore, I decided to spend the night in Biarritz at the Palace Hotel, a massive aging dowager of a resort overlooking the Atlantic Ocean, which was built in the 19th Century for the Empress Eugenie.

I felt like I deserved to treat myself to something special, making sure Quantrolics picked up the tab. It wouldn't completely make up for the night I slept on a bench as a teenager at the Biarritz airport all those years ago, running errands for Steve Moreau, but it might help. Life had come full circle.

14. Reprimand

I got back to Paris the next day still thinking about where I'd been and what it all meant. To distract myself, I spent a little time walking along the Seine, and then around my old neighborhood.

I had dinner alone, at a favorite restaurant in the Seventh, La Petite Chaise, one of the oldest restaurants in Paris. It was a comforting place because nothing much ever changed, and it was exactly the same as the last time I was there, including the four-course Prix Fixe Menu.

Dean was due in the next day. When I returned to the hotel that evening, I checked my email and found a short message from Hans Reinecker. It cryptically told me to meet him at Brasserie Lipp on Boulevard Saint-Germain for lunch at noon the next day. I knew right away what it was about.

Since it was around the same time Dean would be arriving, I sent him a quick message telling him something came up and I had to go to a meeting for work, but said I'd be back quickly. I told him to just make himself comfortable at the hotel, and I'd be right there.

When I arrived at Lipp the next day, Hans was sitting at a small table in the corner of the Brasserie, as far from people as you could get. He didn't look up from the newspaper he was reading, so I made my way over to his table and sat down. He finally acknowledged me.

"Sneak attack?" he asked, as I sat down.

I knew he was referring to my trip down to Biarritz.

"Not an attack," I said, smiling, "More of a 'Gotcha'."

"Touché," he responded, then he said, "You'll want to keep this out of one of your reports."

He'd been reading up on me, and was letting me know it. I wondered where he was getting his information, and Aaron's image flashed in my mind.

"Not sure if I should reprimand you, or compliment you," Hans said, looking at me intensely.

I could tell he wasn't going to reprimand me, and I doubted he wanted to compliment me. Then again, our conversations had been so weird maybe this was as close as he ever got to flattery. After all, not only did I find the strange address in Biriatou, I made it there on my own and actually got into the place too.

"Why were you there?" Hans said bluntly.

"I was there once before as a teenager," I said. "Just thought I'd catch up on an old haunt."

Then I added, "Ever hear of Steve Moreau?"

"Maybe," he confirmed, without confirming anything.

"Turns out he was my mentor, and I didn't even know it."

Hans smirked. "Well at least you come from good stock."

The mention of Steve Moreau seemed to put the whole matter to bed, and another masterful conversation of half thoughts and sentences ensued over lunch. He must have been pleased with the responses though, because it seemed like our unspoken accord held up. I never told anyone, not even Lin until much later, about that side trip down a Country Road in Biriatou. And no one ever asked me either.

When I got back to the hotel, I was told at the desk that my visitor had arrived and was upstairs. The receptionist asked if we could please be a little quieter, and I had no idea what she was talking about. Was she anticipating something?

I began to get excited about seeing Dean as I got into the small two-person, see-through lift. When I opened the door to our room on the 5th floor, I was expecting to melt into a very needed embrace.

Instead, I stopped dead in my tracks as the door swung open. Everything in the room was in a different location, and all the furniture, every stick of it including the bed, had been moved around. I wondered for a minute if I had walked into the wrong room.

Dean walked out of the bathroom. "Like it?" he asked happy with himself, as if everything was perfectly normal.

"What did you do?" I asked, completely shocked.

"I thought I'd redecorate while you were gone," he said as if I would understand. "Better safe than sorry. You never know whose watching you in these small foreign hotels."

"Oh my God!" I bellowed, "When in the Hell did I sign up for all this pseudo spy-world crap?"

All I could think was: Steve Moreau, Colonel McCormick, Hans Reinecker, Quantrolics, Investigative Journalists, CIA, Mossad -- and now we're moving hotel furniture around to make sure no one's watching us? Is this my new normal?

Dean looked at me blankly, as I moved forward and gave him a warm hug.

To cover my outburst, I jokingly said, "I've got absolutely nothing to hide."

"That's not the point," he responded, still holding onto me. "Besides, the room looks better this way."

"Yeah, well I'm not sure Management is going to agree with you."

Dean shrugged. He could have cared less.

Despite the room rearrangement, and needing to move everything back before we left town, Dean and I had one of the best weekends I've ever had in Paris. I'm not much of a tourist, or travel guide for that matter, but as this was Dean's first time to Paris, we did all the sites, all my favorite places, and then some.

Believe it or not, during the many years I lived in Paris, I never really spent lots of time in certain parts of the city. I always thought of places like the Marais, Ile Saint-Louis, Ile de la Cite or the Champs-Elysees as mostly tourist destinations. Now Dean and I were strolling through these areas slowly, through the Quartier Latin, along the Seine and up the Champs, enjoying every moment of it.

Truthfully, I had never known Paris to be a particularly haunted city, and didn't usually have problems there as I sometimes did in places like Amsterdam, Venice or Jakarta. But on those walks with Dean, I was surprised to find out that some of the specific locations we were walking through were a real hot bed of psychic activity.

Spirits communicating with you is quite different from what I personally have always termed "revolvers". When a spirit reaches out and connects with you, it's usually a very purposeful event. They may have some message to give, or need someone to listen to them.

On the other hand, they may be present because they are stuck in-between dimensions, or because they are having trouble removing their energy from the physical realm. Sometimes they are trying to change something that happened to them in physical reality before moving on dimensionally, without realizing they have fallen out of sync with the timeline, which has since moved on.

Revolvers are something different. These are psychic occurrences that were so intense when they happened, they imprinted themselves on the location, and they repeat, or "revolve", over and over again. Spirits, per se, aren't really involved in revolvers, but you're seeing something akin to a photo or video loop, specific to that location, being played-back constantly.

This seems to be especially prevalent when flowing water and stone or brick happen to be intrinsic to the location, which for example, is almost always the case with an old castle or brick building, built near or over water. Those places always seem to have a reputation for being "haunted." The combination of the energy of flowing water, combined with the silica in the stone or brick, acts like film that captures intense emotions and events that happen there. As time passes, the energetic intensity of the imprinted event fades, just like an old photograph, until eventually it is lost forever.

As Dean and I strolled through various Quartiers, revolvers kept passing in front of my eyes again and again. They were powerful and unrelenting. The most intense revolvers are always the most recent, and most of the ones I was seeing now in these neighborhoods had to do with violent scenes from the occupation of Paris by the Nazis during World War II. It made sense. The Germans occupying Paris at the time liked to hang out in all the well-established tourist areas.

At one point in the Quartier Latin, I was startled and watched horrified as a group of teenagers ran in front of me followed by a small band of German soldiers who mowed them down in the street we were standing on with machine guns. It was so extreme I stopped and gasped, and Dean turned to ask me what was wrong.

"Nothing," I said. "Just saw a 'revolver' play out in front of us. A group of teens ran in front of me, and were all gunned down right here. It was incredibly sad."

Dean had no idea what I was talking about, so we kept walking. About 75 yards later, he stopped and pointed up at a plague on the corner of the building. It read, "On this spot in April 1944, a group of 9 French Resistance Fighters were killed by the German Gestapo."

"It's wrong," I said, shaking my head. "It happened back there, and they were all students, not members of the Resistance."

We were next to the Seine, in front of a stone building, in an alley not far from the Sorbonne. The intense tragedy had imprinted itself on that location, and was now like a film loop, playing itself back constantly for anyone with the interdimensional skills to see it.

Anybody who thinks hate, war or other traumatic events are an adventure, or romantic, has not seen a revolver. I'll never forget how vivid that scene came across, and how sad the experience was that had imprinted itself on that location.

When I left Dean, he was relaxed and happy. It had been a freeing time together, with no extraneous worries or commitments, and that helped us bond even more. When I put him in the taxi for the airport, I told him I just had one more stop to make in London, and would see him in Pennsylvania in a few days.

London turned out to be a series of misadventures and bad timing. I seriously questioned if the strange missed and cancelled meetings were all being orchestrated by Hans.

My suspicions were confirmed when I noticed another strange address listed on my sheet that was about an hour out of London. It was nonsensical that there would be an additional remote office there, in a small country village north of the city. The location, and clear attempts on paper to underplay it, reeked of the Biriatou location.

First, I went to the Quantrolics office, located in a modern building near The Tower in the old Warehouse District, which was undergoing gentrification. The office was ultra-modern and fairly typical of the company, in terms of no expense spared, and I said Hello to some of the people I had met in Hamburg as I passed them. Oddly, the person I was scheduled to meet with, Peter Long, who was an engineer spearheading a new push into the English market, which had been neglected in favor of Europe and Asia, called-in with an emergency and said he couldn't make it.

Great Britain was an afterthought because in some way the entire "enterprise" must have been a joint US-British venture. The excerpts I had seen about Steve Moreau was clear in its assessment that he worked for both British and US Intelligence. Quantrolics might be an American-based company, but this was likely a global Intelligence joint venture, at least the secret initiatives. Why worry about spying on yourself?

Since Peter's absence on an emergency essentially cancelled my meeting, as well as my whole purpose for coming to London, I was free for the rest of the day. It was early enough, so I decided it might be a good day for a train ride through the countryside. Why not take an excursion out to a small village an hour away on the line between London and Cambridge, where Quantrolics supposedly had a new field office?

I made my way to the Liverpool Street Train Station, and bought a round trip, anytime ticket to Audley End, after investigating the best way to get to the location outside of town I was ultimately headed to. The train ride was uneventful, if not charming and beautiful, and we passed quintessential, picturesque 14th Century English villages, houses with thatched roofs, 19th Century train stations and all manner of village Pubs and Inns.

From Audley End, I took a taxi to the small village address where I was going, about 5 or 6 miles on the road out of town from the train station. As we pulled up to the house number I had given the driver, I could see it was the British equivalent of the building in Basque Country.

There stood an old farmhouse, this one slightly more off the road with a small car park in front, all shuddered up. A few cars were parked there, but for the most part it looked derelict.

I asked the driver to please wait for me, not knowing what I would find and worried about how to get back. Somehow, things didn't feel right. Suddenly, an older man holding a wrench in his hand walked slowly out from the barn that was adjacent to the large, boarded-up farmhouse. He wasn't dressed like a farmer, wasn't wearing overalls or work clothes, and his shoes looked like fairly expensive cordovan loafers. The wrench looked like either a prop or an anomaly.

He smiled with his mouth open widely as he walked up to greet me.

"Hi," I said, "I'm looking for Quantrolics."

"Your name Nicolay?" he asked, still smiling.

"That's me," I said. "I guess this must be the place."

"Yes and No," he answered, "Yes, this is Quantrolics. No, nobody's here right now."

Then he added, "Mr. Reinecker told us you might stop by, but everyone's gone and the office is all locked up. Sorry about that."

"Do you know when someone might be back," I asked, not really expecting an answer.

"Wouldn't know," he said, "I'm just the handyman."

I laughed to myself. A handyman, working in a dirty barn, without work clothes, in hundred-eighty Dollar loafers!?

Apparently, Hans had gotten to everyone, including Peter Long in London and, especially, here and now. It didn't matter though. Even if I didn't have visual confirmation, as I did in France with Maurice, I knew what was happening intuitively. The fact I was being blocked from seeing anything else now, was just more confirmation. I could tell this had to be where the monitoring for Great Britain's projects was being set up, if it wasn't already in place.

I found myself wondering if and where monitoring for US projects might be located. No one ever mentioned North American Quantrolics projects to me, and the Colonel, Ron Mallick and Aaron Spivak had all been pretty clear that my work, whatever aspect it took on, was focused on international.

Now I began asking myself about the US, and even wondered if there was someone doing "reports" for them like I was. I had briefly touched on some information about the US and North America in my recent Brief for Aaron, but no one had commented on anything. Maybe that was the reason why.

In fact, if there was someone else like me, maybe overlap was all about verifying the information, and in that case, you wouldn't want them comparing notes. In a place where everything was covert and written between the lines, that would be a prerequisite for developing an in-house group of psychics to remote-view situations and future events on the timeline.

In any case, I let it go after I became preoccupied with the message I was given that something was hidden in the first building at Quantrolics headquarters. I had never been in that building, and that would explain why even though Aaron's secretary said I had a good clearance, I didn't have access everywhere. If there was a monitoring center for the US the best place to hide it would be under a building in the middle of nowhere, out in an Amish cornfield in Pennsylvania.

I was glad I didn't send the taxi away, and we drove back to the train station without wasting any more time. It occurred to me after the driver dropped me off that I should have had a pint somewhere in town, to ask around and see if any of the locals had heard of Quantrolics. But it was a bit too early for Ale, and there really wasn't any need.

Instead, I headed right back to London on the next train, and then changed my airline tickets to fly home the following day.

When I got back to the States, I hit the ground running. The first order of business was creating the materials I had promised globally. Everything I had uncovered was still in the back of my mind, but to me, I simply had confirmation on what I had remote viewed and thought I knew. It was present in my thinking, but since it didn't affect me directly, I could put all that on the back burner.

In a very short time, I got used to going to the Quantrolics complex and being underground most of the time. To be honest, I continued to convince myself everything I was doing was for the best, and I was working with the good guys. Dean and I still were living apart, but we saw each other several times a week, and spent every weekend together either in the country, in the city or traveling somewhere.

From years of experience managing marketing campaigns of every sort, I was very fast at creating collateral and other integrated PR and ad materials. Over time, I had learned to do pretty much everything needed myself when necessary, and I was able to design layouts using complex design and CAD programs, gather and prepare images and materials for press and, as a copywriter, even write all the copy.

I designed a series of booklets and ads featuring Quantrolics' technical achievements and capabilities in record time, compiling the high-res images needed, designing all the layouts myself in-house and writing the English, French and Italian copy. The most difficult part was getting good translations that translated the meaning and not just the words literally, so the material wouldn't be ridiculed in nearly seven other additional languages. That effort takes time and attention.

I took Ron Mallick at his word and stuck to the budget, so I didn't feel the need to get approvals or show anything to anyone. I had been led to believe this was my domain, and the covert mentality the company fostered could now be used by me, only in reverse. In many ways, I was good at working behind the scenes in that kind of an environment, probably from years of hiding who I really was and keeping what I really did under wraps.

Anyone who works in the marketing field knows that round after round of corporate approvals is the kiss of death for real creativity, and I was committed to coming through on the promise I had made to Hans Reinecker and other Quantrolics managers worldwide. My actions speeded things up tremendously, and even the limiting budgets weren't a problem for me, although in retrospect I now see that the limits were meant as an intentional handicap for someone who worked in a typical way.

I would find that out soon enough, but even proceeding at maximum velocity, it took me about six months to prepare and complete the program, including printing and distribution in whatever language was required for the foreign office on my list. Another six months after that would pass before anyone could really tell if the program was successful.

Ron was more out of the office than in during the period, and I suspected something related to what the spirit of his mother had told me from day one was starting to take effect. In any case, he took absolutely no interest in any of the materials I was creating. Meanwhile, Aaron would stop by occasionally, but it always seemed like he was just looking for a distraction whenever he did. He would give some inane comment either about the colors or fonts he preferred, demonstrating how totally unimportant any of this really was to him.

The main focus continued to be my Briefs, which I was creating as requested by them on a regular basis throughout the period. There would be about one per month, and the questions had absolutely nothing to do with global marketing, communications or products. Instead, they became more and more focused on specific world events, places and future occurrences, including some extremely esoteric and metaphysical subjects I had never before remote viewed.

I was always happy to comply, since that was what most interested me, and it gave me insight into things that I would never have thought to look myself, let alone inspect from a higher perspective. As I had always said, the right answers hinged on asking the right questions, and that remains as true for life as it does in dealing with someone who is psychically investigating or remote viewing anything on your behalf.

One Brief led to the next. I was asked to follow up on my original Report for Ron and Aaron where I cited possible destruction of a center in New York City. Turned out they had not quite understood my original messaging of the Earth's chakra system and how symbolic focal points of a civilization exists and can be transformative to the culture. However, they had understood what I termed the "Mind Center" of the current civilization, and didn't seem surprised.

I began to suspect they understood because, somehow, they knew in advance what was being planned. I could only assume "they" were privy to the planning, and when I looked at it by myself, my feelings were confirmed. They were not only indirectly connected to these things, they actively understood the information concerning destabilization of the Middle East that would ensue after destruction of the focal point representing the "mind" of the current civilization. They also seemed to grasp how what happened there would serve as a precursor, decades later, for World War III, which would eventually flow out of Iraq into Syria, then later into Israel, Lebanon and Palestine.

Now they were starting to question me more about what I had said concerning the long lead up to another World War, as well as my mention that the West was training many of the terrorists in the Middle East. They asked me to elaborate on what I had said about limited nuclear exchange that would one day occur in conjunction with World War III, and also wanted more details about the breakup of the United States after that conflict. Again, when I looked at it all separately for myself, I saw they were fully aware these things were being orchestrated by factions known to them, and by those who, indirectly, were linked to them as well.

It was starting to be clear they were using me to confirm that the plans they were somehow connected to, and implementing in the here and now, would have the desired effect two to three decades down the line. Confirmation for them lay in what I was reporting I could see on the future timeline, and that seemed to be their main focus of interest.

Somewhat discouraged, I nevertheless ignored inner warnings, and persevered in my work, completing an array of requested Briefings for them. Even well-meaning professionals can suffer some degree of Stockholm Syndrome to the corporate culture they are being indoctrinated into, especially when they consider themselves to be part of the inner circle. It's an easy trap to fall into, and for a time, I was a victim as well.

As a result, I kept my nose to the grindstone and performed as expected, hoping I was doing the right thing. When asked to look at what would take place in the future in Africa, for example, the results were unexpected. I explained that we would soon be going into a mini Ice Age period in the Northern Hemisphere, similar to ones experienced before in the 16th, 18th, and mid 19th Centuries.

This will be particularly poignant following limited nuclear fallout from World War III in the Middle East, but also because of terroristic use of suitcase Nukes in several European cities, including Paris and Rome. That fallout will cause crops to fail, economies to falter, inflation to be astronomical and fuel prices to be untenable.

Severely cold winters in Northern Europe and Scandinavia, at least for a time, will then result in a mass migration from the North to Africa, in reverse of what has been seen for decades. This would quite naturally, cause substantial strife and bitter conflict there.

That answer led to questions as to whether global warming was real. The answer to that was complex because it was a 'Yes' and 'No' answer. Certainly, pollution and man's intervention does heat up the planet, but not as severely as one might expect. In reality, Universal Ascension is mostly responsible for Earth's warming, and the entire Solar System is heating up.

In addition to that, natural global warming leads to more severe heat in summer and colder winters, so this becomes the source of a Mini Ice Age happening as well. This warming, and associative cooling, occurs periodically on the timeline, as the Sun's energy increases. When it is overly dramatic, it is usually in proportion to Ascension's evolutionary energies that are passing through the Sun from the Galactic Center as it journeys through space and time.

Yet, even this was not the primary source of warming. The Brief detailed that it was manmade scalar energy, derived from extraterrestrial technology that was having the greatest impact. Naturally, that report led to the question of why this would be so, and how extraterrestrial technology could contribute to global warming. The response to that question, in my opinion, pushed the limits, and was perhaps as complex as I had ever seen.

Extraterrestrial visitation to the Third Dimension has been going on for hundreds of thousands of years. For the most part, such visitation is interdimensional in nature. Beginning with the end of World War II, and the advent of human nuclear capability, visitation has become more frequent, direct contact has been made and treaties with extraterrestrial cultures have been struck with numerous human world governments, most notably, China, Russia and the United States.

These agreements include the procurement of extraterrestrial technology. Among these, things such as transistors, nanoparticles, quantum devices and related high-tech advancements have been delivered or reverse engineered since being received beginning in the 1950's. Companies such as Quantrolics have benefited enormously from their connections to governments parceling out these technological exchanges from alien groups.

One such significant technology is scalar wave technology, provided to humans with the explanation that it permits numerous communications, defensive and other capabilities. Scalar wave technology also permits weather control and even mood alteration in humans, and in ways similar to the way atmospheric and pressure changes can alter human mood and comfort levels, these waves can be artificially generated and targeted for the same purpose.

Moreover, these energetic pulses can be carried through the atmosphere, and can be used to effect natural weather patterns, as well as natural Earth phenomenon such as earthquakes, hurricanes, volcanic activity and other, prior to this, natural occurrences. Scalar waves can also greatly affect human cellular structure and biology, and even thought patterns, when the correct impulse is applied and when DNA is used as an individual identifier to locate a specific target. This can be so even over great distances, and it is also behind any push to gather and identify individuals and populations by DNA.

In order for this technology to be applicable however, the atmosphere of Earth must be metalized. That metallization acts as a medium through which scalar waves can pass, in order for them to travel from point to point. Metallization of the atmosphere is being carried out through what is termed "Chemtrails", and this is being actively employed by governments worldwide.

As a side effect to metallization of the atmosphere, heat is trapped underneath and not allowed to dissipate, as it normally would. With regard to the global warming, what has been sold to scientists and governments as a means of facilitating scalar wave transmittal, and has also been spun at certain levels as a technique to "block" sunlight and reduce warming, is actually contributing greatly to Earth heating up at the current time. In its wake, the fall out generated from the Chemtrails poisons the Earth, adding Aluminum, Barium and other toxic conductive particles to topsoil and ground water.

But the deception doesn't end there. My Briefing concerning the electromagnetic grid and chakra system of Earth now came into profile, and this new report took a very complex turn.

Extraterrestrials have provided this technology to Earth as a means of curtailing human advancement, reducing global population and blocking human beings from the natural connection they have, through Earth's electromagnetic grid, to their Souls and their higher guidance. Knowing this, Extraterrestrials have given greedy governments seeking military and psychological control of their populations, the means to destroy themselves and their populations. At the very least, for their own purposes, they have in a sense, fenced-in all Souls incarnating in physical form in the Third Dimension.

Their purpose in doing so is manifold. First, is the fact that at times when Universal Ascension energies are at their peak, as they are now, evolution of the entire species is possible. Fencing off the planet, and the human beings in it, by means of poisoning the Pineal gland and manipulation of the DNA, blocks or, at a minimum, curtails that evolution.

Secondly, by fencing off Third Dimensional Earth, they have, in effect, cut physical humans off from the "Soul", and their fundamental guidance and energetic source. Should such a state prevail in the long-term, this dimensional version of Earth will become a fallen paradise.

This is seen on the timeline to have happened once before nearly one million years ago at anther Ascension interval, when a similar attempt at fencing the planet was made. Biblical references, and other spiritual stories of "Fallen Angels", refer to such a period in a distant prehistory civilization of Earth.

The Brief didn't get into why the aliens were doing this, but I was made aware that the Extraterrestrials responsible for this have as their motive the trans-humanization of the physical human body so it is less accommodating to Human Angelic Soul incarnations and more accommodating to their own extraterrestrial Soul race. Part of that process includes altering of Earth's physical environment so it is also more hospitable to the extraterrestrial temperament.

My Report predicted a wave of transhumanistic technology and biological endeavors to be promoted in the 21st Century. Again, these proposed "advances" are founded on technology provided by Extraterrestrial groups. Such biological manipulations will cause future global pandemics, with the solutions being more problematic than the cause, resulting in untold death and destruction.

Unbeknownst to world governments promoting them, the Brief ended by explaining that the primary goal of the alien Soul group in sharing their advanced biological technologies is to depopulate Earth while also transforming the human body's cellular and genetic structure, as well as Earth's physical environment, so it is more hospitable to Souls from their Soul group. Essentially, a bio-invasion of Earth is underway from now through the 26th Century.

I was never asked details about this Briefing, but was told it had been seen by eyes beyond Aaron and Ron, and its accuracy was being evaluated. That was how I knew they were paying attention, and not thinking of my Briefs as fanciful imaginings or science fiction. I was sure they were well aware of the cooperation with Extraterrestrials that called for sharing technologies with various governments of Earth, and needed time to investigate the possibility that the planet's major world governments were being duped.

Based on the information I was receiving the coming decades would be a very scary time. What bothered me most was that I was now forced to understand that perhaps these were not the White Hats I envisioned, nor were they the people I thought them to be. For the first time I started thinking I was working with the wrong side.

Perhaps this was, partially anyway, my fault. I went in eyes wide shut, as they say. What I did was not the kind of simple remote viewing they were used to, where someone draws pictures of a place or an event, and describes what happens there.

Instead, I gave in-depth analysis, background and connections to events and situations, karmic and otherwise, as they were presented to me in the Akashic Records, the energetic imprint of all events, and as they appeared on the future dimensional timeline. I did so with the intention of performing a higher purpose, one that hopefully might benefit people by demonstrating how and why things become events on the timeline in the first place.

What I did was far different from what others did. Other groups I had heard about by now that worked to deliver Intelligence were people trained to remote view by developing the extrasensory perceptions that everyone has to some degree. Reports concerning those groups consisted of them drawing pictures of "targets" somewhere in the nether lands.

To me, that activity didn't seem to give someone a mischievous leg-up, whereas what I offered had the potential to be used in different, even nefarious, ways. Not that other remote viewing methods aren't used for good and don't have validity, especially since those methods are better understood by most people, since everyone is intuitive to a certain degree.

But the skills I offered seemed far more extensive and diverse. Most of all, what I did wasn't relevant to people who knew exactly where they were going, and exactly what they were planning to do. The why or higher purpose of things didn't matter to them.

I began to realize that for them, the relevance of what I offered was in confirming that what was being put in motion in the here and now, probably by factions related to them, had merit. Now they have the ability to see the consequences of their actions, verified by me as seen on the future timeline. It was a subtle distinction, but a distinction nonetheless.

In that respect, I began to feel I was being used by the people I worked for so they could track the success of their efforts based on the results I predicted and what I saw in the future. In simple terms, if you are instigating and putting into motion the covert things that will start a World War, disrupt a region of the world or collapse a Federal government, what better way to see if you are successful then to have someone that can remote view the future for you, by looking at the future events that appear on the timeline.

As the months went on I became more and more concerned about what I was being asked to do. What was of special concern for me was that my Briefings were not being used wisely or for a greater good.

At the beginning, I merely thought those asking the "questions" didn't know what to ask, or didn't know how to interpret my answers. I tried to explain why things happened, and their meaning from a higher perspective. Now I was aware they were using my skills of looking at the timeline to confirm if the nefarious strategies they were implementing today would be successful tomorrow.

My awareness of things was starting to be unsettling. I had no doubt the inner circle at Quantrolics thought they were doing what they had to do to accomplish whatever goals they had based on the philosophies they adhered to. But as someone providing the key confirmations they needed to see if their efforts were on track and working, I was becoming more disillusioned by the day.

For me, understanding the intricate connections that lead to a 911-type event, or that will lead to World War III or the final collapse of the US Federal government, is only relevant if you wish to alter the timeline in some positive way, prepare for the events, or at the very least, push destined events into a more positive polarity through awareness. That awareness could be used to protect yourself and your family, or diminish the impact of challenging events through an understanding of the karmic influences and catalysts involved.

Understanding those connections is vital to pushing for positive, long-term change, and that's how I had always approached the information I imparted to others in the past. I now realized that wasn't the case here. They were simply interested in knowing that the events they were implementing now would put them in control of whatever they sought to establish in the future. I discovered that they were using the information I provided as reinforcement to keep doing, or even intensify, what they were doing, so events I was seeing on the timeline would actually come to pass.

Don't forget, the timeline is dynamic and constantly changing. Having a seer to look in on that dynamism periodically would be invaluable to anyone with the smarts to try and control future events. I could tell that for them, this was a means to achieving and maintaining power.

It was the same with gathering information from every installed project around the globe. Wherever and whoever the actual end-user was, Quantrolics literally had their fingers in nearly every pie. I knew I was being used, but I had little knowledge of where the information was passed to once it left Quantrolics, funneled through the hands of Colonel McCormick, as it undoubtedly was.

It became more ominous and real for me one day when Aaron declared, in passing and without realizing it, that they enjoyed my reports because it was their principal means of seeing if the efforts being implemented worldwide now would be successful. Since none of the Briefs I was being asked to write were about the company, its products or its markets, and all of them were about world regions, governments, terrorists, political factions, war, extraterrestrials and major future events on the timeline, I had to assume he was talking about something much more than just Quantrolics' position in the global marketplace.

Considering that Intelligence Agencies were somehow involved, which had long been confirmed for me, it meant I was somehow looking into global initiatives they were implementing to effectuate geo-political change and even dominate the future. Monitoring various government, commercial and private enterprises globally, as they did through their high-tech surveillance, was merely another facet of their efforts.

Slowly, I became more and more reticent about sharing my skills and wondered what I was doing. Yet sadly, I continued to create Briefs when I was asked, and I did them the only way I knew how -- thoroughly, honestly and truthfully -- retelling accurately what I was seeing or being told. It was my job.

Over time, to compensate for my reluctance I first tried to limit the information I provided. When that didn't work, I threw myself into my supposed marketing role, and began to push hard trying to make that my primary focus.

The international marketing and communications programs and initiatives I had implemented along the way, which no one seemed to pay much attention to, were starting to have real effect. Global recognition and sales were increasing dramatically as developers, architects, corporations and government officials were calling Quantrolics' offices worldwide asking for introductions and capability meetings.

I received email after email from engineers and sales people I had met on my around-the-world tour thanking me. Lin, who had helped the entire time with creating and distributing the materials, told me sales in Asia alone were up several hundred percent from any previous year.

But Quantrolics management wasn't having it. Aaron had stopped his regular visits, and Ron Mallick was missing in action.

Then one day Hans called, something he almost never did. He was speaking in complete sentences, also something he never did, and began half-talking, half-yelling the second I picked up the phone.

"What the fuck are you doing! For God's sake, STOP!" he yelled. "Whatever you're doing, STOP today."

I was confused. What was he talking about? My Briefings? The successful international marketing program that was making inroads? Of all people, he should be the happiest. I had delivered his "cover" and legitimized his efforts in spades.

"Okay, partially my fault," he said, calming down, "I know I told you I needed some cover. But I thought you were mostly bravado. I had no idea what you could do, or that it was even possible to do it so quickly. STOP! You're going to put us out of business!"

I was speechless. What had I done?

"Look, I like you," he continued, "But call this off. Stop the presses...Do whatever you need, but don't send another thing to anyone in any office. Don't place another ad anywhere! Don't speak to anyone who asks you for anything!"

Then he got very serious.

"That's all I'm gonna say, and I'm only calling now to warn you. You're gonna get a call, and I'm advising you to say 'Yes' to whatever they tell you!"

He slammed the phone down with a resounding click.

"WTF!" I said to no one, trying to understand what had just happened.

15. *You Must be Psychic or Something*

Almost immediately, the phone rang again.

"Mr. Nicolay?" an older women's voice asked.

"This is Mr. Spivak, Sr.'s secretary, Marjorie. Mr. Spivak would like to see you in his office as soon as possible," she said.

"Certainly," I said, somewhat surprised. I had never met him, and had no real contact with him or reason to speak to him, but he was the owner of the company. I was being summoned.

"I can come right over. Where are you located?" I asked her politely.

"We're in Building One. You're not cleared for entry to this building, so I will need to meet you at the front door. Shall we say in 10 minutes?"

"I'll be right there," I responded.

I made a quick trip to the rest room and then gathered a small portfolio of printed global marketing materials in various languages. I wasn't sure I would need anything, but felt I wanted something to carry with me for support. Then I made my way up to the surface of Building Three where I was, and walked through the parking lot over to Building One of the Quantrolics complex.

At the entrance of Building One, I barely had to wait 60 seconds before the door buzzed open. A distinguished older woman with perfectly coiffed black and grey hair, wearing a pressed navy suit with a white silk blouse that tied in a large floppy bow at the top, appeared before me. She handed me a pass, and asked me to put it around my neck, then motioned for me to follow her in.

There was no chatting, and I refrained from being overly friendly. Although she was polite, judging from her business-like appearance and deliberate movements, she wasn't the type to engage in friendly exchanges. I tried to open up slightly, saying I had never been in Building One before, but she had no real comment other than to say she heard that a lot.

I could tell right away what was in store for me, if this was the woman Spivak Sr. employed to manage his world. It seemed best to remain silent, and only respond when spoken to first.

This Quantrolics building was very different from the others in the complex, and all the corporate offices were above ground on the main floor. Some even had opaque windows, albeit in the ceiling or high up so you couldn't look in or out. I found myself imagining what must lie underground, several floors beneath. Most likely, this was where you would find all the national monitoring for Quantrolics equipment that had been installed in buildings throughout the United States.

That seemed particularly feasible because the security in this building was off the charts. Security was pronounced in the other two buildings, for sure, but this was another level all together. Armed guards patrolled the main floor of the building as we made our way past them through a labyrinth of hallways.

It was astonishing even to me, and I had seen a lot since being at Quantrolics. This was supposed to be a modern, high-tech company that manufactured and installed sophisticated building control systems globally. Yet here we were, headquartered partially underground in a cornfield out in the middle of nowhere with armed security patrolling the halls.

What was amazing was we were still being told the purpose of the camouflaged buildings and underground offices was to harmoniously blend into the "environment" and be eco-friendly. The reality looked more like a strange mix of extreme paranoia and someone's recreation of a bad 1980's James Bond movie set.

After several more turns, Marjorie led me into a large space that was an antechamber with a good deal of seating, as well as more security. She asked me to please take a seat, and said she would be back momentarily. It was clear that no one here had much patience or fooled around, so I did exactly as I was told.

About 15 minutes later, Marjorie reappeared at the door.

"He's ready for you now. Please go in," she said.

I stood there clutching the materials I had packaged under my arm, and then walked past her into Spivak's office. I heard the solid door close soundly behind me, and for the first time, felt trapped by the situation. My talent for being extremely resourceful was not going to help me out of this one.

The office was enormous and elegant. It put every other office I had seen connected with Quantrolics to shame, including expensive ones in Asia and Europe, as well as Colonel Mc-Cormick's whole-house, suburban office on the Mainline of Philadelphia. I was now standing in the real seat of power.

My first observation was the art collection. The walls were covered with paintings and drawings, and everything was real. The artwork spanned every period and every important artist. Most were originals with very few prints, and the entire collection was knock-your-socks-off sensational. Picasso, Chagall, Van Gogh, Cezanne, Rembrandt, Monet, Gauguin, Goya, Matisse, Mondrian, Bacon, Warhol, Rothko, Pollack, Herring; the list went on and on.

Things were hung floor to ceiling in an old-fashioned way with virtually no wall space left visible anywhere. You could have imagined yourself in a world-class museum. It was a marvel to see.

As I looked towards his oversized desk, I noticed in between us a bronze statue under glass standing on a tall marble pedestal. It was the 'Little Dancer' by Edgar Degas, one of the few cast from the original after the artist's death in the 1920's, complete with cloth tutu and hair ribbon. As I walked forward, I walked over to it amazed, and said, "I used to know someone who had one of these. It even came with a replacement tutu and hair ribbon."

I recognized the statue because it was exactly like one that was kept under glass in the same way at Steve Moreau's house in Monte Carlo. I had seen it a number of times when Anthony and I stayed there, and we used to laugh about the fact that the statue had an extra tutu to wear.

When I spoke, the tall executive chair behind the desk quickly swiveled around 180 degrees to face me, and the man sitting there looked up.

"You mean the Degas?" he said, "I wouldn't be surprised if that's the same one you've seen before. There aren't that many."

I immediately wondered if he was drawing a direct, if somewhat tenuous, connection between himself and Steve Moreau. Was that the same Degas? I looked around at the walls again, completely overwhelmed, and walked over to the desk, closer to him.

Aaron Spivak, Sr. was slightly balding, and had a pencil thin mustache that rode low on his upper lip. It was a holdover from another age, the kind foreign waiters or scientists sported in the 1940's and 50's. His skin looked grey, and because of that he resembled a black and white photo of all the scientists I had ever seen in history books, working diligently on some mid-century military project. If anyone was ever in those pictures, I was now looking at him.

"I see you're a fan of good art," he said. "You'd be surprised how many people walk in here and have no idea what they're looking at, but I see that's not the case with you."

It was true, and he nailed that observation right down. The collection was astounding.

"Incredible," I said, sounding awestruck and trying to flatter him, "In fact, it's quite possibly one of *the* best private art collections I've ever seen."

He was completely silent, and stared at me with his index finger perched across his upper lip. For a second, I wondered if I had offended him by not saying it was the best private art collection I had ever seen.

His ego was palpable, but then again, his intelligence seemed to warrant it. I could tell right away, this wasn't someone you were going to fool with or talk your way around.

This was someone so highly capable and brainy, your only recourse was to be straightforward and direct. He was clearly as cunning and ruthless, as he was brilliant, and probably as informed as anyone could be. Hans' words started to ring in my ears; "…just say Yes to whatever they tell you." I was beginning to understand.

"Please," he said, motioning for me to take a seat in front of the desk he was sitting at, "Let's get down to business."

"I've read these so-called 'Reports' of yours," he began. "Very interesting work, but as I said to my son Aaron, tell us something we *don't* already know."

He laughed slightly, and began speaking in the royal "we" as he looked to see if I had reacted to what he said. After all, that statement had just confirmed the validity of pretty much everything I had ever written for Quantrolics. Coming from him, it was a substantial admission, if not an entirely straightforward one.

"We're not going to clothe this in anything other than the truth," he continued. "You've proven you have the skills you profess to have, and unlike other people here, we also understand that you can look into whatever we say to verify if it's true or not. So, I'm not going to insult you by trying to mislead or delude you. That would be a fool's game, and we are not fools."

"To be honest," he explained, "When you were first recruited, I was reluctant. I couldn't see the purpose of confirming what we already knew would happen in the future, especially now that we have access to the little 'Black Box', which I dare say you know about."

My attention picked up. The only other time I had ever heard mention of a 'Black Box' before was years ago on that fateful plane ride with Levi Steller. He was the only one I ever heard talk about it as being extraterrestrial technology, which was in the hands of Military Intelligence and being used to open dimensional portals and tell the future.

Was Spivak confirming a connection to it? He kept speaking without stopping.

"Frankly, we know there are reasons these things happen, but we don't really care about Karmic influences or metaphysical impact, which seems to be important to you. In fact, when McCormick reached out to you, I worried you may overthink your gifts, or be predisposed to being a goody-goody, and that could be a real danger, especially at the international level."

He shook his head, as if wrong or discounting his statement.

"Even if there's no real indication of that," he said, "Everyone here seems to discount the fact that you can easily see through any cover or smokescreen we create. At some point, you're going to understand exactly who we are and what we do here, as I believe you already do."

He cleared his throat, and took a sip from a glass of something that look like expensive whiskey on ice that was sitting there sweating on his desk.

"McCormick liked what you could do however. He also explained your long history with us, and that it was Moreau who singled you out long ago."

Now his demeanor changed, and I could see he was attempting to be sincere.

"Family and loyalty are something we understand very well here," he said, looking intently at me, "And because of that, I relented and you were invited in."

I began to feel like I was listening to a Mafia Don explain to a soldier why he needed to be eliminated, explaining how much they loved him, while lamenting having to do the deed. I was getting worried, but I worked to relax my face, so no emotions would show.

"Around here, you'll find we have absolute faith in Mc-Cormick," he continued. "He convinced me you have the potential to become both an important asset and a worthwhile operative in the future. We'd even say that in a decade or two, you could be a vital and important figure here at Quantrolics. We're always thinking about succession here."

The conversation was turning, and I began to relax until I heard his voice become cautious again.

"But you've complicated your presence, by bringing so much unwanted attention to us globally. Apparently, you thought a dramatic increase in world sales was something we would applaud, and you didn't seem to recognize the difference between just-enough and too much when it comes to visibility."

Listening, I realized what a farce I was living through. I was being reprimanded for bringing too much attention to the company and helping dramatically increase global sales in an extremely short time frame. Is that possible in any reality?

"Most people in your position would have just sat back, done what they were told and collected the rather fat paychecks we offer. You didn't do that. You went on a hunt, found out what you wanted to know, and then decided you would singlehand-edly pierce a veil that we have spent decades carefully crafting."

His voice was slowing down, as if he was thinking carefully about what to say next.

"Truthfully, it's not your fault completely. I think much of the blame rests with Ron Mallick. But now that he's dead…"

"Ron's dead!?" I broke in, shocked. For a moment it flashed across my mind that maybe Ron had paid the ultimate price for what I had done. Then I recalled the spirit of his mother begging me to tell him that he was ill, and on his way to exactly this fate. I had never had a chance to do so.

"Didn't you know?" Spivak said, coldly. "He died this morning of complications from Leukemia." Then he added, mechanically, "He will, of course, be missed."

I wasn't aware he had died, and his spirit had not visited me. My past experience with those who have just passed over was that it took them time to compose their energetic body, and pull their energy out of the physical body as well as physical reality.

The process is fairly unique to each person, and not written in stone, but most take a minimum of forty-eight hours, some much longer, to learn where they are and how to communicate with lower dimensional fields. Some get the hang of it easily, and some never do, preferring instead to proceed quickly to higher astral planes and dimensional sublevels after dying.

Hearing this now from Spivak, it was as if he was announcing the death of someone he had only met in passing, rather than someone who had worked loyally for him for over 30 years. Suddenly, I was aware that I was witnessing the reason Aaron, Jr.'s Soul had chosen to come into the world and develop the personality challenges it did.

It was clear to me now that with Aaron, Jr.'s personality difficulties always front and center, as a child and an adult, it was a constant reminder to his father of the need to have compassion for others in life, something he seemed uncomfortable with. It was a noble attempt on the part of Aaron, Jr.'s Soul, but whether or not it was successful is anyone's bet.

Spivak continued speaking.

"As I was saying, now that Ron's dead, perhaps we can help you better understand the subtleties of doing just enough, but not so much that you bring attention to our enterprise. Think of it like these works of art we both find so fascinating. Just enough, and never too much. That's what makes anything a great work of art."

He paused again, thinking carefully about where to go from here.

"The fact remains, the attention and notoriety that you've generated in some of our most important world markets, jeopardizes our mission considerably, and it will need to be contained. Because of that, you've forced our hand."

I was getting nervous again. The left side of his face twitched as he continued.

"Do we push you out and discredit you, which we could easily do by calling you delusional, or do we reign you in and let you do what you're fairly good at, all things considered, in secret?"

In part, I knew he was threatening me, and my future was at stake. If they framed me as crazy, either as an International Marketing Executive or based on my other talents, my career would probably be over.

I wondered if I was supposed to answer him. But this was more of a monologue, not a dialogue, and clearly, I was just meant to listen, nod my head occasionally, and, as Hans told me, say "Yes" to whatever was said.

"You know a bit too much for us to push you out in an unfriendly way. And in any case, your work, at least your Reports, have proven somewhat valuable, even if only to confirm that we are accomplishing our long-term goals. Why would we be opposed to having you inform us of what you see on the 'trajectory of the current dimensional timeline', as you say?"

Now I knew he was definitely reading my Briefs. He was using terminology that only I ever used.

"So, this means it's your lucky day," he exclaimed with some finality. "We've decided the answer is to reign you in, not push you out."

I was feeling relieved again, and he continued.

"But there is a caveat. Effective immediately, you are not to do any further international marketing whatsoever. No brochures, no ad campaigns, no conversations with journalists, no discussions out in the field. Nothing. All we want you to do is sit in your office, and write Reports as management requests them. That's all. You can keep the title and the office and the cover, take 5-hour lunches and 4-day weekends, if you like – we don't care. But from now on, you are not to do anything but write the Reports we request of you, without discussing them, or any Quantrolics business, with anyone outside of these three buildings."

I listened calmly, but I knew right then and there this would not fly for me. I liked doing my Briefs, but would I like doing them under these conditions, tied up underground?

And could I really do this for people who, at the top anyway, now came across as elite lunatics, bent on controlling world events and everyone around them, in order to accomplish some unknown future purpose? Did I agree with allowing them to use the information I could provide to confirm that their covert plans would one day be successful?

Then again, I also knew I could never be a whistleblower on the outside. I'd be too easy a target for them, and it wasn't in my nature anyway. That's probably why I had already turned my nose up when the Boston Globe called.

At the same time, no matter how much money they threw at me or how many promises they made for advancement in the future, I knew I couldn't live with being chained to a desk and forced to provide higher information to a group with these ambitions. The idea of all the deceit, sneaking around and the covert activity was also wearing thin. It became clear that the choice I was going to be forced into was a test that had been orchestrated from the very beginning by my Soul.

Spivak wasn't finished with me yet.

"Make an appointment to see Bill Perna as soon as possible. I can't say you'll love him – he doesn't appreciate art like we do - - but he'll be able to teach you a few things about life here. You report to him from now on."

I knew the name Bill Perna and had seen him once or twice in
Building Two, where his offices were right next to Aaron Jr., but
I had never met him officially. He was the Chief Operating Officer, one of the three members of the Executive Team that ran
the company.

With Ron dead, only Aaron and Perna remained. I figured
Perna would take over Ron's areas temporarily, but then got the
hit that the company was going to be reorganized and my rota-
tion would be permanent. I was told right there by my guidance that in the future there would only be two divisions at this
company: Engineering, Product Design and Development,
which had always been the sole domain of Spivak, and everything else under Perna.

Perna had a reputation as a no-nonsense executive who had
spent years in the military, then went out in the field at
Quantrolics before being put in charge of National and International Sales and Installation. Of course, I assumed that meant
he was also the person in charge of all global covert monitoring
in places like Biriatou in Basque Country and outside London
in Audley End, not to mention what I suspected was hidden by
tight security under Building One. I also knew for a fact that
Lin, as well as Hans, reported to him, yet neither of them had
ever mentioned any interactions, which I now found strange.

From the two times I had seen him, I remembered clearly that
no one I had ever seen at Quantrolics looked more like an undercover agent, a detective, a cop, a Secret Service man, or a
CIA, NIA or DIA person than Perna did. His look was so iden-
tifiable as some kind of operative, that I was certain he stayed
underground in Pennsylvania because no matter where he went,

even a five-year-old could out him.

I stood up to leave, but decided I should at least have one opportunity to say something.

"Thank you, Mr. Spivak," I told him in a confirming, soft-spoken tone, "And I look forward to seeing this stunning art collection in a museum someday."

He looked up at me one last time, and paused.

"Yes indeed, it all goes to the National Gallery when I'm gone."

Then he smiled and looked back down continuing what he was doing, as he said, "You must be psychic or something."

It was Friday, and I had a lot to think about. I had planned to leave early anyway, since I was driving down to stay with Dean for the weekend in Philadelphia, so I decided Spivak's offer to me of four-day weekends could begin right away.

Before leaving, I went back to my office to drop off the collateral materials I was still clutching under my arm. They were useless now. No sooner had I arrived back there than the phone rang. It was Lin.

"Hi," she said. "Everything Okay?"

"Sure," I said, "I just got back from meeting "Senior" for the first time. Did you hear about Ron Mallick?"

"I did," Lin answered, "The news is making the rounds now. I don't know if you remember, but you mentioned it to me a while back. Something about what his mother said to you."

"I remember," I said. "But I never told him about it. Maybe it's for the best."

Lin's tone changed.

"I'm actually calling on behalf of Bill Perna, who just called me. There's some kind of meeting Monday morning at 10 in the large Conference Room in Building Two. Bill wanted me to ask you to join the meeting. I'll be there too, and I hear Hans and a lot of other people are being asked to fly in from Europe and Asia over the weekend. I'm not sure what it's all about, but it must be pretty important."

"I think I know," I said, "They're going to announce a reorganization. Perna is inheriting two- thirds of the kingdom, at least anything outside of engineering and scientific development."

Intrigued, I added, "Frankly, I wouldn't miss this one for the world. Do you want to meet here for coffee first, and then we can walk over there together?"

"Absolutely, see you then," Lin said, "Have a good weekend."

"You too," I said, hanging up the phone.

16. All In

A lot had happened in one day. Ron Mallick, the call from Hans Reinecker, my meeting with Spivak, the announcement about Bill Perna. I was going to need to think long and hard about what Spivak had outlined for me.

On the one side there was the continued extravagant income, ability to keep using my skills and relative autonomy, albeit as an occasionally chained-up eunuch. On the other side of the equation was the potential of a career in shambles with no guarantee it could be salvaged if Quantrolics dedicated its enormous resources to demolishing it.

There was also the possibility of more intense retribution down the line, and the possibility that my relationship with Dean would be over for good. Above all of that, there was no guarantee I wasn't working for the wrong side, helping a strange and possibly nefarious covert mission.

Oddly enough, probably since I was on my way to see him for the weekend anyway, my first thought was to test the waters with Dean. At least that would indicate which side of all this he fell on. If everything he had said that first drunken weekend together was true, he had a stake in this and might have something to lose.

Of course, that's if they cared at all, which maybe they didn't. I pulled my thoughts back, to make sure I wasn't giving myself too much credit for being someone important to them.

In fact, my feeling was that even if I happened to be a long-term investment for them, how important was I to them really, as either an asset or an operative? Didn't Spivak say something about having the mysterious extraterrestrial "Black Box" for predicting the future and he didn't originally know why they would need me? And he certainly had made it clear now that I had little to no value to them as International Marketing professional.

I limited my thinking to the intuitive and psychic talents they were really after, and knew I would have to weigh their treatment of me and their goals, against my personal moral and spiritual code. I always prided myself on being objective, independent and non-aligned with any dogma, society or political apparatus, including any specific metaphysical societies or spiritual philosophies, so this was an important self-trial. Quantrolics was looking more and more like a cult with high priests, dogma and a mission attached.

The idea of being non-aligned hit home when I remembered for the first time something that had happened to me as teenager, right before being shipped off to Switzerland. I was walking down 63rd Street on the East Side in Manhattan with my mother around 6pm one evening. We had just parked our car in the garage down the street, and were headed home for dinner, when we passed three people standing in front of a large 19th Century townhouse, not far from where we lived.

It was a beautiful old, double-wide Gothic Revival townhouse from the 1870's, one I had admired when passing a thousand times. It was even more intriguing because the most interesting looking people were constantly coming and going. But it had no signs, and no identification. I assumed it was some adjunct law office, or a Consulate that was secondary and didn't need or want to be recognized.

The three people out front greeted us warmly, as if they knew us. Even though neither my mother nor myself had ever seen them before, they said they had been told to wait for us by their spiritual leader. The Guru had told them they were to invite us in, and inform us that we were to have the rare honor of being introduced into their Society.

My mother was suspicious, and naturally refused to take one step inside. Still, she was willing to listen a bit more to their explanation while standing on the street, with me standing at her side. She asked them what exactly their Society was, but in answering, it seemed like they were mostly addressing me. She would ask the questions, and they would point the answers looking in my direction.

They said they were members of the Gurdjieff Society, an international organization founded on the spiritual and philosophical beliefs of their founder, George Ivanovich Gurdjieff. They explained that they do not recruit members ever, and were composed only of those individuals who were true spiritual seekers of enlightenment who had been guided to find them. They said they only invited the people who were directed to them by spirit, and their Society was a completely secret one that had existed this way for over 35 years.

It was an exciting statement and I was enthralled, but my mother was anchored to the sidewalk. Suddenly, she asked something I thought very reasonable: Why had they stopped us, not knowing who we were, if they never recruited outside members and only invited those directed to them by Gurus or spirit?

Their answer seemed profound. First, they explained that the path of their Society allowed for accelerated spiritual transformation and transcendence. Although many were already dead, their various philosophical leaders and guides were in touch with them through channeling and mediums. They said that in a meeting that was taking place at that very moment upstairs, the three of them had been told to stand on the street and wait for a mother and her son who would be passing by, and invite them in. The Medium at their meeting had said that although both have clairvoyance abilities, the son would soon be initiated on a path of accelerated spiritual growth, and he would benefit from their association.

I knew from the past that my mother would not take kindly to anything that exposed her talents, let alone the skills she knew I had inherited. As all mothers naturally would, she moved to protect me, and her response to them was polite, but definitive.

"Thank you for your kind introduction," she said, "But we do not adhere to any dogmas or philosophies, religious or otherwise. We entertain the wisdom found in all, and take what is valid from each, but our path is our path, and we choose to remain objective and free from the karma of any group or any form of organized indoctrination. In any case, we wish you well, and thank you for speaking with us."

I was proud of her response at the time, but disappointed because I would have loved to go into the building and find out more. I believe now that, exactly as they said, it would have "accelerated" my transformation exponentially.

Had I not been sent to Switzerland immediately afterwards and stayed at home instead, I would have gone back to visit them by myself once I had the chance. In that way, I wondered if my path had been forcibly turned towards the doorstep of Steve Moreau, Colonel McCormick and Quantrolics. If Switzerland and Quantrolics had never happened, if the Colonel had never called me, I probably would have followed a different road to awareness and spiritual enlightenment. I wondered if I was being redirected now.

What my mother taught had always remained with me. There are no doctrines, dogmas, cults, religions or other philosophies that must be adhered to in order to become open, conscious or aware. One is not preferable over any other, or favored by the divine for access into Heaven. Falling into those traps will only lead to control by the very doctrine or dogma that professes to give you freedom and enlightenment.

I had always made that belief a cornerstone of what I did with my skills. I was told early on working with Karen that those who were meant to discover the information and guidance I could offer would find it on their own. In many cases, this occurs by agreement at a Soul level prior to the current physical lifetime.

Now it weighed heavily on me, since Quantrolics had actively sought me out, and especially since they had now made their intentions clear. They wanted to cajole me into using my talents, for profit, in a particular way that was not a matter of my growth, nor was it something that would benefit their own growth, wisdom or fulfillment.

The beliefs and methods they were committed to may not have been published anywhere, or formally established and taught, but they had established a dogma and cult around their beliefs nonetheless. And I was being asked to follow it blindly now, and to do their bidding as well.

The reward for doing what they asked and remaining silent would be a chained-up existence, softened by a satisfying paycheck and a three-day workweek. I would need to decide if that was what I really wanted. It was not lost on me that that when you boiled it all down, the struggle to do what you believe in, whatever it might be, versus doing what you must to survive, was a dilemma every person must face at some point in their life.

One question still remained unanswered for me. It was the question that I sensed Levi Steller was struggling with when I met him that fateful night. He had talked about how "they" had created the persona he became, which he knew wasn't truly who he was, and I had never forgotten his melancholy stare as he said those words. I wondered now if he was somehow expressing to me that he regretted his choice.

Nothing I had seen as yet, despite the covert nature of it all, looked wrong from a spiritual or higher perspective. It was what it was. Yes, they were spying on people and world organizations. Yes, they were everywhere and had their hands in directing things towards a particular kind of future that they favored. Yes, it was all being kept secret and undercover.

But was any of that wrong? Or was it *my* contribution to what they were doing that would be wrong, particularly if I didn't agree with what they were asking, not to mention the future they had in store for me as well as everyone else.

I thought about it over and over, and every new doubt led to a new question and inner debate. I knew in my heart that something wasn't quite right, but my brain and my Ego were still insisting that I evaluate things very carefully.

After all, hadn't I been told repeatedly that there is no right, wrong, good or bad, except in the eye of the beholder. Things exist and are draw to you electromagnetically through vibrational resonance for a reason. That has to mean nothing is "wrong" except superficially and subjectively based on the standards that you and those around you have established. But what if those standards are not your own truth?

Even so, I was aware that what is problematic in these situations is when you bring something into your life, and participate in it in some way, after you have become aware it runs against your core beliefs or desires. That becomes the real story of life, especially when there are karmic implications attached.

It was getting confusing, and I was going to need a clear sign. This choice would require some revelation that could not be misinterpreted, and I would need to experience something that demonstrated without question which truth resonated for me. My future hinged on it. All I could do now was ask that the Universe show me a clear sign before I made an all-encompassing and potentially life-changing decision.

The response from my guides came quickly. I was told that a sign would come very soon, and it would be clear and unequivocal. Once I had seen it, I was told I would make my decision.

But I was not told what the sign would be, or what decision I would make. I wondered if it had been established as only a possibility, as some things are, or as a destiny and fait accompli, as others seem to be fixed on the timeline. Since the timeline is dynamic and changing constantly, especially when it results from an individual's free will, you often see diverging trajectories that split-off from the timeline, but one inevitably rejoins the main timeline trajectory at some point later.

I was assured by my guides that the decision would be mine alone to make, and I was also told to remember that there are no good or bad choices in life. Each path has its own consequences, to be sure, and all trajectories on the timeline represent different opportunities for Soul growth. What was important for me to understand now, was that I had come to a turning point in my spiritual mission and, as a consequence, I was facing a choice that would influence the way in which my future life path would unfold from this point forward.

Holding onto faith, that a sign as well as an answer would come, I turned to a related but different matter, and headed to Philadelphia to see Dean. I would need to explain to him what was happening, so I could factor him into whatever choice I would make. In turn, he would be required to do the same concerning me.

When I got to Dean's place, he was happy and excited, but was rushing around finishing what he needed to do to close up the house. Without telling me, he had planned a surprise for the weekend. He told me we were on our way to the shore, to an apartment he had rented not far from the beach in the Pines on Fire Island in New York.

Normally, it would have been a very pleasant surprise, but right now it was about the last thing I wanted to do. I wondered when I would find a good time and place to have a long heart to heart with him.

Driving wasn't ideal for that kind of discussion, especially considering my original experience with him during that long car ride back from New York when we first met. And now, if things turned south because of the dilemma with Quantrolics, I couldn't make a quick exit, and just head home.

Things would have to wait, displaced by a mad rush to beat the traffic and make the almost four-hour trek out to Long Island. Even so, we made the trip in record time, and caught the last Ferry out. Since no cars are permitted on the small island, we walked the long distance to the edge of the Pines, where the studio apartment Dean rented was downstairs, under a large A-frame house. It had been a long day, so we went to bed right away after having a light supper.

At 3:30 in the morning, I sat straight up in bed, startled and wide-awake with my heart racing. There was a man in his late-twenties standing at the foot of the bed weeping. I looked over at Dean, who was sound asleep, and realized this wasn't someone in the room from our dimension. This was the spirit of someone who had passed over recently.

As I listened in between his sobs, he said over and over again how sorry he was for doing it. Apparently, he had taken his own life by drowning himself in the ocean less than a week ago.

Aside from the deep regret he felt at having taken his own life, the story he told related how depressed he became when he gave up his dreams to be a singer and stage actor in New York. Feeling he was a failure and would never be able to do what he loved most, he became more and more depressed, trapped in a life he didn't want as a service representative, answering inane complaints day after day.

When his boyfriend of 2 years broke it off while the two of them were visiting the island the previous weekend, it all proved to be too much. Alone and in despair that same night, he walked into the ocean and never walked out.

I could feel his pain, and all I could think to do was to pray for him to be guided into the light, and comfort him by telling him the world will understand. While there is absolutely no punishment, eternal or otherwise, for taking one's own life, as so often expressed in religious literature and dogma, the traumatic action can carry the need for heavy karmic balancing going forward.

That is because having faith that life has purpose from the standpoint of your Soul, regardless of the challenges you face, is usually part and parcel of the life lesson being experienced. To be sure, there are times when the ending of one's life in this manner can be something preplanned by the Soul as a great sacrifice the individual makes to provide profound and unique opportunities for friends and loved ones to achieve expedited Soul growth.

Those who have been personally touched by the suicide of a loved one are never truly the same, as they will attest. Often, this can also be the case when young, innocent children pass away, either by accident or through illness, or even when still in the womb. Because of the dramatic grief it causes, it is sometimes difficult to understand that from their Soul's perspective, they have offered a learning experience to those around them that is unparalleled in its importance and sacrifice.

But putting such a sacrifice aside, as well as genetic physical, mental and emotional imbalances, which can also be a part of a scenario planned in advance by one's Soul, the taking of one's own life as an adult usually indicates they have fallen into the unfathomable depths of the negative polarity of their life lesson. Since such an ultimate act of free will negates their Soul's life lesson by cutting it short, reincarnations on the same Soul Wheel as the current lifetime will now play a significant part in balancing any emotional, energetic or karmic burden that results. From that perspective, suicide places a heavy burden on the individual's Soul and their reincarnated selves.

Through my thoughts, I did my best to show the young man love and understanding, telling him he would be fine and that there was no punishment waiting for him or any need to regret his actions now. I pointed out to him that he should ask for higher guidance, and follow the light when and if he was attracted to it. I attempted to explain that this was how he would proceed to higher astral planes, where he would be shown how to better understand his actions as they related to his consciousness growth and the desires of his Soul.

At the same time, I realized how sad it is in modern society that the art of passing from the physical body into higher dimensions is no longer taught or available to us, especially since everyone must someday face that journey. I determined then and there that I would one day write a book as a handbook to death and dying to assist others in some small way.

He seemed to accept the forgiveness I offered him. For several minutes more, I continued to do my best to comfort him, asking for his guides to be present and show him the way.

As soon as I had finished my silent soliloquy, the stereo in the small apartment turned itself on spontaneously, and blasted the music that was playing that moment on the radio. The station was playing the Bryan Adams hit, "Heaven", which I recognized from the 80's. It kicked in just as he sang the lyrics, "…and I'm finding it hard to believe, we're in Heaven".

Dean jumped out of bed, panicked.

"What's happening," he said, woken from a deep sleep.

"Nothing," I said, getting up and turning the radio off. "We had a visitor. I'll explain it all tomorrow. Go back to sleep while you still can."

Dean went back to sleep easily, but I couldn't sleep the rest of the night. The sadness I felt in the young man lingered. I wondered if maybe this was the sign I was told to expect, since his story was about not being able to do what he loved and wanted to do, which led to his severe depression and, ultimately, his demise.

It wasn't my story, but could it be one day? If I were chained up at Quantrolics, using my talents only the way they instructed, would I be headed in that same unhappy direction? I continued to roll the questions over and over in my head for the rest of the night, without ever finalizing whether or not this was the sign I was waiting to receive.

The next morning over coffee outside on our deck, I told Dean exactly what had happened, including that the stereo turned itself on as the young man left. As soon as I was done telling the story, we heard shouting as people ran down the walkway off in the distance. Then the man who owned the house above us came slowly down the stairs.

"They found him!" he said looking at us both.

"They found who?" Dean asked.

"The body of the guy who went missing," he answered, "It just

washed ashore. They've been looking for him all week -- he must
have drowned."

Late that afternoon, Dean and I took a walk on the beach. I was
still mulling over everything, including the meaning of the paranormal visit I had received the night before. I hadn't intended
to open any new fronts, especially because we were having such
a nice day, but as we stopped for a moment to sit on the beach
and look out at the ocean, I decided it was time.

"I need to talk to you about something important, maybe even
life changing," I said.

"This sounds serious," Dean said, brushing it off as he often
did. "Whatever it is, I'm sure we can handle it."

"Handle – that's the magic word," I said, opening up the line
of thought.

Dean looked at me confused.

"There are some major changes going on at Quantrolics. Ron
Mallick, who I reported to and who basically gave me full autonomy, died yesterday. It looks like they're going to completely
reorganize, and he will probably be replaced by someone I don't
really know -- someone I'm not sure I want to know either."

Dean listened attentively.

"And on top of all that, I was called in to meet the big 'Boss'
yesterday, Spivak Senior."

"Wait a minute," Dean said, "You mean you met with the old, mad scientist himself yesterday? Not many people get into that office!"

He acted stunned, and was trying to be funny.

"Yeah, I did, and boy you should see his art collection," I said. "But it wasn't all fun and games. Essentially, I got reprimanded for increasing sales dramatically and bringing too much visibility to the company overseas."

Dean laughed, understanding the same irony that I found shocking.

"But it gets worse," I said. "I can keep the job, title, salary and everything, but I am told I'm not to do anything else ever again, other than sit in the office and write Briefings and analysis exactly as they request them. In other words, I'm to be tied up in that underground fortress, and perform like a trained monkey using my precognition skills whenever they ask me to. Spivak commanded it, and now I'm supposed to submit fully to their will."

I heard myself for the first time talk about it out loud, and realized that what I was saying was an indication of how I really felt.

"So, I'm thinking of calling it a day there," I said, almost as if I had just made the decision.

Dean was speechless, but in a strange way he looked relieved. I could tell I needed to continue explaining.

"But if I leave, they could make it very difficult for me. Should that happen, it might take some time for me to get out from under it. They've been watching me since I was seventeen, so who knows what they're capable of doing. They could forget about me tomorrow, or they could follow me around for years," I said.

He still didn't speak.

"None of that is the worst of it to me though," I said, lowering my head.

"I don't want to jeopardize what we have," I told him, "And I'm worried it might impact our relationship in a number of ways."

I cleared my throat to explain.

"You probably don't remember it, but when we first met you let it slip you were my 'handler'. In fact, you were worried I was going to ruin your life because of it."

Dean remained stone faced.

"I'm not completely sure what you meant, but if that is still the case," I continued, "Then this could jeopardize our relationship, not to mention your career, because of whatever you've been asked to do for them."

Suddenly, Dean looked as if he understood, and began to shake his head back and forth.

"I'm not going anywhere," he said, "No matter what you decide to do, and no matter how they retaliate, if they actually do, we're in this together now."

I could breath again. It was exactly what I wanted to hear.

"Thank God," I said.

But I still had questions.

"So then, were you really asked to 'handle' me?"

Dean smirked.

"Depends on what you mean by 'handle'. Did they come to me and say, 'Will you be his handler?' No, not in those terms. Did Louis Lidner, who I know worked for Spivak in the past and whose wife works at the firm, come to me and say we need you to meet someone connected to Quantrolics? Yes, in a way. Did they mention that Quantrolics was looking to 'handle' some situation with you? Maybe. Did they throw some lucrative legal work my way afterwards -- Yep, definitely!"

I was still somewhat confused, so I waited for him to finish his explanation.

"But it all changed after we spent time together, after your emails when you went to Asia and Europe, and after we were in Paris. If that was 'handling' someone, I guess I decided it was a matter of fate, and I convinced myself Louis brought us together knowing it was the right thing to do. No one ever asked me for anything, and they certainly never questioned me or requested a report on you."

He added, almost jokingly, "And I'm not the kind to continuously write reports – I've got too much to do already. Truthfully, I figured they forgot all about it once you were working there, and once we were seeing each other and practically living together."

He was grinning widely now. I put my arm around his shoulder to let him know where I was coming from.

"I haven't made any decision about what I'm going to do yet, but I wanted you to know what was happening in case it would impact you at work, or worse, impact our relationship. And I guess I just wanted to know if you were in or not."

"I'm all in," he said, putting his head on my arm.

It was one of the best weekends we had ever had. Everything was finally out in the open and on the table.

All that remained was for me to decide what I would do. But first, I would need to go to that meeting at Quantrolics on Monday morning.

17. Seeing the Light

After a perfect weekend, Monday morning was rainy and dreary, similar to the first day I ever drove to that out of the way cornfield, and passed through the gates into the Quantrolics complex. Now, I was recognized by the guards easily, and they had the gates drawn before I was even close to the guardhouse. I wondered how much longer that would continue to be the case.

I walked past Ron's old office, and Sarah was sitting at her desk in the office antechamber, working as if nothing had happened. I went in momentarily to give her my condolences.

Ron had his faults, and he certainly tried that weird stunt to hypnotize me once, but he never did try again and he allowed me a maximum of freedom in an environment that could have easily done the complete opposite. I was appreciative now, but like with so many things in life you really don't know are good until after they're gone, it was too late to thank him. Since I knew Sarah had worked with Ron for years, I was sure she felt his loss as much as any member of his family did, and hoped she would respond to the empathy I tried to show her now.

When I got to my office, Lin was waiting for me. I was glad to see her, and wanted a chance to speak before walking over to Building Two for the meeting.

"So, what's Bill Perna like to work for?" I asked to open up the conversation, after sitting at the desk.

"It's hard to say," she answered, "In over a year, even though I supposedly report directly to him, I've only met with him two or three times, and that was when someone like Ron or Aaron was present. Mostly he acts uninterested, and just leaves what you want to do up to someone like Aaron."

I laughed at her response.

"So, you mean he's so secretive and clandestine, he doesn't even like meeting with the people who report to him directly."

It was more of a statement of fact than a question.

"Well, he definitely prefers hanging out in the shadows, and he's not all that touchy-feely, at least as far as I can tell," she said, looking around to make sure no one was listening behind her.

"Yeah, like a Vampire," I said, only half joking.

"But he does understand being out in the field, even though he's never out there anymore. From what I hear, he spends more and more time with the Spivak family these days, so I wouldn't be surprised if you're right and he's somehow going to be anointed today."

"I wonder if Spivak Senior will be there?" I asked.

"Probably not," Lin said, "Spivak never goes to anything other than technical meetings concerning new inventions or patentable devices. That's top-secret stuff, so it requires an unbelievable clearance."

"I have no doubt," I said.

Then we became more serious, and I looked at her as if to tell her to read between the lines.

"I don't really care what they're going to announce today, but I'm not sure I'm okay with what they're up to. And I'm definitely not okay with what Spivak Senior outlined as my future on Friday. Oh, and heads-up – they're not too happy with either of us about the increase in global sales and higher company visibility."

"Yes, I know," Lin said. "I got a call from Hans this weekend, and he never calls me. He'll be at the meeting today. He told me to keep my head down, say 'Yes', and everything would be fine."

"Sounds just like him," I laughed. "But seriously, I'm having doubts about what they're doing here. Are we working for real people, at a real company? And are they the kind of people we should be working for?"

Lin thought for a minute about what I was suggesting, and then answered.

"I've wondered about that ever since our trip to Asia last year. It's pretty hard to discount some of this stuff, and since then I've seen even more things that tell me you're probably right. It doesn't make a whole lot of sense."

I shook my head in agreement. Lin was questioning things too, even if she wasn't as far along as I was in drawing her own conclusion. Then again, she didn't have the full benefit of knowing some of the things I did.

"Well," I said, standing up, "I guess we'd better go see what it looks like from inside the belly of the beast. Maybe we'll get some answers there, and find out for certain who and what we're dealing with."

There was a stream of people going into Building Two and the small main entrance of the building couldn't handle the influx. As per protocol, each person had to scan their ID as we walked through the door, so the line was moving slowly to get inside.

As soon as we got through to the other side, I saw Hans Reinecker standing not far from me, waiting for the elevators to go down to the second Sublevel. It was clear we were all headed to the large Conference Room, which was really more of a small auditorium, for the same meeting. Hans walked over to us, and shook our hands.

"Welcome back to Pennsylvania," I said. "How was your trip?"

"Unexpected and unwanted," Hans said, sounding just like himself.

I looked around, and Lin had vanished. She always seemed to do that whenever Hans was around, so I was on my own with him waiting to get into the elevators.

"I want to tell you something," he said, sounding earnest. "When you first got here, I didn't think much about it. But after that little escapade you pulled in Biarritz, and then outside of London, I could see we were dealing with someone who knew their way around. We don't get lots of naturals around here, but I've come to realize you're the real thing."

I felt uncomfortable, but flattered. I listened quietly, and then thanked him for sharing the observation he was making.

"I know the powers-that-be aren't very happy right now with the way you plowed ahead," he continued, "But I want you to know that I appreciate your effort – even if you do have the tendency to go too far."

He said the last part with a grin, but then became sincere again, speaking under his breath as he often did. I could tell he was about to say something he wanted me to take note of.

"If you need it, I've got your back," he said.

He walked directly into the elevator when he finished the sentence. I let him go, and walked into the elevator allowing a few people to get in front of me. When the elevator stopped two sublevels down, I walked out slowly to see if he would catch up, but he was already speaking with someone else, so I made my way to the meeting alone.

Hans always spoke in riddles and innuendo, so what he said as we walked into the elevator startled me. It could have been a simple "thank you" for what I did to provide materials that would make his team look legitimate and cover covert aspects of their operations. Or, it could have meant that things were about to get dangerous for me. I really wasn't sure.

When I walked into the Conference Room, I could see that the crowd was leveling off, and wasn't as dense as it might have been. I realized this meeting was being attended mostly by upper and middle management, whereas almost all regular staff, and people who didn't have a direct report to Ron, Aaron or Bill, had been left out.

As people milled around waiting for the meeting to start, I saw Hans talking to Bill Perna. He motioned for me to join them, and I walked over cautiously. Hans took the lead.

"Bill, this is EM. EM, Bill Perna," he said, introducing us.

Bill spoke first, and out of the corner of my eye, I noticed Lin watching us.

"I've heard a lot about you, and I'm looking forward to working with you in the future," he said, rather perfunctory.

Then he added, "I've read some of your Briefings. Very interesting stuff. I can't say I understand it all, but I'm sure in time you will teach me how to understand them better, so we can use your insights to our best advantage. Perhaps we need more people like you. Who knows, maybe it even warrants a whole new division composed of people just like you."

He was looking for a reaction, and possibly a buy-in.

"That's an interesting thought," I acknowledged, leaving it at that.

"I think it could be worthwhile" he responded, "But I'm told there's still some debate about whether or not the 'why' of these things really matters. Most professionals who do what you do just give the what, not the why. In my mind, the verdict is still out on which is more valuable, or if both are equally important."

"I appreciate that," I said. "For me, when it comes to a remote view of something, the why is what makes the what happen. But I guess it really depends on your perspective, not to mention your purpose in obtaining this kind of information in the first place."

Perna looked at me intensely, as if I struck a nerve and he understood what I said had a double meaning. His eyes grew smaller and his eyebrows tightened. It was clear he knew how to speak in between the lines as well as Hans did, but I realized his abilities were more sophisticated and at least doubly elusive.

"I hope you'll enjoy our presentation today," he said, "There's a very important message in it -- one I'm counting you will understand and fully embrace."

My heart began to pound. He was telling me something in code again, but I wasn't sure what. Had he just informed me that the "sign" I was waiting for was forthcoming? Could that be the revelation I was told to expect by my Guides, or was it just pure coincidence? He had my full attention now.

"Good luck," I offered, "And by the way, congratulations..."

"Whatever for?" he asked slyly, looking at me intently.

"In case congratulations are in order," I responded.

Then I decided to throw him a curve ball.

"I was with Mr. Spivak yesterday, and he filled me in on some of the coming changes."

Perna smirked. I knew what he was about to announce to the company, which hadn't been made official yet. It wasn't any extraordinary prediction on my part. Common sense could see it coming, and Spivak had mentioned parts of it. But I was hoping either he thought I remote viewed it, or that by inferring I had a relationship with the Spivak family he might back off somewhat when dealing with me going forward. It was worth a try.

Aaron called the meeting to order, and after a brief, rambling introduction about the value of family and the global force that Quantrolics was beginning to represent, he turned things over to Bill Perna. Perna took the podium, and immediately referenced Ron Mallick's contributions and many years of service. He led everyone in a moment of silence.

It was something Aaron probably should have done, but was incapable of doing given his usual detached and impersonal nature. Instead, the job of mourner-in-chief went to Perna, who without question understood the value of igniting sympathy in the mass consciousness of a crowd. He pushed all the right buttons now.

After the moment of silence to honor Ron, the meeting took off. Perna began by giving a brief description of the current structure of the company. That segued into a sermon about how consolidation of divisions always creates a stronger bond and union within a company, and that led to the announcement of division consolidations.

Finally, he rested the consolidation decision squarely on the shoulders of Aaron Spivak, Sr., who was revered by this group, and the Board of Directors. It was, according to Bill, through their wise judgment and good graces that they ordained the time was right to place Perna in charge of it all.

Bill Perna would now be Chief Executive Officer and Chief Operating Officer, in charge of all worldwide sales and installations, global and national marketing, and communications and strategic planning. It was a neat package that placed operations of nearly the entire company, national and international, under the complete control of Bill Perna.

The only thing remaining outside of his control were the engineers and physicists working for Spivak Senior on the proprietary inventions he was creating to be installed globally by the company. Aaron, Junior remained President of the company, and both Aaron and Perna reported directly to Aaron's father, Chairman of the Board of Directors, as they did already.

Perna went on to explain that nothing would change, except that any direct reports to Ron would now report to Perna. Bill Perna would oversee the smooth merger and future operations of the two divisions, with the assistance of Aaron Spivak, Jr., the company's President, and there would be no downsizing or layoffs.

In fact, he said that a transitional period over the next year would serve as precursor for the potential augmentation of global personnel and expansion of the company in the future. The room erupted in applause.

At the same time, a collective sigh of relief filled the air and the nervous energy that had been present transformed itself into relaxed relief. You could see the shoulders of nearly every person in the room adjust to their usual stance, and everyone became super-malleable, now that they imagined the worst had been called off.

I remained silent, but dubious. Nothing at this place ever happened without some hidden agenda. Even if this part of the meeting had mostly been calm and peaceful, I was waiting for the other shoe to drop.

It was easy for me to see that Bill Perna's background practically mandated expansion of covert operations for the company as an Intelligence Agency front. But everyone in the room, except for a handful of people like Hans, seemed blind to that fact.

The reorganization would be a bonanza for people like Hans, who knew exactly where the bodies were buried.

I wasn't the only one who felt that way. When I looked across the room at Lin, she was shaking her head back and forth slowly. Meanwhile, everyone else had thrown caution to the wind, and they put their full weight behind the announcements.

I wondered if this group somehow had their true guidance severely shunted or blocked. How could they work here, and not understand what was really happening, or at least have some suspicion? Or worse, did they know and approve?

While people spoke softly to their neighbors expecting to be on their way shortly, I braced myself. It was evident the audience had been primed by Bill Perna for something else. I had watched enough Hypnotherapists operate and prepare people for hypnotic trance to know that this was only a precursor, relaxing the crowd for something more important to come.

At the same time, I realized I wasn't any closer to a decision, and there hadn't been a real revelation, as I expected. As my thoughts looked for something tangible, Aaron quieted the room for a second time and Perna walked back up to the podium.

He began by telling a long, drawn out parable. It was a classic technique similar to the one Ron had pulled out of his hat when he was trying to hypnotize me at our first meeting over lunch.

The story meandered, and was essentially the story of a village at war with itself over diverging belief systems. One day, a stranger arrives who introduces all the villagers to a completely new belief system that incorporates all the things they can accept and follow from that point forward. It ended with the villagers making the stranger their King.

For anyone who knew where they were coming from, the story was as transparent as it was hokey. The stranger was a metaphor for Quantrolics, purveyor of a new belief system that would supersede all others and save the day. In gratitude, the people would name it "King". I had to ask myself if anyone would believe this stuff.

Believing it or not wasn't the purpose however, and I watched as the group became more and more mesmerized, suggestable and enthralled, anticipating a happy ending. When the story concluded, maintaining the same vocal tone as before, Perna introduced someone whose talents he praised endlessly, referring to him as his "right hand man".

Damon Danker worked directly under Perna, responsible for all planning and operations in North America. As a result of the reorganization, he would now include all worldwide planning and operations as part of his role.

I had never seen him before, and few people had. There was a second or two of hushed mumbling following his introduction, and I got the inner message that he was relatively unseen since he spent all of his time deep underground in Building One. That meant he was also the Master of a location where few of us had clearance, where security was overboard, including armed guards, and where I was sure all North American surveillance was taking place.

Danker was about my age, with dark hair and chiseled features. He was one of the most handsome men you ever saw. His good looks were complemented by his cultured style and expensive clothing, all of which matched his calculated mannerisms, poise and sophisticated way of speaking.

As he walked to the podium, a change came over almost every person in the room and you could feel their pupils visibly dilate. I had seen this kind of person before. He was the type that succeeded in life with little to no effort. People automatically accepted whatever he said as truth, and would follow him into an abyss with complete abandon just because he asked them to.

To me, he looked like the epitome of a perfect cult leader. Even now I could tell that, to a person, few if any in the room imagined that this striking, well-spoken youthful man could also be the most manipulative, guileful and ruthless character you'd probably ever meet.

I laughed to myself, as a James Bond reference rolled through my mind: "All the women wanted him, and all the men wanted to be him". Then I laughed again because I couldn't remember if that description was from an Ian Fleming quote, or an ad for cheap Tequila.

It would have been more of a joke if it weren't so disturbing. We were entering psychopath territory now. Good looks aside, judging from his energy all I could think was if you shaved his head, you'd find horns. To me he was what a demon would look like, if demons wore Armani.

After shaking Perna's hand, Dankor gave a brief background explanation of what he was about to play on the large video screen that hung on the wall behind him. The gist of it was that Quantrolics was no longer content to merely place its high-tech building control systems in commercial, government and corporate headquarters around the world. They would now strive to move into the consumer market, and work to put whole-home "control" systems in every household, everywhere.

With that he introduced the new Quantrolics corporate video his people had prepared for this meeting. It was entitled, "*We Control Your World*".

I was taken aback and felt like someone had punched the wind out of me. Here it was. They were no longer merely satisfied with placing their control systems, which they claimed to install for security, HVAC, lighting, doors, shades and audio-visual equipment, in public and government venues to spy on the likes of embassies, banks and corporate headquarters. Now they wanted to infiltrate and create the potential to access and monitor every private home in the industrialized world.

Someone might be able to justify spying on governments, banks or other international businesses, since you could easily excuse that away by saying it was common practice and part of the quid pro quo nature of international espionage. But there was something about the audacity and entitlement expressed by this new expansion into every home that could not be explained. The purpose of this must be to secretly eavesdrop on entire communities and populations in the future.

The whole thing was astounding. How could anyone justify installing something in private households that had the possibility to record and send back information to a central monitoring location without anyone knowing it? Sure, there were mobile phones following most people already, but they knew it and could easily turn them off. A secret purpose and use focused in the home was different. This was an unacceptable extension of an already dubious endeavor.

And who was to know what add-ons could be included or put

into play in the future. I'd already written Briefings about the electromagnetic grid system of Earth, and the ways in which the Soul communicates with each individual through their glandular system and DNA, how DNA can communicate with itself at a distance, and how DNA can be used as an electromagnetic identifier to locate an individual using scalar techniques.

Were they using my Briefings as a guide to things they could form high-tech inventions around that would interfere with everyone at a higher, spiritual level? Based on what I knew, it appeared that not only would they be on the road to controlling the physical component of what makes people human, they would be also be entering the realm of cutting people off from their spiritual connection.

Even if they hadn't figured that part out yet, what would prevent them from using the technology they were installing from doing so at some point, or at the very least from gathering information on every household? With the kind of covert associations and backing they had, could they be trusted not to use the technology they installed that way?

And what if Mad Scientist-Spivak was inventing a process whereby every human's rightful communication with their Soul, through the auspices of the planet, could be usurped, or supplanted by third party messaging or blocking? What if technology existed already that could be used to subjugate natural thought patterns, so a person had no idea the thoughts they were experiencing were not their own inner and personal guidance? And what if the ability for someone to do that from afar was sitting in the living room, waiting to be activated and used whenever it was needed by whoever controlled the equipment and technology?

Such tech would give unlimited access to the thought patterns, desires and will power of nearly everyone, everywhere, at any time. Now or in the future, it would provide any maniacal government, not to mention any terrorist, cult, fascist or other organization, the ability to alter thoughts and emotions in any group with the flick of a switch.

The problem was, according to what I was being told, to what Lin had suggested and to existing Quantrolics patents, the technology was available already. All it needed was an outlet, some slight modifications and installation at precise locations, under the guise of convenience and electronic whole home control.

Whoever the backers standing behind the front of Quantrolics were, this would allow them secret, unlimited and unprecedented access to anyone, almost anywhere. Without ever knowing it, entire populations could be enslaved, or at the least, fenced-off from their natural and God-given connection to their own thoughts, and even their Soul. Considering Quantrolics had fairly deep Intelligence Agency, including possible CIA, DIA and DOD connections from behind the scenes that I had already uncovered, something was very wrong with this scenario.

If the title, "*We Control Your World*", wasn't awful enough, my feelings of doom went from bad to worse once the video began. It clearly used all kinds of subliminal messaging, including imagery that tugged at your heart, with happy families at home peacefully enjoying the technology, and joyful office workers going about their daily chores with mindless ease.

There was little if any mention as to exactly how all this takes place, other than through the mystery of advanced technology. The video started off as an in-house propaganda piece to con-

The Metaphysician / Memories of a Psychic Operative341

vince everyone that Quantrolics was on the cutting edge of something enormous.

Based on its superior technological advancements, the video suggested that Qunatronix was on the side of good, right and the future. To accomplish its goals, the help of every employee was enlisted, and each person needed to offer the company their full and unquestioning allegiance, so it could complete its goal of working for the betterment of mankind.

Next, it made the case that Quantrolics' building and home control technology would ease humanity's suffering, and bring joy and comfort to men, women and children around the world. I cringed as one teenage actor in the video smiled joyfully and said to the camera, *"Bring on the Controls!"* It would have been laughable if it weren't so nauseating.

As a crescendo was reached towards the end, the video's message became overpowering. With intense background music building underneath, the narrator dramatically announced:

"Our state-of-the-art building and home control systems are a marvel of ingenuity and science, and a look at how man's world will be controlled in the future with the help of our technological achievements."

Then came the video's defining and definitive final statements.

"Our systems control it all. We control where you work -- We control where you live – We control your safety and comfort -- We control what you see and what you hear – We control the light – We control your world..."

Finally, sounding like it was commanding the obedience of

every person in the room, the voice boomed, *"... We control the future – We are Quantrolics."*

The room was completely silent. Everyone had become entranced. After a moment of absolute quiet, the group broke into a second round of massive applause.

I was astounded and looked around the room full of clapping people, saddened and shocked. No one seemed to hear what I had heard. This video was not talking about giving everyone control of their environment or their "world", as it implied. It was talking about controlling them.

In a parade of the despicable, as bad as every statement it made seemed, it was the last statements that stood out as the most egregious I had ever heard.

"We control the light... We control your world... We control the future."

Perna, Dankor and whoever else was involved in this had snuck these statements into their finish, and it was the most serious head-on confrontation with pure evil I had ever seen. Immediately, I was aware that this was the spiritual revelation I had been told to expect. It was as clear to me as the nose on my face, or the horns on Dankor's head.

From the very first time Karen and I had received higher information from Samuel, we had been told that everything comes down to Sound and Light energy. Sound and Light are the primordial substances linked with creation. The vibration of Sound and the frequency of Light bring life and physical realities into existence.

In particular, Light is the full experience of the God force and a focal element and building block of the Universe. Light is what augments and is a hallmark of consciousness. Light is the defining frequency of higher dimensions, and the reason Light is always seen emanating from higher dimensional Beings. Light is wisdom, knowledge and quintessential universal structure. Light, is the reason we say someone reaches en-"Light"-ten-ment.

Where there is Light, darkness cannot exist, and in the absence of Light, there is void. The Creator said, "Let there be Light, and there was Light".

Teachings on the importance of Light in higher metaphysics are as numerous as they are profound. To state that you "control" the Light, or any aspect of it, is akin to stating you control life and all creation. It is a declaration of Godhood. It is an affront to consciousness and higher spiritual learning.

I was certain there was no accident here. References to controlling the Light had been placed there purposely, if not solely for people like me.

This was further confirmed by the second part of the statement, *"We control the future"*. That mention was a direct reference to exactly what I did. Had I inadvertently given them access to such a claim?

For the first time, I felt like a pawn being played in their intended mastery of the Light, their manipulation of the timeline and, ultimately, their desire to dominate world events. This wasn't a group of engineers, scientists and secret agents spying on the other side in a game of hide and seek. This was a group of mad and demonic characters looking for ways to control everything and everyone by using high technology to manipulate ancient principals of the metaphysical and spiritual world.

They were all being exploited by hidden forces and potentially supervised by out-of-control deep states and governments. Most likely, when you backed it up even further, those forces were under extraterrestrial influences seeking to block "Light" energy from being received by Human Angelic Souls incarnated on Third Dimensional Earth. This, at a critical time, when Light energy is increasing on the planet to ensure Universal Ascension and the evolution of mankind, as well as the Solar System.

It was difficult to believe they didn't realize what they were doing. Regardless of whether they did or not, it was totally unacceptable.

I don't remember leaving the Conference Room. The next thing I was aware of was being back in my office in Building Three, and sitting down at my computer to write a letter of resignation. I addressed it to Aaron and Bill Perna, with copies to Hans and Lin.

In it, I chose to be as cryptic, brief and as complimentary as I could be. I simply said that in view of the reorganization, I felt it was a good time for me to pursue other opportunities. I thanked them for giving me the chance to work for Quantrolics, but said I felt I needed to focus on my professional marketing career rather than my "special" talents at the current time.

I made sure not to be indignant or condescending, and had only praise for what they were doing. It was an attempt to keep them from worrying about my motives for leaving, or thinking I was planning to escape and become a whistleblower, or announce exactly what they were doing to the world.

Within minutes of hitting send, the phone rang. It was Lin.

"I saw your email," she said, "And I wanted you to know I understand completely. What we saw today was pretty revealing for anyone with even an inkling of what is really going on. I think it was your only choice."

"What will you do?" I asked her.

"The writing is probably on the wall," she said, leaving it at that.

It sounded like she didn't want to say anything else, in case someone was listening on the line. Lin had always been one of the few people I truly respected there, and I was sure her integrity and inner wisdom wouldn't abandon her now. She would arrive at the same conclusion I had in good time. For me, there was no way to remain, silently participating in it all, knowing what I knew and seeing it flaunted in front of our eyes.

"I'm not giving any notice," I said. "I doubt they want it anyway, so as soon as I gather up my stuff, I'm going to take off. See you soon."

"Sounds good," Lin answered, "I'll be in touch."

I was gathering up the last of my things when Aaron walked in.

"What happened!?" he said forcefully, "You want more money, bigger office, staff? Done and done!" he blurted out, as only he could.

I was probably one of the few people who understood and empathized with him, even though it wasn't easy sometimes.

"No, nothing like that, Aaron," I said. "I've always been a loner and an independent contractor. I think I work best on my own. No offense intended. I just have some personal goals I'd like to achieve, and I think this is the right time, what with the reorganization and everything."

He was still upset. I think he liked having me to talk to at times, and this impacted him the way it would if someone you thought was your friend was rejecting you. The conversation took a turn.

"It's not that easy," he said, slightly threatening. "You can't just leave. No one just leaves!"

It began to revolve between a tantrum and a threat. Suddenly, I recalled what Dean had said to me on the beach that had completely calmed me down, and decided it would be appropriate here as well.

"I'm not going anywhere, Aaron," I said. "I'll be around, and we can work together on a freelance or contractor basis, whatever you and Bill Perna want. When you really need something, a Briefing or an opinion on something, you can call me, and I'm happy to come over and do that with you. I just would rather work as an independent contractor than in-house, that's all."

It clicked. Aaron relaxed.

"I'm glad to hear that," he said. "I'd hate to think what could happen if you decided to work for the competition, or worse, share what you know with anyone."

It was half a warning and half a threat. But I was fine with the way he backed down, since he had given me the rules for leaving without really knowing it. I'd be fine if I just went on my way, and didn't talk to anyone, ever, about Quantrolics. Just list the company on the resume like any other, with the marketing job description, and move on peacefully and quietly like a distant cousin.

Aaron added one last poke.

"Good. And it's best if you don't talk with any more Boston Globe reporters, if you get my drift."

They probably knew all about that before I did, and he was letting me know it. Maybe the call was a test after all, who knows? With that Aaron left the office, satisfied with himself.

I gathered my last few things, and left Quantrolics for a final time. As I rode through the gate and waved to the guards, who knew me now, I was certain that by tomorrow morning, my name would be scrubbed from their sheets and any connection I had ever had with Quantrolics would be buried forever.

When I got home, I called Dean to tell him the news. He expected it, and wasn't surprised. I told him I needed to get away for a bit, and asked if he would mind if I moved in with him in Philadelphia and stayed a few weeks, while I took a break from it all.

We were practically living together at that point anyway, and he sounded excited about the possibility of my being there on a more regular basis. I was sure getting away would be a tremendous help to smoothing out my transition and deciding what to do next.

Quantrolics immediately locked me out of email and website access, and I didn't hear a thing from anyone until Lin called about two weeks later to say she had also resigned. I was happy for her, and after some conversation asked if maybe she wanted to collaborate on creating a consultancy or venture of some kind together. It seemed a natural idea and progression for us both.

After all, we were on the same page, had the same interests and both of us were now well aware there was a covert global battle going on between what could be considered good and evil, or light and darkness. Perhaps we could do our part, and take up the mantle helping to educate and enlighten people, without exposing too much about what we had been through and knew.

We would need to be discrete. Understanding who they really were also meant understanding what they were capable of doing.

I was now living in Philadelphia with Dean during the week, and the two of us would ride out to the country house to spend the weekends. Things were working out well between us, and Lin and I had had some preliminary meetings about what we wanted to do going forward.

Then about two months later, I was walking through Rittenhouse Square in the city when I realized that I had forgotten something at my previous appointment. Without any hesitation, I turned around on a dime to quickly retrace my steps. As I looked up, about half a block away, I saw two faces that I recognized from Quantrolics.

I didn't know these two personally, but I had passed them many times on the Quantrolics campus. They stuck out to me because every time I saw them, they reminded me of *Mutt and Jeff*, an old newspaper comic strip that my father used to point out to me because it was his favorite as a child.

One of the two was tall, lanky with a mustache, and the other was short, stocky and had a beard. One had a darker complexion, and the other was so pale his face could have been powdered. The odd thing was, you never saw one without the other nearby.

There they were, standing right in front of me now. They realized that I noticed them, so they turned towards each other quickly in a comical attempt to act as though they were just standing around in the park talking, hoping I hadn't seen them following me. I actually laughed, and as fast as I could, practically ran up to them.

"Hi guys," I said, "You're from Quantrolics, right?"

They looked completely startled, and fumbled to say Hello, asking me if I worked there too, as if they had never seen me before. They really were *Mutt and Jeff.*

"Yeah, I used to work there," I said, without waiting for them to respond.

Then as I turned, I saw Aaron Spivak about half a block away walking straight towards me through the park. I forgot about those two immediately, and walked up to him.

"Aaron, it's great to see you," I said, taking his hand, "Are you with *Mutt and Jeff?*"

He looked at me confused, pretending to have no idea what I was talking about, but welcomed my friendly acknowledgment. Maybe he expected I would gristle at the idea I was being followed, but truthfully, I wasn't bothered at all.

"Just passing through," Aaron said. "We didn't want you to forget about us, and thought we'd remind you that we'll always be around somewhere."

We exchanged a few banalities about life at Quantrolics, and he said he would call to ask for a Report sometime soon, which I doubted. Perna would never allow that, and I even imagined they were already off forming a division of people with skills like me, albeit people with less ethics, just as he had mentioned when we met.

The encounter with Aaron was brief, but one that was meant to send me a sign that I was being closely watched. Truthfully, I was flattered that it came from a fairly high level through the appearance of Aaron, and not just *Mutt and Jeff.*

These occasional run-ins happened for nearly a decade after I left Quantrolics, but it didn't really concern me and I never felt threatened by them. I could spot them as easily as if they had Quantrolics tattooed across their foreheads. Over time, I just became used to it.

It wasn't until much later in the game when I began to feel psychotronic and frequency-type undefined physical attacks that I questioned if they were targeting me with technology implemented since my departure. There were times when my entire body would literally vibrate, and at night sleeping I could feel myself almost levitating off the bed sheets with waves of energy passing through me.

Doctors could find no physical explanations, and everything was completely normal. When I remote viewed the situation, I was told it was due to my extreme sensitivity to frequencies and electromagnetic fields that existing around me. I was told there had been a dramatic increase in the electromagnetic, EMF and other unseen frequencies generated in the environment. This would require new methods on my part to properly ground my physical self because of these energies.

I was reminded of what Samuel had once said about vibrational energy that passes through all physical bodies. When this kind of scalar and vibrational frequency energy is compiled and compressed, it is like sending a lightning bolt through a thin copper wire.

We are the thin copper wires in that metaphor. Regardless of what the government and its scientists say concerning safety with the proliferation of these wavelengths in the environment, at some point, especially for those who are sensitive, the element heats up and becomes inflamed.

In addition, just as I was originally told, secret plans to block and fence Human Angelic Souls from receiving "Light" and spiritual energy, and eventually bring about the de-evolution of mankind, were proceeding worldwide. These efforts were being facilitated and expanded through the use of new technologies that include 5G and other EMF fields, scalar waves, new methods to metallize the atmosphere, chemical poisoning of the Earth, food and water, and the introduction of bio-modified bacteria and viruses into the environment. Newly created pharmaceuticals and vaccine technologies, said to counter the bioengineered bacteria and viruses being introduced into the world are also taking a toll, predisposing humans to transhumanistic and intuitive-deadening effects, as well as accelerated biological de-evolution.

The only good news here for me was that I was not being singularly or individually targeted. I have been careful to shield myself, as best as one can, from the devastating effects these newer technologies are having on everyone, robbing living Beings on the planet of their divine connections. But it is one of the greatest tragedies of our time that people are not aware, choose to be in denial or are motivated by greed on how these technologies are being used against us, despite the fact that we are told constantly when they are introduced that they will make life easier and more efficient.

Right after my "chance" meeting with Aaron in the park, I realized these visitations would always be present somewhere in the background. But I also felt I didn't need to make it particularly easy for them.

I hadn't really considered it before, but now I decided it might be best if I sold the house in the country. It was just too close for comfort to Quantrolics, and that weird underground complex in the cornfield. Besides, who knew what might have been planted on the property during our long weekday absences.

After speaking with Dean about it, and some consideration as to the memories the house had for me, I called a local real estate friend and put it on the market. Excited, but also saddened by it, the house sold in less than 48 hours. I was told it was being purchased by a local, who I had never heard of before, and when they didn't come to the closing and the house was purchased in the name of a Trust, I wondered if Quantrolics had a hand in the purchase.

In any case, the buyer wanted the house almost immediately, so in record time I had to scramble to find somewhere to move a whole house full of antiques and a barn stuffed with equipment and odds and ends. Since Dean and I had already decided we liked spending weekends in the country, I woke up one morning and decided to take a long drive far from where the old house, as well as Quantrolics, was located.

As I drove, with no idea where I was going, something kept pushing me in a certain direction. I continued driving until I was much deeper in the countryside than I had ever been, rambling down small rural roads for what seemed like hours.

Then, driving over a hill, it was as if I had driven back in time. I found myself in a beautiful hamlet of rolling hills and farmland in a place called Raubsville.

It was picturesque and quiet, and there was no question I had been guided there. I drove down a small country lane that seemed particularly deserted, took a left at a fork in the road and several hundred yards further saw a sign posted at the end of a driveway that read, "House for Rent", with a number to call.

You couldn't see the house from the road, so I drove up the driveway, which was a long and winding, tree-lined dirt road up a steep incline. At the top of the hill, there in front of me was a run-down, but beautiful, grey cut-stone house from the late 1700's, with white pillars and a portico over the front door. It needed work, but it was completely intact, and the enormous structure, crowned by its massive slate roof, looked solid and secure.

Sitting in the car, I could see a woman dressed in white standing at the window on the second floor looking out at me. Then I noticed a man mowing the high grass in front of the house. When I looked up at the window again, the woman was gone, so I decided I'd try to talk to the man on the mower.

I got out of the car, and waved to him as he shut off the machine and stepped down from it. I quickly walked over to where he was standing on the front lawn.

"Hi," I said, as friendly as I could, "I'm interested in renting the house. Do you know who owns it?"

"That would be Farmer John," he answered.

"Farmer John?" I laughed. "For real, his name is Farmer John?"

"Well, that's what we call him around here. His family picked up the place with about five hundred acres at auction during the Depression, when the original family went belly-up and died out. It's one of the largest farms around here, and since he's the one that farms it now, we call him Farmer John."

He sounded like a history buff, and since I was one as well, I let him talk.

"They don't make houses like that anymore. Townspeople have called it 'Raubsville Manor' since when it was built in the 1770's. This was an original land grant from William Penn himself. They built the manor house right over the original log and stone cabin, before there was even a town."

He began wading through the history of the township as well.

"That was in the days when the Lenape Indians still camped on the other side of that mountain. The settlers had lookout posts built up on the hill behind the house, in case of Indian raids. You can still see ruins of the stone towers they used when there were attacks. Must have been a hard life."

The place was absolutely ideal. Tranquil, hidden away, stately and secure. I was fascinated by the house, its history and the setting.

I didn't need to know anything else about it, or even look inside. Right then and there, I decided to rent it.

"Who's the woman living there?" I asked, "I saw someone in the upstairs window."

Somewhat surprised, he shook his head back and forth slowly, and pushed out his lower lip.

"No one living in that house now. John really should live there, but his wife refuses to step one foot inside the place, so he lives in a small house he built in the 80's for him and his family down the street."

It sounded odd, so I dug a bit deeper.

"That's strange," I said. "Looks like it could be a great place with a little TLC. Why won't his wife live there?"

"Lots of strange things happen here," he said, still shaking his head back and forth.

"Will you need a gardener?" he asked, changing the subject.

"Yes, probably will," I said, in agreement.

Then I tried to steer the conversation back.

"What kind of strange things?"

He shrugged.

"Too many to talk about."

I got the feeling he didn't want to scare me away now that he thought I might rent the place and need to hire a gardener. He climbed back on the riding mower and prepared to start it up again, but hesitated and motioned for me to come closer.

Suddenly, there was an abrupt change in him, and his tone became hushed. He acted like he had something secret he wanted to tell me.

"People say the place is haunted…"

Then just as abruptly, in a normal voice he said, "…But that's another story entirely."

I smiled. If I had knowingly planned it, the place could not have been more perfect.

THE END

Coming Soon in "The Metaphysician" Series:

The Metaphysician 2.0

The True Story of the Haunting at Raubsville Manor

About the Author

E.M. Nicolay is a gifted internationally-known psychic, remote viewer and author dedicated to helping people access higher guidance and metaphysical wisdom. His first book in "THE META-PHYSICIAN" Series is a semi-autobiographical account of his work as a remote viewer and precognitive operative for a covert intelligence agency contractor. His "ESSENCE PATH" series of textbooks are a deep-dive into higher levels of metaphysical learning, prophecy and spiritual awareness.

Other Books by E.M. Nicolay
www.essencepath.com

Wheels of Creation: A Guide to Life After Death, Reincarnation & the Journey of Your Soul

The Samuel Sessions: A Collection of Sessions, Essays, Transcripts and Revelations for Achieving Higher Spiritual Guidance, Understanding the Nature of the Multi-Dimensional Universe and Discovering your EssencePath

Timeline Collapse & Universal Ascension: The Future of Third Dimensional Earth and Fifth Dimensional Terra

The System Lords and the Twelve Dimensions: New Revelations Concerning the Dimensional Shift of 2012-2250 and the Evolution of Human Angelics

Fear, Faith and Physical Reality

Discovering Your EssencepathPath and Other Quintessential Phenomena

Made in the USA
Middletown, DE
09 November 2024